NO DEBT
NO SWEAT!

Other Books by Steve Diggs

Putting Your Best Foot Forward
Free to Succeed

STEVE DIGGS

NO DEBT NO SWEAT!

CATCHING UP
GETTING AHEAD
AND ENJOYING LIFE

BROADMAN
&HOLMAN
PUBLISHERS

NASHVILLE, TENNESSEE

0–8054–2744–9

Published by Broadman & Holman Publishers,
Nashville, Tennessee

Dewey Decimal Classification: 332.024
Subject Heading: PERSONAL FINANCE \
SAVING AND THRIFT
LS/02/110.LS/02/110.P/02/2000.P/03/4084.P/03/4508.P/03/2000.B/04/2500(PER.).B/04/5500/P/06/5000

Author Photo: Jerry R. Atnip

An Important Note to the Readers of This Book
This publication is designed to provide accurate and authoritative information
with regard to the subject matter covered. It is sold/provided with the understanding that the author and the publisher are neither one engaged in rendering financial, accounting, legal, or other professional advice. If such advice or professional
help is required, you should seek the services of such a competent professional
person. Also, you must read and accept the information in Appendix 1, Important
Things to Know and Accept Before You Read This Book.

1 2 3 4 5 6 7 8 9 10   09 08 07 06 05 04

To my best buddy—
I love you, Darling!
And all four of the Little Ones
Who aren't so little any more.
Keep holding the torch high!

Contents

Part II
The ABCs of Christian Money Management

Part IV
The Future: Saving, Investing, and Getting Ready for Retirement

Acknowledgments

To say thanks isn't enough, but here goes:

Appreciation to Mike Root, who has been an ongoing Barnabas in this mission to get the No Debt No Sweat! message out. Others who deserve to have their backs patted are Joe Beam, Dave Clayton, Len Goss, Karen Hodge, Jerry and Lynn Jones, Jim Taylor, Weldon Rickman, Willard Tate, and especially Bonnie Diggs for her endless encouragement and patience.

Special thanks to my elders who oversee this ministry and give me spiritual counsel:

Ron Cunningham, Junior Grimes, Wayne Holt, Kent Johnson, Wayne Pyle, Bill Reeves, Jim Thweatt, and Ernie Scarbrough.

Megathanks to the Antioch Church of Christ family that has patiently served as guinea pigs for this whole endeavor.

Finally, thanks to my Lord and Savior Jesus Christ, who gives purpose to it all.

Preface

The book you're holding is titled *No Debt, No Sweat!* for a good reason: That's my philosophy of life. Actually, I conceived the title in the mid-1990s when a publisher first asked me to write this book. At the time I declined because I was just too busy. Today I'm glad I waited.

In the last several years my views have matured, and my beliefs have crystallized. The truth is, I see some things differently today than I did a few years ago. For one thing my view of debt has changed. Today I'm less of a fan of borrowing. I don't believe that we should try to leverage our way to prosperity. Am I totally opposed to debt? No. But as the years have passed, so has my willingness to encourage a lot of borrowing. I've come to this belief the hard way—through the school of hard bucks (if you get my drift).

But, if you think this book is simply about getting out of financial debt, you may be disappointed. Yes, that's a big part of what we're going to be discussing in the next nineteen chapters. But, if all you take away are some slick tricks for paying down debt, then I will have failed in my mission.

When I speak of debt, I'm referring to more than just the money we owe to someone else. Debt is bigger, broader, and badder than just that. Debt is all of the painful things we deal with rolled into one short, benign, little word. Debt is pain. Debt is confusion. Debt destroys relationships. Debt is sitting bolt upright in bed at three in the morning wondering how to get through the next day. Debt is slavery. It saps the joy and peace out of life. It sucks the delight from a person.

As a person who has made more than his share of mistakes, I come at this not as an expert but as a fellow struggler. Most of what I've learned I've learned the hard way. But the danger when one writes a book is that some people will assume the writer is fully accomplished. Those who know me best will happily put an end to such an erroneous assumption.

My goal is to encourage you to develop a set of healthy life skills. I want us to look for answers on a holistic level. We will explore ways to bring clarity and balance to all areas of our lives. Whether it's paying off a car loan that's more than the value of the car itself, figuring a way to finance college without robbing the retirement fund, or learning to walk more serenely with God—it all has to do with what enslaves us.

In this book you are going to find practical ways to cut expenses (without selling the kids). I'll teach you how to buy a home and a car that you can afford. And we will explore ways to mentor our children so they won't make the same mistakes we did. We'll talk about the best ways to buy insurance while keeping our eyes on God and trusting him for ultimate protection. Later we'll discuss the dollars and cents of investing in down-to-earth terms—unlike the jargon you've heard all your life. I'll use simple, clear examples that will illustrate the techniques of the great, long-term investors. We'll discuss how to overcome the temptation to let greed drive our investing decisions. Finally, we'll look at some doable, real-world solutions to retirement planning. These will be ideas you can use right now—even if you're starting late.

So, if you're ready, there are three things to grab:

1. Grab your husband or wife, squeeze each other tight, and ask God to bless you as you read together—whether you're presently hopeful or hopeless.
2. Grab a pencil so you can mark up this book and begin your "things to do" list.
3. Grab a Coke.

Part I

Living for the Beautiful Bye and Buy in the Nasty Now and Now

Getting from where we are
to where we want to be
with financial and spiritual integrity

1

Failure, the First Step to Success

THE YEAR WAS 1958. What a time! America was feeling her collective oats. It was the year *Billboard Magazine* began its Hot 100 chart reporting hits by the likes of Pat Boone, Rick Nelson, the McGuire Sisters, and the Platters. *Gunsmoke, The Danny Thomas Show,* and *Tales of Wells Fargo* captured our tele-attention in the evenings. The Brooklyn Dodgers and the New York Giants grand slammed their way to the West Coast. And America stepped boldly into space with the launch of her first earth satellite, *Explorer I.*

But not everything was so successful. That same year also saw the launch of one of the most highly promoted cars that Ford Motor Company had ever produced. Of course today, for many people, the word *Edsel* is almost synonymous with the word *failure.* But it didn't start out that way. Designed to be an innovative, niche filler in the Ford lineup, the Edsel featured a host of new styling and technical ideas. One of the most talked about was the push-button system in the center of the steering wheel hub that controlled the automatic transmission. Even the name was special—chosen from nearly eight thousand options supplied by Ford employees, the ad agency guys, and renowned poet Marianne Moore. And talk about promotion (or,

3

maybe I should say, hype)! In the late summer and fall of 1957, it was everywhere. National television ran ads promoting the new car with Bing Crosby, Frank Sinatra, Rosemary Clooney, and Louis Armstrong. Two-page spreads in national magazines heralded the coming of the car to end all cars. In a film shown to Edsel dealers nationwide, Mr. Ford announced, "Gentlemen, the Edsel is here to stay!"

But, alas, the Edsel simply didn't sell. One person described the car's sales chart as the drawing of a dangerous ski slope. Why? Well, that depends on whom you ask. There were complaints about the price being higher than comparable automobiles. After all, Ford introduced the car about the time America was going into a recession. Buyers' tastes were changing, too. Big, bold, bombastic cars were giving way to smaller, more fuel-efficient rides. Others complained that the parts simply didn't fit—hoods wouldn't open, and trunks wouldn't close. And then there was that nagging complaint that the all-new transmission didn't fulfill its mission either.

So after three disappointing years and millions of lost dollars, Ford discontinued production of the Edsel.

So What Does the Edsel's Failure Have to Do with You?

Well, actually it may have a lot to do with you. I realize that many of you who are reading this book are financially healthy and are looking for investing concepts. There will be lots of that later. But there is also another group of you who are hoping to find some answers and relief from money problems that are tearing apart the fabric of your lives. If you are like many Americans today, you started your early adult life planning for success. You probably dreamed of having the financial resources to enjoy a comfortable lifestyle with enough money in the bank to care for and house your family. You, no doubt, planned to have enough set aside one day to buy a home, send the kids to college, and retire with dignity.

Yet despite all those early "plans," if you are like about 70 percent of American families, you have experienced living from paycheck to paycheck. For you the American dream long ago became a gothic nightmare. If I'm describing you, maybe you'll identify with some of these struggles:

- You know all too well what it feels like to sit bolt upright in bed in the middle of the night not knowing how you are going to pay the rent.
- More than once you have hesitated to answer the phone for fear of another harassing bill collector.
- You've ordered yet another credit card because the others are already maxed out.
- You dread talking about money with your spouse because it always ends in a fight. And, even worse, there are times when you haven't been totally honest with each other about money and spending issues.
- Even when you're at church, a Little League game, or a school play you find your mind drifting to the money problems you're facing.
- When a good cause comes along, your heart breaks because you have nothing to contribute.

If you can relate to any of these scenarios, this book is for you. Just like the Edsel, you had "plans" for success, but somewhere along the way things got off track. Ford Motors turned the Edsel experience around and learned from its mistakes. Today, with scores of automotive hits to its credit, Ford is one of the most successful carmakers in the history of the world. By learning from your mistakes—and then having the courage to do things differently—your future can be a lot brighter than your past.

Learning the tricks of financial success isn't hard; we're not talking about being Web-master smart here. No, instead, you and I are going to walk through this financial maze together. I'll show you how, by understanding and following some simple concepts, you will be able to get your financial house in order and then take off like a bullet with a tailwind!

Like Fish in a Barrel

You may have noticed that in the previous paragraphs I have been putting the word *plans* in quotation marks. That's because, if you're like most people, you really have not had a clearly conceived plan for managing your money. And without a plan there is no way to have maximum financial success.

Everybody on the other side already has a plan. Car dealers, advertisers, real estate salespeople, telemarketers, credit card companies—all have plans to extract the money in your wallet and transfer it to their corporate piggy banks. And unless you are more prepared and dedicated than they are, you'll lose and they'll win. No, I'm not saying that these are bad people. But as a consumer you have to be *dollar smart*. You need a spending, budgeting, and investing plan that you stick with, no matter how good that new car smells or how low that introductory interest rate is.

Believe me, these people are smart. Retailers study us. They know that most people turn to the right when they enter a store and then proceed counterclockwise. That's why store owners frequently put their highest profit items in that "sweet spot" directly to the right-hand side of the front doors.[1] Have you noticed the trend toward larger shopping carts and fewer hand baskets in grocery stores? Experts tell us that bigger carts give us the perception that we aren't buying as many items, while hand baskets get heavy and cause us to hurry to the checkout line faster.[2]

Grocers know that shoppers will buy higher priced items if they put them on shelves at eye level and that we'll pass up equally good, less expensive items if they are out of easy reach on lower shelves. It's no accident that there is always a clutter of stuff for sale at the cash register; merchants know that we're most likely to make impulse purchases when checking out.

Brian Wansink, an expert in the field, says people like stores with lots of variety. People perceive a store to have lots of variety when there is some degree of jumble and a lack of predictability. That may explain why you might find picture frames next to socks at a T. J. Maxx and why Campbell's Soups are never in a logical order.[3]

Have you ever gone into a store and seen some horribly expensive item and wondered who would ever buy it? The answer may be, no one. But the retailer figures that it will lead you to assume that you're getting a bargain on your purchase.[4] An old real estate trick is to heat cinnamon in the kitchen. It puts potential buyers in a homey, buying mood. Some life insurance people are notorious for using emotional stories to scare prospects into buying their products. And how many cars have been sold on payment plans that lasted longer than the cars?

Next time you pass the corporate headquarters of an insurance or finance company, go up and inspect the building closely. You may find that it's not mortar you're looking at between the bricks; it's the dried blood of customers trying to make their payments! For far too many people, the drive-up windows at the bank are there so their cars can see who owns them!

America's Great Closet Sin

Like most of the problems we face, financial pain has its roots in the bad decisions we have made all along the way. As with most bad decisions, we are filled with shame and fear that others will find out. To admit financial failure is to admit that something in our lives is out of control, and we don't like to do that. So instead of bringing the problem into the light where it can be addressed, we try to hide it from others and often from ourselves. Things go from bad to worse until, finally, the house of cards falls in on itself. That's when what we had hoped would remain a private struggle suddenly becomes public.

God really does know how we tick. Over the years I have become convinced of two things:

1. As long as I deny or excuse any sin in my life, I continue to fall further behind. Only when I face my sin can the healing (changing) process begin. Sin is like a cancer; until it is recognized and isolated it can't be treated. And just like cancer, a sin ignored doesn't go away; it continues to grow until it finally consumes and destroys the whole body!

2. There is strength in numbers. Sometimes the only way to deal with a problem is through confession and accountability to other believers. James tells us to "confess your sins to each other and pray for each other so that you may be healed" (5:16).

Just yesterday I was visiting with a broker friend of mine who told me about a man in his church. He had known this man for a long time, but they had never really been close until they began attending a men's prayer group together. Gradually in these meetings they got to know each other and began to open up. Eventually my pal's friend felt safe enough to share a dark secret with the other men. He admitted that despite a healthy income he was deeply in debt and saw no way out. The wolf wasn't just at the door; he'd already strung a hammock on the porch! Thankfully, the other men in the group rallied around him, and since then they have helped him through his difficulty.

You're Not the Only Rat-Race Refugee

My point is simply this: People with money problems are frequently in denial, and believe me, denial is not a river in Egypt! It's a broken, dysfunctional way of life that's no fun. Financial turmoil is the great silent pain of many in today's Christian church. It depletes our energy and destroys our vigor. Money problems weigh us down until we're no good to others, ourselves, or God.

The devil knows this, and he uses it against us. He's like a roach that does its best work in the dark. If he can divide and make you feel alone, like you're the only one with this problem, he wins.

The good news is that you're not alone. Americans spent the 1990s piling up debt. People found that a teacher could live like a tycoon with the help of enough credit cards and an occasional home equity loan thrown in for good measure. So now we find ourselves awakening with a financial hangover in the first decade of the new millennium. If the old adage about misery loving company is true, the following will leave you delirious:

- Total household debt (credit cards, mortgages, auto loans, etc.) went over 100 percent of total disposable income for the first time in 2000.[5]
- We charged over one trillion dollars on our credit cards in that single year. This was more than we spent in cash![6]
- The kids are following their parents' lead. The average graduating college student has a credit card balance of over $3,300.[7] That doesn't include the $15,000 of student loans that also have to be repaid, or the car loan, or the bill consolidation loan.
- Money problems are the leading cause of divorce in America.
- Credit card debt exploded in the 1990s. As of September 2000, the average balance per household (for all credit cards from banks, stores, gas companies, etc.) stood at $8,562 compared to $2,985 ten years earlier in 1990.[8]
- Although most Americans overestimate their level of financial assets and wealth by up to twenty-five times,[9] the typical family in the U.S. has net financial assets (counting retirement accounts) of just $9,850.[10]

- In the typical household, consumer debt is more than 50 percent of total financial assets. Percentage-wise the level of family debt increases significantly over the average in the lowest income households.[11]
- Unbelievably, one survey showed that 27 percent of us believe that our best shot at getting a million dollars or more over our lifetimes is by winning a lottery! John Anderson, co-CEO and president of Primerica, points out that the chances of winning a big lottery jackpot are ten to twenty million to one, but the typical family could probably accumulate hundreds of thousands over the years by saving a few dollars every week and avoiding the gambling.[12]
- Fifty-six percent of U.S. citizens are failing to set aside enough for a comfortable retirement.[13]
- Fifty-nine percent of the people surveyed say they expect a lower standard of living in their retirement years.[14] (Do you really think all those senior citizens working at Wal-Mart and McDonalds are there for the social interaction?)
- Sixty-four percent of families earning a moderate income ($20,000–$50,000) say they live from paycheck to paycheck. The number goes up to 79 percent among lower-income families.[15]

Where Do I Start?

I have always admired Vince Lombardi, the legendary Green Bay Packers coach who took the team to five NFL titles and two Super Bowl victories. When he died in September 1970, he was the NFL's winningest coach. Lombardi had the ability to take complicated concepts and reduce them to ridiculously simple terms. The story goes that at the beginning of season practice each year, Vince would stand before his squad of the toughest, most seasoned players in the league, pick up a football, hold it before the men, and say, "Gentlemen, this is a football."

This was his way of reminding rookies and veterans alike not to forget the basics. He knew that all the strategy in the world wouldn't win games until these guys got the fundamentals between their ears.

It's the same way with financial problems; you have to understand the fundamentals. Basically, there are two things to remember: First, if you're swamped with debt, you aren't alone—the vast majority of Americans (even Christians) are in the same trap. Second, there are some productive steps you can take to get your financial house in order. Things didn't get bad overnight, and you aren't going to fix them overnight, either. But by getting back to the basics, we can chip away at the problem and chart a course for a more financially secure future.

Why We Borrow

I will have more to say about this later, but for now please understand that I don't believe that debt is always evil or sinful. However, the Bible does teach that debt can be bondage, or slavery. Proverbs 22:7 tells us, "The rich rule over the poor, *and the borrower is servant to the lender*" (author's emphasis). When our lives are controlled by the monthly payment schedule, debt has become the master.

There are two things you should ponder before going into debt:

1. *What are my motives?* Why are we borrowing money? All too often we buy things we don't need, with money we don't have, to impress people we don't like! Folks, this is dumb behavior! A lot of borrowing happens for all the wrong reasons.

Often there is an element of greed involved. Over and over again, the Lord warns us to avoid covetousness and greed. In Luke 12:14–15, Jesus gets right to the point here: "Watch out! Be on your guard against all kinds of greed; a man's life does not consist in the abundance of his possessions."

A first cousin to greed is vanity. Frequently people go into debt trying to keep up with other people in the neighborhood (or, sadly, even at church) who have a more lavish lifestyle. When I teach classes on money management, I like to ask the audience what they think is the most expensive thing they will ever own. Of course, I get all the usual answers: "Our home?"

"Nope," I say.

"College for the kids?"

"No," I tell them.

"Retirement?"

"Not even close,"

By now I usually have their attention. That's when I write three letters on the overhead: EGO. You see, there is nothing in the world more costly than an out-of-control ego. It makes us do stupid things that we end up paying for for years to come. How many people do you suppose are making payments on boats, expensive cars, prestigious private schools, second homes, and extravagant clothing because their social position or circle of friends expected it?

2. *What is my ability to repay?* The problem with borrowed money is that it has to be repaid. Today's instant gratification becomes tomorrow's bondage.

It is so dangerous to presume on the future. Murphy's Law always kicks in at the least-expected and most-inopportune moment. Just when you think you'll be ready to make that first payment—BOOM! The bottom falls out. Either the baby needs some new, exotic medicine, or the central heat goes out, or the transmission gives up the ghost, or well, you get the point.

Again, Scripture gives us helpful guidance in this area:

> *Now listen, you who say, "Today or tomorrow we will go*
> *to this or that city, spend a year there, carry on business and*
> *make money." Why, you do not even know what will happen*
> *tomorrow. What is your life? You are a mist that appears for*
> *a little while and then vanishes. Instead, you ought to say,*
> *"If it is the Lord's will, we will live or do this or that." As it*
> *is, you boast and brag. All such boasting is evil*
> *(James 4:13–16).*

As Christians we must pre-act so we aren't forced to react. We need to "count the costs" (Luke 14:28 NKJV) before we launch into any venture that will commit our future earning power.

God Wants You to Experience Freedom

Know this above all else: God is on your side; he's pulling for you. It doesn't matter whether you are reading this book for investment ideas or to find a way out of smothering debt—God's ways work. Remember, "Make sure that your character is free from the love of money, being content with what you have; for He Himself has said, 'Never will I leave you; never will I forsake you'" (Heb. 13:5).

God wants His people set free from every form of bondage, including financial. Only then will we be at our best for others, ourselves, and the kingdom work we're here to do!

In the next chapter I'm going to challenge you to refocus your view of money and what it means in your life. I'm going to share with you some of the personal struggles I have had with this topic and some of the conclusions that make sense to me.

2

The Great Balancing Act

*IT'S BEEN THE BETTER PART* of forty years now, but I can still remember a large jug of liquid that my dad stored in the utility room of our basement. I can't even tell you what was in the container. I don't remember its color or size. I don't even remember if it was made of plastic or glass. But I do remember something about the label. There was a picture of a human skull and crossbones on it. I remember learning that was the universal sign of poison. It was the manufacturer's way of warning everyone—literate and illiterate, adult and child—not to swallow the stuff inside. It was clear that unless I wanted to assume room temperature prematurely, I had better not mess with that bottle of liquid!

The Skull-and-Crossbones Part

In a less literal yet equally important way, I want you to think of this chapter as the skull-and-crossbones part of our visit together. This is where I hope to challenge you to get a God's-eye view of money. I want to warn you of some of the pitfalls that money can lead to. Because to leave you with a book about money, controlling debt, and investing for the future can be like playing with a beautiful candle in a room full of dynamite. It is so easy to turn virtue to vice and allow a healthy interest in asset management to become an unhealthy focus on materialism.

Hopefully, we can explore the way God wants us to view money and material goods without going to either of the extremes that are so prevalent in today's church. Without a godly viewpoint we are easy prey for those who preach a nonbiblical theology of money. Usually it plays out in one of two extreme teachings: On one end of the spectrum are those who pitch a form of Christian prosperity that isn't much more than a sanitized form of greed, and at the other extreme are those who would urge a vow of poverty. As is the case with God and all his creation, balance in the area of money is critical.

Jesus' Lifestyle

Jesus had a curious approach to money. He didn't seem to care whether a person had a lot of it or not. Jesus looked at hearts, not checkbooks. From the widow and her mite to the numerous street people, the Gospels are full of stories about Jesus befriending and ministering to the poor. He associated with lowly people and recognized their value before God, even when the rest of society, including established religion, viewed them with contempt. He championed their cause and urged his followers to love, feed, clothe, and show them hospitality.

Jesus also had wealthy friends. I have long suspected that Mary, Martha, and Lazarus must have had a large home in order to accommodate Jesus and his disciples when they came into town for a visit. And let's not forget the story in Luke 8:3, of "Joanna the wife of Chuza, Herod's steward, and Susanna, and many others who were contributing to their support out of their private means" (NASB).

Apparently, women who had both pedigree and piles of cash financed Jesus' ministry! And do you remember Matthew, one of Jesus' disciples? He was a tax collector and, based on his ability to entertain, probably pretty well-heeled financially. At Jesus' death, a wealthy disciple named Joseph supplied the burial chamber.

In his parables Jesus made use of wealthy people. It took financial resources for the good Samaritan to minister to the injured man beside the road. The Bible says that he "brought him to an inn, and took care of him. And on the next day he took out two denarii and gave them to the innkeeper and said, 'Take care of him; and whatever more you spend, when I return I will repay you'" (Luke 10:35 NASB). This good man had more than good intentions; he had the resources to check his injured friend into a hotel. And, folks, we all know that you can't stay at a Hilton for free!

The Gift of Giving

Sooner or later you will run into some well-intentioned Christian who implies that your ability to earn money is somehow less worthy than the ability to preach the good news or serve in a foreign mission field. When that happens, don't retreat into a cave feeling like a spiritual pygmy! Simply ask the good brother to tell you where he thinks the money comes from to finance great ministries, pay the missionaries' salaries, build Christian schools, and feed the hungry. Then flip over to this spot in Romans 12:3-9:

> For through the grace given to me I say to every one
> among you not to think more highly of himself than he ought
> to think; but to think so as to have sound judgment; as God
> has allotted to each as a measure of faith. For just as we
> have many members in one body and all the members do not
> have the same function, so we, who are many, are one body

_in Christ, and individually members of one another. Since
we have gifts that differ according to the grace given us, each
of us is to exercise them accordingly: if prophecy, according to
the proportion of his faith; if service, in his serving; or he
who teaches, in his teaching; or he who exhorts, in his exhortation;_ he who gives, with liberality; _he who leads, with
diligence; he who shows mercy, with cheerfulness_
(NASB, author's emphasis).

Here Paul lists seven spiritual gifts. Many Bible teachers believe
that all Christians are blessed with at least one of these gifts. If these
gifts are distributed throughout the community of believers, then the
fellowship will be strong and healthy. The fifth gift in this list is
the gift of liberality. (The New King James Version renders it by saying that if his gift "is contributing to the needs of others, let him give
generously.") Well, excuse me, but doesn't it just make common
sense that if one gives liberally he first has to have something to give?
And in order to have something to give, it is reasonable to assume
that this individual probably is good at making and investing
money.

About Rivers and Reservoirs

As I've gotten older, some things have changed for the worse. My
forgetter works better than my rememberer. I need glasses to find
my glasses, and I've finally gotten to the point where I can comb my
hair with a towel.

But some things have changed for the better. One good thing
that I'm beginning to realize is that most of the time it's bad to go to
an extreme on any issue. As we've seen, Jesus wasn't for or against
money. His focus was on our hearts. Accordingly, I believe Jesus
wants us to be rivers instead of reservoirs.

Just as a river allows fresh water constantly to flow through, we need to hold God's blessings loosely. We can, and should, enjoy the material gifts God brings into our lives. But we need to "be ready for every good work" (Titus 3:1 KJV), ready to share and pass what we have on to others. Instead, too often I have been more like a reservoir. When blessings came into my life, I hoarded them. I wrapped my arms around them and refused to honor God by passing those blessings on to others. Why? Sometimes it was born of selfishness. Other times it was due to a lack of faith on my part that the same God who had given me the original blessing was able to continue flowing future blessings into my life. And just like a reservoir, I became stagnant and dead in my heart.

Paul's Advice to the Rich

Like so many others of the baby boom generation, I grew up in a middle-class home. We weren't poor. My father had a successful business. But we certainly weren't rich. My parents had all the normal financial pressures. So in the late 1970s when my own young business began to take off, I was faced with some real issues. Suddenly we were making more money than ever, and I felt guilty! It was a legitimate, honest business, and I treated people fairly. *So why*, I wondered, *am I feeling so uncomfortable with this money?* I found myself wondering if maybe I should just give most of it away, keeping only enough to live on. Maybe I shouldn't aspire to owning a home, or being able to eat in good restaurants, or driving a nice car. I was conflicted. I was miserable.

Then one day when I was visiting with my friend, Dr. Rubel Shelly, the dark clouds began to lift. He took me by the spiritual hand and shared God's advice for people who have money:

> *Command those who are rich in this present world not to*
> *be arrogant nor to put their hope in wealth, which is so*

*uncertain, but to put their hope in God, who richly provides
us with everything for our enjoyment. Command them to do
good, to be rich in good deeds, and to be generous and willing to share. In this way they will lay up treasure for themselves as a firm foundation for the coming age, so that they
may take hold of the life that is truly life (1 Tim. 6:17–19).*

Wow! What a clear, terse, concise teaching! It was as though the
hand of God had lifted a huge load off my shoulders! With God's
Holy Spirit as his inspiration, Paul had laid out an entire doctrine of
wealth management. In just a few sentences he had brought common sense and balance to an internal struggle that had sapped me
of peace and joy. This passage makes clear that there were a number
of wealthy Christians in the Ephesian church where Timothy minis-
tered. In the first century this city was vibrant and prosperous. As a
matter of fact, the tourist trade was so successful that the city fathers
opened the first world bank in Ephesus.[1] Obviously, some of these
wealthy Ephesians had accepted Jesus. So the question for these new
Christians was, how does one balance the calling for character with
an abundance of cash? Let's go through this gem of Scripture one
point at a time.

*First, Paul signals whom he's writing to: those who "are rich in this
present world."* It's almost as though Paul is trying to keep some
good first-century Christian folk from misunderstanding him. He is
not talking about heavenly or spiritual wealth here. No, in this case,
Paul is speaking to people who have a lot of zeros on their bank
accounts!

And before I leave this point, let me suggest that the rich people
to whom Paul is speaking would probably include most of us today.
Although you may not think of yourself as wealthy—compared to
most of the world, especially in Paul's time—we are all filthy rich! If
you have a bathtub, you're better off than 70 percent of the rest of

the world. Only 30 percent of the world's population can read, and only one person in a hundred owns a computer! If you have never faced the horror of war, the pain of imprisonment, or the pangs of starvation, you are ahead of 500 million people throughout the world. If you have clothes in the closet, food in the fridge, and a place to sleep, you are richer than 92 percent of the rest of the world!

Next Paul gives two "not to" commands. He says that those with money are not to be "arrogant" or to "put their hope in wealth." Here he warns about some of the dangers that are inherent with money and material possessions. How many times have we all seen rich people who have arrogant, prideful, boastful spirits? This condescending attitude by the rich toward those of lower financial position is condemned over and over in Scripture. (Check out James 2:1–12.)

Equally dangerous is the tendency to trust in money. Despite the phrase on our money, "In God We Trust," the cold, hard fact is that most people trust more in the money than they do in God. Money is deceptive. We become convinced that with enough of it all our problems will go away. Be honest, haven't you ever fantasized about receiving a huge inheritance or winning a big sweepstakes and never having to worry again? Satan tells us that with enough money we can buy our way out of every problem, hedge against every risk, and insure for any catastrophe. So we buy the lie and gradually rid ourselves of any perceived need for God. This may be why Paul points out in the first letter to the Corinthians (1:26–31) that not many wise, influential, or noble will come to Jesus. They have glutted themselves on all the goodies and pleasures this world has to offer. They have "put their hope in wealth" and convinced themselves that they just don't need God.

But now Paul turns his attention to the positive side of wealth. Without any explanation or apology, Paul says that it's OK to have nice things. He says that God provides us with "everything" for our enjoyment! Presumably this includes financial blessings. Wait a minute, Paul. Are you saying that it's not only OK to have money but, that it's also OK to spend some of it on ourselves and have a good time? Yes! Contrary to popular belief, our God is not a god of austerity and scarcity. Our Father has an abundance. And if he has blessed you with financial resources, it's all right to enjoy his blessings!

Paul's last directive is a positive one: "Command them to do good, to be rich in good deeds, and to be generous and willing to share." It is perfectly fine to enjoy some of your wealth personally. But Paul also reminds us of the greater good we can do with our wealth. Not just as a suggestion but also as a command, Paul tells wealthy people to do good. Then to drive his point home, he turns the phrase and tells rich people to *"be rich"* not just in money but in good deeds. Instead of just being known for their wealth, they should also be known for their good deeds, their readiness to share what they have.

One of my heroes is a man named Bob Nash. Bob is low-key and sort of bashful. He would be the last person in the world to brag about himself. But I think he is a spiritual giant. Not because he can outquote the preacher from the Bible or because he has all the answers in a religious debate. No, his strength comes from a different direction. You see, Bob has built a successful company that supplies an important service. He's spent years learning the ropes and has put in a lot of long, hard hours when he would rather have been relaxing. Because of his diligence and God's blessing, Bob has prospered financially. Today Bob drives a nice car, wears stylish clothing, and can afford to do pretty much what he wishes. But the first thing that comes to my mind when I think about Bob Nash is his generosity. Bob is always ready to give when someone at church is hurting or when one of our missionaries has a need or whenever any other good work presents itself. In my mind Bob *is* the man that Paul is talking about who has been blessed financially and has become rich in good deeds.

Like a loving counselor, Paul seems unable to leave the topic without reminding his readers of the blessings that follow such a lifestyle. Notice how he promises that when we share our earthly prosperity we are setting aside eternal treasures in heaven.

Fringe Benefits of Being a Steward

Back in the old days, say a couple of thousand years ago, being a steward in the king's palace was a plum job. Granted, the guy had a big responsibility. He had to keep up with the king's business and do his bidding. Also the steward really didn't own anything of his own.

But who cared? The fringe benefits were great! The steward got to live in the king's castle. He ate the same food as the king. His wardrobe was filled with princely suits. He was chauffeured in the king's own late-model chariots with the six-way speakers pumping out tunes from the king's personal CD collection. All in all, not a bad life.

It's much the same today. As Christians we must remember who really owns the money and the things we possess. They don't belong to us; they belong to God. He owns everything. *It's all his stuff!* But just like the stewards of old, we get to enjoy God's blessings in our lives. The key is always to *hold things loosely* and *hold God tightly.*

The Critical Balance

Before we go into our next chapter, please remember this: If we allow anything to get between God and us, we are in trouble. In today's materialistic, money-driven society, Christians must be cautious. The culture tells us that our value and worth are based on our wealth and clout. All around us we see friends, coworkers, and even other Christians who have built lives focused on acquiring the stuff of this present world.

One of the places in Scripture that always makes me tremble when I read it is the parable of the sower in Matthew 13. Here Jesus analogizes the way five groups of people respond to God's message by comparing them to various types of farmland soil. One of the soil types was thorny ground. Speaking of this person, Jesus says this "is the man who hears the word, but the worries of this life *and the deceitfulness of wealth choke it [the word], making it unfruitful*" (v. 22, author's emphasis).

Wealth can be a blessing from God, but it is also a burden. With money comes responsibility. Jesus warns us that "from everyone who has been given much shall much be required; and to whom they entrusted much, of him they will ask all the more" (Luke 12:48b NASB).

Christians with money have temptations and spiritual battles that other people don't face: How much is too much? How will I teach my children not to love and trust money? Where is *my own* faith—in God or in money? How can I avoid elitism and remain close to hurting people?

In upcoming chapters I hope to share some of the concepts that my study and experience are helping me understand. I certainly don't claim to have all the answers to questions about money. You and I will be fellow strugglers in this study. So let's make a deal. As we progress through the coming pages and talk about controlling debt, managing our income, and planning for the future, I'll pray for you, and you pray for me. Together we'll seek the Father's heart and direction in matters of money and finance.

Part II

The ABCs of
Christian Money
Management

ALL RIGHT, I'LL ADMIT IT. A title like the one above isn't very creative. But don't assume that I'm the kind of guy who goes into Baskin Robbins and orders vanilla. No sir-ree! I'm always up for something different. Why, I'd probably get a scoop of chicken ripple if they had it! After all, I ran an ad agency for over twenty-five years. Our stock-in-trade was in coming up with fresh, creative ways to present ideas and products. I understand the benefits of a well-turned phrase. Many times I have sent artists, writers, and other right-brain sorts back to the drawing board with directions to bring back something with more pizzazz.

But there was something else that I used to tell my staff: "It isn't creative if it doesn't sell!" They understood my point: No matter how innovative the design, an advertisement is worthless if it doesn't communicate a clear benefit. Haven't you ever seen a great television commercial that captured your attention? Maybe you even told a friend about it. But when she asked you what it was advertising, you drew a blank. Such a commercial fails in the communication process.

So even though the ABC title may be a cliché, I'm sticking with it because it says what I want to communicate. In this chapter the ABCs stand for the following:

Acknowledging Who Owns Our Money

Budgeting Our Money

Controlling Our Money

I am convinced that if we can get these three concepts under our belts, 90 percent of our money problems will evaporate. Most financial problems have far less to do with knowledge than with behavior. So as I share some data with you on these three points, I also hope to help you get rid of some of the "stinkin' thinkin'" that leads to destructive financial behavior patterns.

If you're ready, let's go.

3

Acknowledge Who Owns Your Money

THE YOUNG MISSIONARY had looked forward to this day for more than five years. Finally he was back in the States ready to visit with Mr. Jackson. Mr. Jackson was more than the young missionary's mentor; he was also his largest financial partner. As Mr. Jackson's secretary ushered him into the office, the missionary remembered other visits when the two had prayed and discussed the people he was teaching and baptizing. Mr. Jackson always loved these stories of Jesus' power to change hearts and save souls. The young missionary often suspected that, had the businessman been a bit younger and in better health, he too would be serving God from the mission field.

Mr. Jackson was on his feet behind the big desk, offering a warm handshake and his ever-present smile. The meeting began with the usual pleasantries, but soon the conversation turned to the mission work. As the discussion finally began to wind down, the two men knelt together on the floor in front of the desk and prayed. Never one to waste time, Mr. Jackson was immediately on his feet, reaching across the desk for his personal checkbook. When he had finished writing the check, he tore it from the pad and handed it to his missionary friend. The young missionary looked down at the check and tried not to gulp too loudly. He could hardly believe Mr. Jackson's generosity. It was a check for $50,000!

"This is way too much," protested the missionary.

"Not at all," responded Mr. Jackson. "My business has been doing well, and I can afford it. Besides, your needs are great, and your work is vital. It is my way of helping you reach the lost for the Master."

With the words barely out of his mouth, Mr. Jackson's secretary opened the door and leaned in. "There's a call on line four. You'd better take it right now."

As the businessman picked up the phone, the young missionary looked through the huge picture window behind the desk. His eyes canvassed the acres of manufacturing buildings on his friend's corporate campus. As he looked across the parking lot filled with hundreds of employee cars, the missionary remembered the hard years of work that had built this enterprise. But his daydream ended abruptly when he noticed Mr. Jackson's troubled face and heard him say, "Are you sure it's that bad? OK, call the board into an urgent session. I'll meet your team downstairs in five minutes."

As the businessman hung up the phone, the missionary said, "I don't mean to pry, but it sounds like there's a real problem?"

"That's an understatement," said Mr. Jackson. "Right now, I really need your prayers. That was my chief financial officer calling with some pretty sobering news. It appears that our entire shipment of raw rubber from South American has been destroyed. Our international insurer doesn't cover this type of loss, and without that rubber next season's production will fall by over 90 percent." Then, somberly, he added, "This may put us out of business!"

"I'm so sorry. Besides my prayers, which you will have, what else can I do?"

"I'm going to have to ask that you return the check," said Mr. Jackson.

"Of course," said the missionary, handing back the piece of paper, "I understand."

Taking the check, the businessman tore it in half and dropped it in the trash can beneath his desk. Then, without saying a word, he pulled his checkbook out again, opened it, wrote another check, and handed it across the mahogany desk.

Somewhat surprised, the missionary looked at the new check and turned pale. It was a check for $100,000! "I don't understand," he stammered, "you just asked me to return the $50,000 check when you got the terrible news. Why are you giving me twice as much now?"

Mr. Jackson leaned forward and rested his chin on his large hands, and, speaking in a low, deliberate voice, he said, "You're right, I just got some devastating news. Humanly speaking, there's nothing I can do to fix the problem. So now it's between just the Lord and me. I want him to know where my trust is."

What faith! I doubt that mine is that strong. Is yours? But if we're ever going to get it right, we have to understand what Mr. Jackson understood. He got the big picture: We really don't own anything; it's all God's! Just like King Solomon of old, Mr. Jackson realized that we come into this world without anything, and we will one day check out without anything. All the stuff in the middle is just on loan.[1]

Three Great Principles of Godly Giving

Once we realize that all we have is God's, then the question is one of stewardship. What are we going to do with that money? Serious Christians have always realized that a portion of their money should be given to godly causes. Over the years I have grown to believe that there are at least three great principles of godly giving.

Principle 1: God expects us to give from our firstfruits. Firstfruits giving is taught in Scripture starting in the Old Testament with references well into the New Testament. I'm no theologian, but my understanding is that firstfruits sacrifices had to do with God's expectation that his people should always set aside the first part of their crops and produce as a thank offering for his goodness. Additionally, these firstfruits were to be unblemished, the best available. Simply put, the idea was that the *first* and the *best* always belonged to God.[2]

Godly giving today is at its best when this principle is kept in mind. In addition to the Scripture references you will find in the endnotes for this chapter, another passage has become the marching orders for the Diggs family over the years: "Honor the LORD from your wealth, and from the first of all your produce; so your barns will be filled with plenty and your vats will overflow with new wine" (Prov. 3:9–10 NASB).

Years ago our family made the decision to give to God from the top. By that I mean that God gets the first part of our income. We would give up a lot of other expenditures before we would fail to give our gift to the Lord. It also means that we give from our gross income. When we determine the percentage we plan to give, that percentage is based on gross income before we deduct taxes, Social Security, or Medicare withholdings.

Am I trying to lay down a legalistic formula here and say that everyone has to do it just like us? No. But I am suggesting that every Christian needs to spend time in prayer and soul-searching to determine how best to honor God from his or her financial wealth.

The best time to formulate your giving strategy is now. I have learned the hard way the importance of planning our giving *before* life's pressures come to bear. It's much easier to hear God's prompting without the stress of too little money or the temptations that come with having too much money. If we wait until we have financial stress in our lives, it's too easy to compromise and excuse a selfish attitude.

One strategy that helped us was to open a separate bank account to set money aside just for spiritual giving. We even titled it the "first-fruits" account. This way, when we received income, we deposited a percentage of it directly into our firstfruits account where it sat until we needed it. This little discipline helped us in two ways: First, it kept us from accidentally mixing God's money with our other funds and spending it. Second, it served as a clear, tangible reminder that those dollars were spoken for. They belonged to God; they were our first-fruits to him.

Principle 2: Giving should be a joyful experience. Has anyone ever given you something with a scowl on his face? You knew he really didn't want to do it, but someone else was forcing him to release the goods. Maybe it was your little brother when your mom forced him to share the ice cream. Possibly it was a dishonest client when the judge ruled in your favor in a civil case. Or maybe it was a sales manager who resisted paying your commission until his boss told him to do so. Sure, you ended up with the money, but you went away feeling like you needed to take a shower!

If you have ever had such an experience, then imagine how God must feel when his children—the ones he has gifted with life itself—are too selfish to share with others. The simple point is this: We have been given so we can give. When we fail to understand this, we break the heart of God!

Paul opened the window to God's mind this way: "Each one must do just as he has purposed in his heart, not grudgingly or under compulsion, *for God loves a cheerful giver*" (2 Cor. 9:7, author's emphasis, NASB).

Maybe it's a slight exaggeration, but to help me remember this point, I have written the word *hilarious* in the margin of my Bible next to "cheerful giver." This helps me stay focused when it comes to giving. And it helps me overcome my natural tendency to find excuses not to give.

The Unwelcomed Test

I remember a time when God gave me a "giving" test that I only got 50 percent right. It was in the 1970s. Bonnie and I had just begun the business, and dollars were fairly tight, but we were glad when an old college buddy and another missionary came to our home for a visit. Actually, it was more than just a visit. It turned into a two-week stay while they met with churches in the Nashville area to raise funds for a bus ministry they were starting. As the days passed, it became increasingly obvious that they were getting nowhere fast. At the end of every day, I would ask about their success; and every day they told me the sad news that no one had offered to help.

I'm not exactly sure which day it happened, but finally my gray matter kicked in, and I realized that maybe they wouldn't get any of the money they needed—and I'd be the only one left to help! So with a greater sense of urgency, I began inquiring about their success every night. And every night they confirmed the worst.

Finally the day came when they had to leave, and I was faced with a dilemma. Either I could shake their hands and send them off, knowing that they would not be able to start a bus ministry, or I could take a large percentage of the company's resources out of the bank and give them the $3,000 they needed.

What to do? Did I really believe all those things I said about trusting God and putting him first? I was really struggling before the Lord on this one!

Today some of the details have gotten a little fuzzy, but I believe it was Bonnie who finally challenged me to do the right thing. So I wrote the check, and just as they were about to leave, I handed it to them. To tell you the truth, the check almost stuck to my hand. I could hardly let go of it. But I did.

I said I only got 50 percent on the test. On the one hand I did give the money, but on the other hand my heart wasn't really in it. God is good, and he can do his work even when our motives aren't the best. Our friends were able to build a ministry that blessed many other people.

Beating the Devil at His Own Game

Through the years I have improved a lot in this area. There are still times when I'm selfish and greedy, and at those times God still has to deal with me. But I'm doing better and enjoying it more. One little trick that helped me through some financially stingy days was this: When I heard of a need, immediately I would think and pray about it. Then I would determine how much I thought I should give. If the devil tempted me to back down, I doubled the amount I was planning to give! Believe me, that little method works!

Principle 3: We should give as we have been given. God doesn't expect us to give what we don't have. There is no place in Christian giving for competition or comparison with others. Each Christian's giving is a personal experience based on his or her financial ability. From the earliest days God has made allowances for the financial disparity among his people. In Old Testament days the better-heeled Jews were expected to bring a sacrificial lamb, while poorer followers were permitted to bring less expensive doves and pigeons.[3]

I think of Matthew 6 as the "when you" chapter. On three different occasions in that chapter Jesus says, "When you," in referring to the Christian disciplines of giving, praying, and fasting. In each case he gives his followers directions on how to give, pray, and fast. Interestingly, Jesus makes a strong point of the personal, private nature of each of the disciplines. Listen to what he says about giving:

> _When you give to the poor, do not sound a trumpet_
> _before you, as the hypocrites do in the synagogues and in the_
> _streets, so that they may be honored by men. Truly I say to_
> _you, they have their reward in full. But when you give to the_
> _poor, do not let your left hand know what your right hand_
> _is doing so that your giving will be in secret; and your_
> _Father who sees what is done in secret will reward you_
> _(vv. 2–4 NASB)._

Since our giving is never to be done for human acknowledgment or praise, the only one left to please is God. And he doesn't care how many dollars you give compared to anyone else. Paul says it well in 1 Corinthians 16:1–2: "Now concerning the collection for the saints, as I directed the churches of Galatia so do you also. On the first day of every week _each one of you is to put aside and save, as he may prosper_, so that no collections be made when I come" (NASB, author's emphasis).

Should a Christian Tithe?

I want to address three issues before leaving this topic. I mention these because they are points on which I respectfully disagree with some other writers. Feel free to consider my conclusions, pray about them, and then do as you believe is right.

Issue 1: Should a Christian tithe? I am fully aware that many writers today teach that Christians should tithe, or give 10 percent of their money to God. Because of the battle I've fought in my own life against legalism, I'd like to share a few thoughts about this teaching. While I accept full responsibility for my comments, I am borrowing some ideas from Alger Fitch's excellent book, _What the Bible Says About Money._[4]

Since man first began to relate to God, the question has been, What and how much should one give? Much is said in the

Old Testament about tithing. Contrary to what many people believe, tithing did not originate with the Law of Moses. Early in the Genesis account we see Abraham tithing to Melchizedek the priest.[5] Additionally, the concept of tithing isn't found only in the Bible. Various pagan cultures, such as the Greeks who worshiped Hercules and Apollo, also tithed. Arabians, Egyptians, Babylonians, Phoenicians, and Romans were familiar with tithing as well. Suffice it to say, God's people were expected to tithe. By the time of Moses, tithing was the law of the land for the Jewish nation.

I find it curious, however, that when we come to the New Testament there seem to be no directives to any of the newly formed Christian communities about tithing. Paul has a lot to say about giving yet never mentions the word *tithe* in his directives to the Christian church. Other first-century records are silent on the subject as well. In second-century writings, when tithing is mentioned, the emphasis is on followers' giving more than the tithe because of the grace they have received.

Back to my earlier point: I hesitate to bind on others what I don't see clear and concrete teaching for in the New Testament. However, in each of our lives, we must be totally open and honest before God. And I must tell you that in our family we like the concept of tithing for several reasons.

First, by tithing we have some structure, or purpose, to our giving. As Paul told the Corinthians, our giving should be planned, or "purposed."[6] I know me, and I know that without a plan, or structure, I find excuses not to do as I should. Tithing keeps me focused and precludes me from shirking my God-ordained responsibilities.

Second, tithing is a divine concept. Admittedly, as Christians we are under grace and not the Law. But as Fitch points out, "For a Christian under the Gospel to give less than a Jew under the Law, is not an evidence of grace but of disgrace. . . . The tithe is an appropriate starting line for those in the race, but an inadequate goal at which to stop running forward."

Third, as one old sage put it, "The greatest danger with tithing is that some good church folks might use it as an excuse to stop at a tenth."

Today's church is dreadfully out of step with God's heart on the topic of giving. Estimates suggest that the average Christian today is giving less than 3 percent back to the Lord—with many giving nothing at all! Friends, this is terrible! Barry L. Cameron says that if godly people faithfully tithed there would be an extra $219 billion available every year for kingdom purposes. Based on the estimated 350,000 churches in America, that's an additional $625,000 for each one.[7] Wow! Think of what could be getting done!

Issue 2: Must I give only to my church? Another of today's popular teachings is that one's offerings should be given only at his home church. I suppose some of this is a reaction to all of the televangelists of the '70s and '80s who urged people to send them their tithes. Local churches in many areas suffered because of this.

Without question it makes logical sense that a Christian's first and primary commitment should be to the fellowship of which he is a part. That is why when I'm traveling and visit another church, generally I save most of my contribution until I'm back home and can give it to my home church. After all, it's my home congregation that depends on me. It needs and deserves my support.

So, if you are one of those people who excuse not giving your contribution to your home church because you "just don't agree with how they spend the money," then something needs to change. Either it's time to find another congregation that is more in line with the truth, or maybe it's time to do a "check up from the neck up" of your own commitment level.

However, with all of that said, let me put a little different spin on the subject. As I've already mentioned, I fear anything that turns an act of love and charity into an act of obligation and legalism. As an active member of my own congregation, I know what our budgetary needs are. And generally speaking, I'm pretty much aware of whether we are meeting those needs. At times when we are falling short, our family gives a little more than normal. When we are meeting and exceeding the budget needs, I feel more comfortable giving some of my money to other efforts. While my first obligation is to my church, I try to keep my eyes wide open to other opportunities the Lord shows me from day to day. I don't want to be like the priest and the Levite who, likely on their way to a church service, couldn't find the time to show compassion to the man along the road who had been robbed and beaten.[8] One thing that appeals to me about Jesus is the way he moved and walked freely in the Spirit—always ready unto every good work.

I want to see the poor people that God puts before me. After all, more than twenty of the Hebrew psalms center on God's love and care for the poor. John, one of Jesus' closest disciples, wrote: "But whoever has the world's goods, and sees his brother in need and closes his heart against him, how does the love of God abide in him?" (1 John 3:17 NASB).

But it's not just the poor who need our help. What about the missionary you may know who has barely enough to keep body and soul together? What about the young woman who would go to school to become a Third World doctor but doesn't have the funds? What about the flood victims who have lost their homes? What about the fledgling radio ministry that reaches into China?

Issue 3: High Purposes Versus High Pressure. Finally, let's contrast some of today's high-pressure, coercive fund-raising techniques with the way God encouraged his people to raise money. Notice how the passage in 2 Corinthians cited earlier begins with the teaching that giving should be on a free-will basis. There are several refreshing passages in Exodus where God encourages giving without today's tacky tactics:

> *Tell the sons of Israel to raise a contribution for Me;*
> from every man whose heart moves him you shall raise
> My contribution *(25:2 NASB, author's emphasis).*
>
> *Take from among you a contribution to the Lord;* who-
> ever is of a willing heart, let him bring it as the Lord's
> contribution *(35:5 NASB, author's emphasis).*
>
> *Everyone whose heart stirred him and everyone whose*
> *spirit moved him came and brought the* LORD's *contribution*
> *for the work of the tent of meeting and for all its service and*
> *for the holy garments (35:21 NASB).*

And look at the results when human manipulation and high pressure are replaced by people with a holy goal and a heart for God:

> *They received from Moses all the contributions*
> *which the sons of Israel had brought to perform the work*
> *in the construction of the sanctuary. And they still con-*
> *tinued bringing to him freewill offerings every morning . . .*
> *So Moses issued a command, and a proclamation was*
> *circulated throughout the camp, saying, "Let no man or*
> *woman any longer perform work for the contributions*
> *of the sanctuary." Thus the people were restrained from*
> *bringing any more. For the material they had was sufficient*
> *and more than enough for all the work, to perform it*
> *(36:3, 6–7 NASB).*

My goal here isn't to be critical of Christians who are charged with raising the funds needed for kingdom work, but I have to wonder if sometimes we don't slip into the world's way of doing business. Honestly, I don't always know where the line should be drawn in these efforts, but I do know one thing: Greater good is accomplished when prayer takes precedence over strategy.

Some Personal Blessings of Godly Giving

Without question one of the greatest blessings that comes from giving is the way it frees the giver from the tyranny of money. When we give our money away, it's no longer *our* money. It's hard to remain a slave to a master who is no longer present.

Giving helps us stay involved in others' lives. In today's high-octane world we tend to stay busy and focused on ourselves too much. Our comfortable cars have great radios that insulate us from people who are hurting. Our homes have become personal fortresses that all too often are used to close out the world. Giving is a good way to become involved in the lives of other people who have needs that we can address.

Giving brings personal joy. If you are unaware of this fact, it may be because you've never chosen to give sacrificially. History books are replete with stories of greedy, crusty old businessmen who spent their lives making and hoarding money only to die in misery and solitude. I have nothing against people leaving money for good works after they die, but the best time to give is when you can get the enjoyment of seeing others benefit from your gifts.

Have you heard the story of the unpopular pig? He was jealous of the cow in the pen next to him because everyone loved the bovine's gentle spirit and kind eyes. Grudgingly, the pig admitted that the cow gave lots of milk and cream but maintained that pigs give more. "Why," the chubby little guy complained, "we pigs give ham and bacon, and people pickle our feet. I don't see why you cows are so much more popular."

Gently the cow said, "Maybe it's because we cows give while we're still living."

Finally, I want to discuss the relationship between giving to God and receiving blessings back from God. You will never find anyone who has less patience than I have with what I call the Gospel Greed

Merchants. This has been a pet peeve of mine for a long time. In my earlier book *Free to Succeed*, I had several things to say about this teaching. You know the type of people I'm talking about. We see them on television, hear them on radio, get their periodicals, and sometimes run into them in our own churches. These are the people who raise money by playing to greedy hearts. They talk of God as though he is nothing more than a cosmic game-show host who pays off like a heavenly slot machine. The more you give, so the message goes, the more you will get back. Some of these folks have even gone so far as to promise percentages of return. If you give a certain number of dollars, you'll get such and such back in return. Whether we call it the "name it and claim it" theology or prosperity religion, I believe it's wrong!

Today's problems with money and ministry aren't new. There have always been people who wanted to get paid for their good deeds. In 1 Timothy 6:5, Paul talks about the "constant friction between men of depraved mind and deprived of the truth, *who suppose that godliness is a means of gain*" (NASB, author's emphasis). Just a few lines later in verse 10 (NASB), the apostle warns, "The love of money is a root of all sorts of evil, and some by longing for it have wandered away from the faith and pierced themselves with many griefs." Several years earlier, in Luke 12:15, Jesus had warned, "Beware, and be on your guard against every form of greed" (NASB).

My greatest concern is that prosperity theology can lead to perverted motives. When I make a contribution, it should be to please God and help others, not primarily for a personal return on my investment. When I give in order to get back more, all sorts of wrong motives come into play. Suddenly, what should be a loving act becomes an act of selfishness and personal promotion.

However, to leave this subject here would be unfair and unbalanced. I believe the Bible does indicate that God blesses those who give.

"Give, and it will be given to you. A good measure, pressed down, shaken together, and running over, will be poured into your lap. For with the measure you use, it will be measured to you" (Luke 6:38).

Is God sending us mixed messages? Is he the author of confusion? Not at all! Do I have answers to all the ins and outs on this issue? No. But I have spent a lot of years thinking about it, and I do have a few observations (that are subject to change as I study and learn more) that make sense to me today. First, I believe that God is perfectly capable of searching and knowing each of our hearts. And while the principles he wants each of us to learn are the same, I don't believe he always uses the same methodology with each believer.

For example, as the father of four children, I want each of my kids to accept certain common principles. However, because each child has a different personality, I have to approach each of the four in a different way. It's not that the principles I'm teaching vary from one child to another; it's simply that I use different methods to teach the same principles because each child responds differently.

God works with us in the same way. He wants to bless each of us with as much as we can handle, but he loves me too much to give me a blessing that I'm unable to control and that could lead to spiritual destruction. So if he blesses and challenges each of his children differently, while always teaching the same principles, doesn't it follow that God is able to give different children different blessings too? For instance, Christian 1 is blessed with the ability to sing while Christian 2 wonders why he can't carry a tune in a bucket. Maybe it's because God knows that Christian 2 would use the gift of music in a worldly way. And God loves him too much to allow him to lose his soul because he mishandled his gift.

I wonder if it isn't the same way with financial issues. Rather than asking God to give us wealth, maybe we should pray for him to search our hearts and bless us only with those things we can handle. Then if wealth comes your way, your mandate is to give and steward those monies properly. And to the degree you show yourself a worthy administrator of those blessings, God is able to bless you with more. The following passage seems to support this view:

> *Now this I say, he who sows sparingly shall also reap sparingly, and he who sows bountifully will also reap bountifully . . . And God is able to make all grace abound to you, so that always having all sufficiency in everything, you may have an abundance for every good deed . . . Now He who supplies seed to the sower and bread for food, will supply and multiply your seed for sowing and increase the harvest of your righteousness; you will be enriched in everything for all liberality, which through us is producing thanksgiving to God (2 Cor. 9:6, 8, 10–11 NASB).*

Note how Paul suggests that God gives financial resources to those who are already using what they have in the right way. If one gives bountifully, with a cheerful heart, void of selfishness, God may be more inclined to continue flowing blessings into that good Christian's life. Maybe this is why some Christians are convinced they cannot outgive God—because they have tried and failed!

The only place in Scripture that I know where God tells his people to test him is on this same topic in the Old Testament Book of Malachi. Speaking on God's behalf, Malachi came on the scene about 430 years before Jesus. Despite hundreds of years of prophetic teaching and exhortation, the Israeli culture did not bear the evidence of their labor. Most of the people were corrupt—as were many of the priests. But God was still in charge, on the throne, sovereign. In chapter 3, Malachi confronts the people about their selfish hearts and ungiving spirits:

Will a man rob God? Yet you are robbing Me! But you say, "How have we robbed You? In tithes and offerings. You are cursed with a curse, for you are robbing Me, the whole nation of you! Bring the whole tithe into the storehouse, so that there may be food in My house, and test Me now in this," *says the* LORD *of hosts, "if I will not open for you the windows of heaven and pour out for you a blessing until it overflows. Then I will rebuke the devourer for you, so that it may not destroy the fruits of the ground; nor will your vine in the field cast its grapes . . . and all the nations will call you blessed, for you shall be a* delightful *land" (vv. 8–12 NASB, author's emphasis).*

There is so much to say about this passage, but for my purposes at this time, note the following two points:

1. God is upset that his people have "robbed" him by not giving as they should.
2. He tells them to change their ways and to test him to see if he does not bless their giving in three ways: a blessing from heaven, crop protection, and honor from other nations.

To Revisit an Earlier Story . . .

Do you remember the two missionaries I told you about earlier in this chapter? Despite the struggle that went on in my own heart, God took my mustard seed-sized faith and blessed it. After those missionaries left, life went back to normal, or so I thought. It never occurred to me that God would respond to our gift the way he did. Over the next several weeks, it was as if God had opened the windows of heaven! At the agency we had an influx of new accounts and blessings that was totally unexpected. The $3,000 gift was more than replaced by God's abundant hand! Humanly speaking, there was absolutely no rational explanation.

Why did God bless me when I had had such an internal battle and had almost not given the missionaries my check? I don't know for sure. But maybe God realized that I had not given out of greed or simply to get more in return. Maybe he looked into a young man's heart and saw potential. And like the loving Father he is, God used my paltry gift to teach me a lesson in grace and abundant giving that I'm able to share with you more than twenty years later.

The Bottom Line Is the Bottom Line

Ultimately, what really matters is what really matters. Or as one tongue-tied linguist put it, "The bottom line is the bottom line." The bedrock principle that we must remember is summed up in Jesus' words, "It is more blessed to give than to receive" (Acts 20:35). My goal is not to get it backwards.

4

Budget
Your Money

 *WE HAD TALKED* until there really was nothing more to say. Marty (I frequently don't use people's real names) sat in my office thoughtfully reflecting on what we had just discussed. He was either going to have to make some tough changes in his life, or things were going to go from bad to worse. His life was upside down, his personal relationships were faltering, and his finances were in a mess. This particular evening we had spent most of our time discussing the latter. At twenty-eight years old, this college-educated bachelor was so loaded with debt and financial obligations he didn't know which way to go. Like so many others, Marty had no real idea how much he was spending each month. Since he had failed to control his money, his money was now controlling him.

Contrast that with Phil and Penny. I had known these two good folks for some time. They had all the job stresses and personal challenges that any couple with college-age children does. A few days after attending a class I had taught on financial management, Phil came up to me with a big smile and said, "I just want to tell you about something good that has happened in our lives. After your class on budgeting, Penny and I decided it was time to give it a try. And guess what?"

"What?" I asked.

"We found money we didn't know we had! After preparing a written budget like you suggested, we've found $300 per month for savings, and we've been able to increase our giving by $40 per month!"

The Lay of the Land

The primary reason most families get into financial trouble is because they haven't made adequate plans not to. Relatively few families crash and burn financially because of a medical catastrophe, a bad business investment, or because they are swindled. The vast majority of Americans who are in acute financial pain are there because of poor planning and virtually no record keeping. I suspect that less than 10 percent of all households in this country work from a planned, written, monthly budget. And without such a document your family finances are a disaster looking for a place to happen.

No one would start building a home without a blueprint. Would you leave on a long road trip to a new destination without a map or at least some directions? I'll bet even Tiger Woods wouldn't play a tournament without walking the course first. Yet every month, all over the country, people get their paychecks and spend them with no written plan. Then when the money runs out before the month does, they're back in the same old downward spiral of stalling bill collectors and living on credit cards.

Budgeting, Dieting, and Root Canals

In this chapter I want to share some practical thoughts on the *B* word—*budgeting*. Yeah, I know. No one likes to budget. We associate it with pain and austerity. Budgeting means scrimping, having to say no to all the things we want to do. Budgeting, dieting, root canals—they all sort of go together, don't they?

Believe me, I know how you feel. I don't like budgeting either. But I learned a long time ago that there are usually two ways to do anything, the right way and the easy way. Although I call it the easy way, it's actually only easy in the short term. As we discussed in chapter 1, those "easy monthly payments" have destroyed many families' financial health. When you think about it, isn't this the root of a lot of our pain: putting immediate gratification ahead of long-term planning? Ever since Esau sold his birthright for a bowl of Jacob's stew, people have been making bad long-term decisions to enjoy short-term gains.

There's a Lot in a Name

Marketing people learned a long time ago that names mean a lot. They affect how we perceive the world around us. For instance, instead of calling them "used cars," some auto dealers use the phrase "pre-owned automobiles." Television reruns are called "encore presenta-tions," and credit card fees are called "service charges." Recently the network news reported that federal nuclear energy officials want to put a high-level nuclear waste dump in the Yucca Mountains just north of Las Vegas, Nevada. As you might suspect, the good citizens of that area aren't enthusiastic about the plan. But not to worry. The government boys aren't going to call it a nuclear waste dump; they're calling it a "repository." Ah, that makes it seem so much better, doesn't it?

Instead of calling it a budget, why not find a word that speaks to the benefits that come from budgeting? After all, a budget allows you to manage your wealth so it's there when you need it. It gives you the freedom to live life with joy, peace, and dignity instead of dodging bill collectors and never having the money to invest, save, or give away. So why not look at the positive side of having a budget? Why not think of it as your personal financial freedom plan? Ah, sounds better, doesn't it?

Why We Don't Budget

There are about as many reasons for not budgeting as there are people without budgets. But most of these "reasons" probably fall into one of three broad categories:

"I don't know where to start!" These are the folks who feel overwhelmed by life and the money pressures they are facing, and one more straw will be enough to break the camel's back. They want less stress and confusion. From their perspective, doing a budget is just one more complication they don't need! What these people fail to realize is that a budget is the first step toward relieving their pain. Just as it's painful to lance a boil, it's the only way true healing can begin. The good news is that a budget is simple and not very time-consuming. A few minutes spent in the budgeting process just before the month begins can bring financial balance and tranquility for the month ahead.

"I'm not a geek. Money stuff confuses me!" This is like saying, "I'm not a chef, so I'm not going to eat." To handle your income properly doesn't require any special classes or degrees. All it requires is a little basic knowledge and a willingness to change one's behavior. It's not a question of whether your income is going to be spent. The only question is, Are you going to control the spending, or is the spending going to control you?

"Budgeting is such a downer; it's such a negative thing to do!" I take special exception to this complaint. The source of stress in our lives comes from the feeling that we don't have control over our environment. As long as the steering wheel in your car functions properly and allows you to turn it as you wish, you're relaxed. But how would you feel if the steering wheel suddenly stopped responding as you are driving down a mountain road? That loss of control would lead to a lot of stress, wouldn't it? It's the same with budgeting. When a person seizes control and begins to take charge of his money, something wonderful happens. There is a rightful sense of

power and control, a sense of having control over what happens in life. All in all, it's a pretty good feeling.

Another Way to Look at a Budget

Allow me to present the other side of the case for budgeting. The following list of budget benefits is only a beginning. You could probably add other points to the list, but for starters here are some of the pluses of having a budget:

- No more creditors calling the house at all hours.
- Never having the waiter come back to the table to inform you that your credit card "is over its limit and didn't clear."
- Using cash in the bank to pay for a Hawaiian vacation.
- Never having to stall one creditor to pay another.
- Never regretting the gifts you bought for Christmas when the January bills arrive.
- Always having money on hand when a worthy need comes along.
- Never having another fight with your spouse over money issues.

Five Keys to a Successful Budget

Five things will help any family develop a successful, long-term budget, or personal financial freedom plan:

1. Teamwork is important. The most important human relationship in any person's life is the one you have with your spouse. If you are married, you and your partner are one. This means that, ideally, all the important, life-shaping decisions should be made together. In my opinion, it is a real mistake for one person in a marriage to take ownership of the money and budgeting.

When this occurs, usually one of two things is at play: In some cases one person simply refuses to be involved because of disinterest or confusion about money issues. By behaving this way, the person leaves his or her mate stuck with having to make all the decisions alone. This is an unkind way to treat a person you love.

In other cases one of the partners is dominant and wants to control the other person, and money is one way of doing this. More often than not this occurs when a husband wants to show his wife who's boss. When a marriage has this sort of problem, the issues usually go far beyond money. There may be a need for spiritual and marital counseling. But for the purposes of this book, suffice it to say that no loving mate should use money to control and dominate his or her spouse. Many couples actually find that by coming together on money management issues they strengthen their relationship and grow even closer.

Before moving on, I do want to put a sharp point on one thing. While I accept the biblical concept of male leadership within the family, I do not believe that it necessarily follows that the husband is always the best money manager. I bring this point up because a lot of Christian couples struggle with it. As a matter of fact, Bonnie and I did. Before we were married, we both wanted to prepare ourselves to be the best wife and husband we could be. So we prayed, took a marriage course in college, got counseling, talked to successfully married people, and read books. One of the books I read made a big point about how the husband should handle all the money and pay all the bills. So, being too young to discern good advice from bad, I took the author's comments to heart. I told Bonnie that after we got married I would be handling the money and paying the bills. Being smarter than I am, Bonnie realized this would save her a lot of grief, so she readily agreed with my idea.

To make a long story short, it wasn't long before I realized that I'd made a mistake. I was working lots of long hours starting the company, and I had all the budgeting I could do with the business. I swallowed my pride and asked Bonnie if she would mind handling the bill paying at home. Thankfully, she agreed, and the rest, as they say, has been history. For the past twenty-five years my best buddy has overseen our monthly financial matters and kept things in far better order than I ever would have.

My point is this: In every relationship one person usually has more ability and interest in money management than the other. There is certainly nothing wrong with allowing that person to use his or her natural gifts in the marriage. But, whichever person manages the money, he or she should remain humble and open. And, conversely, the other mate should not ignore his or her responsibility to be a partner by remaining involved and engaged in the budgeting process.

2. Learn what your true income is. Few people really know what their true income is. By "true income," I'm referring to the actual number of dollars your family brings in each month. These are net dollars after withholdings have been made for taxes, Social Security, and so forth. This is reliable income that isn't dependent on unpredictable overtime, bonuses, or wishful thinking. The only way to have an accurate, workable budget is to know exactly how many spendable dollars you have available.

3. Do your budget on a monthly basis. I like to encourage people to prepare a new budget every month. As you'll see in step 5, this won't be a matter of reinventing the wheel each month since your budget's format will already be in place. But by preparing a monthly budget, you gain at least two benefits:

- It forces you to review and rethink your spending habits regularly.
- It encourages good husband-wife communications.

Many couples find that the best time to prepare the next month's budget plan is in the last three or four days of the present month. This way the budget is finished before the new month begins, but by doing it on the eve of the new month, they have a good idea of what's just ahead financially.

4. *Do your budget in written form!* This may be the most important yet the most overlooked of any of the five steps. Whether it's a contract, a new law, or the history of a nation, it is never considered definitive until it is written down. Any concept, until it is reduced to writing, is just an idea that is open to revision.

If your family budget is going to have life-changing impact, it deserves to be written down. By putting a budget in writing, it becomes an important document that is taken more seriously. There are at least two benefits to a written budget:

Clarity. A written budget can be reviewed and discussed by all parties involved. Everyone can either accept, reject, or suggest changes. Open and informed discussion is easy, and no one is able to say later that he or she didn't understand.

Commitment. Once final changes are made and agreed on, it is easier to commit to a budget that is in written form.

5. *Prepare your budget in order of priority.* Many people have found that the best way to prepare a budget is to ask themselves the question, "If I don't have enough money to do everything I want to do right now, where will my first dollars go?" Then they prepare a budget in order of priority. Different people will have different priorities. What is critical in one family may be viewed as simply important, or even optional, in another family. In our family's hierarchy of priorities, we place our basic sustenance (food, shelter, clothing), our giving, and our moral and legal commitments to others (debts) at the top of our list. This is a personal matter of soul-searching and prayer for every Christian, and it will vary somewhat from one family to another.

Following is a budget outline that you may find helpful. However, as you develop a personal budget for your family, please rethink the order of priorities. Do they make sense in your situation? Have I included elements that don't even apply in your family's situation? Are there items that you should include in your budget that aren't part of this one?

Personal Financial Freedom Plan

Family Budget for: _____ *For the Month/Year of:* _____

EXPENSE	$ AMOUNT	% of INCOME
Giving		
Church		
Mission Efforts		
Ministries We Support		
Other		
Shelter/Housing		
Rent		
Mortgage (1st)		
Mortgage (2nd)		
Homeowner's Insurance		
Property Taxes		
Maintenance & Repairs		
Home Improvement		
Yard Care		
Exterminator		
Furniture		
Other		
Utilities		
Electric		
Gas		
Water		
Sewer		
Garbage Collection		
Computer/Modem		
Telephone (Hard-wired)		
Cell Phone		
Long Distance		
Other		
Food		
Groceries		
Necessary Restaurant Visits (i.e., for business)		
Other		
Clothing		
Child 1		
Child 2		
Child 3		
Child 4		
Mother		
Dad		
Other		
Debt Service (Hopefully, in time, this section will become shorter and shorter.)		
Car 1		
Car 2		
Bank Credit Card		
Educational Loan		
Store Credit Card		
Other		

EXPENSE	$ AMOUNT	% of INCOME
Transportation		
Gas/Diesel		
Oil Change		
Tires/Repairs/Maintenance		
Car Insurance		
License/Tax/Tag		
Parking		
Toll Road Fees		
Next Car Set-Aside (No More Car Loans!)		
Other		
Medical		
Health Insurance		
Doctor Visit &/or Co-Pay		
Dentist Visit &/or Co-Pay		
Optometrist Visit &/or Co-Pay		
Eyewear/Dentures/etc.		
Drugs &/or Prescriptions		
Therapy		
Other		
Other Insurance		
Life (Dad)		
Life (Wife)		
Life (Children)		
Disability		
Umbrella		
Long-term Care		
Other		
Children		
Allowances		
Child Care		
Baby-Sitters		
Lessons		
Athletic Teams		
Activities/Field Trips		
Lunches		
Birthday Party Gifts		
Future Weddings		
Other		
Gifts and Presents for Family and Friends		
Christmas		
Birthday		
Wedding		
Anniversary		
Holidays		
Other		
Education		
Homeschool Curriculum		
Private School		

EXPENSE	$ AMOUNT	% of INCOME
Education (continued)		
Uniforms		
College		
School Supplies		
Public School Expenses		
Adult Study Courses		
Other		
Entertainment and Goofing Off		
Cable TV		
Recreational Eating Out		
Vacation		
Magazine/Newspapers		
Films/Tapes		
Parties		
Play Money		
Other		
Savings and Investments		
"Murphy Fund" (Goal: $2,000)		
"I Don't Need This Job" Fund (Goal: 6–12 Months' Expenses)		
Investments		
Other		
Miscellaneous		
Dues/Membership Fees		
Toiletries/Personal Care		
Barber/Beauty		
Dry Cleaning & Laundry		
Postage/Mailing/Delivery		
Pet Expenses		
Other		

Understanding the Personal Financial Freedom Plan Chart

As you develop your first month's PFFP, you may have all sorts of questions. Not to worry—a little experience and some trial and error go a long way here. But to help you through some of the land mines, the following thoughts may be beneficial.

Don't be overly optimistic. Things often cost more than we expect. Murphy's Law has a way of kicking in at the worst moment. I always prefer to err on the side of caution. Instead of underestimating an expense, learn to overestimate your expenses. This is a good way to avoid unpleasant surprises.

Be kind to yourself. Doing a budget is a little like starting a diet. How many times have you known of someone who began a diet with such strict limitations that she simply gave up and quit trying? The same can happen with a budget. If you start on a budget that allows no fun or play money, it probably won't last long. Be reasonable, enjoy life. Just remember the importance of moderation.

Don't forget the "set aside" items. A number of the items on the PFFP work sheets are what I call "set aside" items. These are expenses that don't occur every month. Items like property tax and vacations may come around only once a year. Others, like buying a car, may only occur every few years. Still others may pop their heads up every few months. If you don't force yourself to follow a monthly "set aside" discipline, these expenses will catch you unprepared.

It's important to distinguish between what is essential and what is optional. I'll never forget a young divorced mother of two who came to me for some help with her finances. Despite a good job she seemed to stay in financial distress. She needed to change a number of behaviors, but the one I remember most was her cable television. She just could not seem to understand that cable TV was an unnecessary expenditure. The idea of getting only the local channels, which was all most of us had as kids, wasn't an acceptable compromise. She was happier dealing with debts and creditors than living without cable!

This is why I placed "Cable TV" under "Entertainment and Goofing Off" instead of "Utilities." Also you will note that I put "Necessary Restaurant Visits" under "Food," while including "Recreational Eating Out" under "Entertainment and Goofing Off."

Don't read too much into the progression on the worksheet. For instance, just because "Car Insurance" shows up after "Oil Change" doesn't speak to its relative importance.

How Much to Spend on What

The following suggested maximum spending levels are presented as just that, suggestions. I have developed these percentages based on the thoughts of other financial advisors as well as my own real-life experiences. While they may not all fit in your particular situation, maybe they will encourage thought and conversation as you plan your budget. These numbers are presented in a broad-brush fashion and will apply best to average income families. If your income is higher or lower than the average, these percentages may need to be adjusted. Also, unusual circumstances (i.e., unavoidable medical bills) can skew some of these percentages significantly higher or lower.

- Housing (including mortgage, insurance, taxes, utilities, repairs/maintenance, and related expenses): best if 25 to 33 percent of "true income"
- Food: 10 to 15 percent
- Clothing: 5 percent
- Transportation (including cost of the vehicle, maintenance, insurance, fuels, and legal fees): approximately 15 percent
- Entertainment & Goofing Off: 5 percent
- Debt Service: 5 to 8 percent (or less if possible)
- Saving/Investing: 5 to 15 percent
- Medical/Health/Dental: 5 to 8 percent (Obviously this may not be as easily controlled as some of the other items.)

Patience: Your Best Friend

Good things usually take time. And that is certainly the case when it comes to developing your PFFP. You may find that it takes three or four months before the various categories of your plan begin to work in harmony. You will have to put more in some categories and take money out of others. Like a master craftsman you'll gradually fine-tune your PFFP into a highly accurate, customized document. If you stick to it, gradually you will develop an invaluable worksheet that serves as your financial map to a more predictable and secure future.

Six Tricks of the Trade

Before I tie a ribbon on this chapter, let me share six ideas that will give you a real leg up as you develop and implement your family's PFFP.

1. *Devote your effort to God in prayer and make at least a six-month commitment.* It takes time and effort to change bad habits. As you launch into this new lifestyle, realize that there is a spiritual battle going on. At present the devil has you exactly where he wants you—frustrated, worried, at odds with your mate. Bring this new approach to controlling your money before God and give it to him. Make up your mind not to become discouraged, not to turn back. Make a personal commitment to stay the course for at least six months. This will give you the needed time to get past the first few months of confusion. It will also give you time to begin enjoying the benefits of your new lifestyle.

2. *Balance your checkbook every month.* Nothing mucks up a financial management plan quicker than an out-of-balance checkbook. Developing a PFFP while your checkbook is out of balance is like trying to win a triathlon with an anchor tied to your waist!

3. *Develop an "agreement purchase amount" with your spouse.* Happy marriages have good communication. I have recently been working with a couple in a Midwestern state whose finances are in terrible condition primarily because of the wife's uncontrolled spending habits. Without her husband's consent—and in some cases, even his knowledge—she has racked up over $30,000 in short-term debts—including a new car! I'm happy to tell you that, thanks to a lot of prayer, some good Christian counseling, and a lot of patience on the husband's part, their marriage is on the mend. But the debt problems are probably going to require at least five years to repair.

I like to encourage couples to agree on a maximum amount of money that either partner can spend without the consent of the other. The amount will vary based on your age, maturity level, and financial capabilities. For instance, if you're young newlyweds with limited incomes, you might decide that any purchase over $20 requires mutual agreement. However, a wealthy, middle-aged couple might agree that it's OK if one buys a car without notifying the other.

4. *Avoid the "impulse market mentality."* It's amazing how many budgets get blown out of the proverbial water because of what I call the "impulse market mentality." This is the temptation to run into a quick market and grab a snack and a soft drink—or some other impulse item. This is a special temptation to folks who spend a lot of time in their cars, like salesmen. No, I'm not against snacks and soft drinks, but I am against throwing away $100 to $200 monthly! Think about it. If you run into a quick market two times a day, that's sixty stops per month. And, if each time you buy a drink and a candy bar for $2, that totals $120 in the course of a month! That's $1,440 per year!

5. *Use ATMs cautiously.* ATMs are great. I use them myself. But you need to remember at least three things: First, ATM usage makes record keeping more difficult. It's easy to make an ATM withdrawal and forget to stub your checkbook. A few oversights like this can lead to an overdraft charge from the bank that resembles a payment on the national debt!

Second, avoid using your credit card at ATMs because it is so easy to over-withdraw. One study showed that while the average ATM card withdrawal is $53, the average credit card withdrawal is over $120!

Third, when you do use your ATM card, try to use it at your own bank. When you use your card at another bank's ATM, most of the time there will be additional charges.

6. *Consider destroying any credit card that you don't pay off in full each month.* I know that carrying a credit card balance is almost an American institution, but if you are ever going to get out of debt and stop letting your money manage you, a good starting place is with your credit cards. I'll have more to say about this later, but for now, suffice it to say that credit card debt has proven to be a real financial killer for many families.

The Diggs Family's Secret Weapon

All right, are you ready to hear what Bonnie and I consider an important element of a successful budget for the typical family? First, let me tell you that it's not complicated; it takes about five minutes to implement. Second, it costs little—less than a dollar. Third, this secret weapon really isn't a secret at all. As a matter of fact, it may be the single most recommended budgeting technique of all time! Money counselors and financial planners everywhere recommend this little management technique.

What is it? It's the world famous "envelope system." We have found that the best way not to overspend is to have a series of envelopes, each with the name of one of the monthly expense items listed in our Personal Financial Freedom Plan. The envelope system works best with those smaller items that can easily spin out of control and blow the budget. For instance, you might have an envelope for some of the following: restaurants, allowances, gifts, groceries, and gasoline. Then, on payday, cash your check and put the allotted amount of money into each envelope. As the month progresses and you deplete the money in that envelope, you know you have reached your allowable spending limit, so you stop spending.

From Need Money to Seed Money

I like to think of the money allocated to our PFFP as our "need money." This is the income required each month to pay the bills and carry life forward. Now, as you turn the page, get ready for something different. In the next chapter we are going to begin looking at ways to control our money rather than allowing it to control us. This is where I will begin showing you how to use your surplus dollars to get ahead. I think of these dollars as the "seed money" for a more secure and prosperous future.

5

Control Your Money, or Your Money Will Control You!

RONNIE WAS MORE than an acquaintance, but we weren't close friends. So until we bumped into each other on the street that day, it hadn't occurred to me how long it had been since we had seen each other.

"Hey man, where have you been keeping yourself?" I inquired lightly.

"Well, Steve," he began slowly, "I've just gotten out of prison."

Then with sadness in his eyes, the young man began to relate a painful story. Ronnie told me about the successful business he had owned. He was earning $5,000 per month making keys and doing lock work. And his business was growing. But, despite all he had going for him, Ronnie had thrown it away. Instead of controlling his money, he had allowed his money to control him. In the hope of making an easy score, Ronnie had begun leaving his business early to play video poker games. The habit soon became an obsession. Before long he was spending (and losing) over $1,000 a week on the machines! Eventually, he was left broke, hungry, and without gas money. Too late, Ronnie realized that it had all happened because of his greed and lack of self-control.

A Very Common Problem

Most of us don't lose everything we have, and most of us don't wind up in prison. But, in a more general context, can't you relate to Ronnie? Haven't there been times in your life when you lost control of your money, and a sense of desperation gradually destroyed your joy and peace? If not, you're a better man than I! I can remember a number of times when I was too lazy to maximize my earning potential, or I overspent and found myself in financial quicksand. Maybe you are there right now. If so, this chapter is for you. My purpose is to make the case that one of two things is going to happen. Either you will control your money, or your money will control you! It can all be summed up in one statement, or truism:

Money is a wonderful servant, but it is a terrible master!

A Typical Story

Over the years I have seen a lot of get-rich-quick schemes come and go. I have seen good people like Ronnie swallowed up in systems that wouldn't work, couldn't work, and didn't work. Most of these people didn't fall into gambling or criminal behavior. Most of them are more normal, typical, everyday people like you and me; but they ended up equally broke.

Many are more like my friend Dennis. The two of us grew up together; we were best friends. Dennis always dreamed of financial tranquility but was never willing to pay the price. As college men the two of us decided to spend a summer doing sales work together. It was a great opportunity to be productive and earn the money we needed. But, since we would be working without supervision, to be successful we had to be self-starters. Dennis began with great intentions, but as the summer went on, he lost his desire to succeed. Although success in our jobs required getting up early and working late, Dennis spent many of his days either sleeping in or visiting a theme park in a nearby city. Needless to say, the summer was not a financial success for Dennis.

After college the same cycle continued. Dennis went from one job to another. The combination of his poor work habits and inability to control his spending kept Dennis in constant turmoil and financial distress. He owed money to friends, banks, and family. It wasn't until the early nineties that Dennis finally woke up and decided he was tired of this sort of existence. He made the hard decision to change his lifestyle and his spending habits. He decided to take control of his professional and financial lives instead of allowing them to control him. Happily, today Dennis is settled, successful, and in control of his financial household.

Three Ways to Achieve Financial Freedom (Without Using a Mask and a Gun)

When people ask me for help getting their financial house in order, I tell them that it is a matter of learning to control their money. I only know of four ways to do it. I strongly advise against one of them since it involves the use of a mask and a gun. The other three options are totally legal, incredibly simple, but frequently overlooked.

1. Spend less.
2. Earn more.
3. Invest wisely.

I know, it's so simple. You didn't need to buy this book to learn something so basic, right? I'll grant you, conceptually speaking, this is no-brainer stuff. But in my experience not one person in twenty is willing to follow these simple steps. Have you ever wondered why doctors smoke cigarettes and insurance agents don't buy coverage? It's not because they believe smoking is safe or that living without insurance is wise. It's because they don't have the intestinal fortitude to do what they know is right!

Until you make a personal commitment to the three steps above, financially speaking, your life isn't going to improve.

I like this simple three-step approach because, for me, it answers all the questions. Spending speaks to what we're doing with what we already have. Earning involves the actions we can take to improve our standard of living. And investing focuses on future planning. Taken together, these three steps will determine how well we control our money.

An Old Adage

I heard an old adage years ago. Frankly, I couldn't tell you who shared this with me if my life depended on it. But I owe a huge thank-you to whomever it was. It's a short, little phrase that has blessed our family's financial planning. It also served as a cornerstone policy during the years when I owned different companies whose survival depended on sound financial management. This little phrase has reminded me numerous times of the danger of borrowed money. It has helped me control my spending. It has confirmed my decisions to maintain conservative fiscal policies in the businesses that I built. And it has been the bedrock principle behind what we have taught our four children about money.

What is this incredibly powerful axiom? Simply this: *Bank deposits must precede bank withdrawals.*

As you are no doubt beginning to realize, I don't claim to be a particularly brilliant guy. My mind works on a fairly simple level. Alan Greenspan has never dropped by for monetary advice. My banker friends have never asked me to join a policy panel. And some people are probably amazed that my brain generates enough electricity to keep my legs moving. But when it comes to nononsense, real-world-tested philosophy, that one little phrase makes me feel like a dime standing up to a nickel. When you sweep away all the debris of graduate-level financial schools, that's the bottom line!

Four Tricks for Controlling Your Money

Although I have already mentioned some of these, and will mention others later in the book, I want to share four tricks of money control. These tricks are not difficult to understand, but they are all tough to do. As we have already discussed, financial management is less about head knowledge than about behavior.

1. Learn to recognize and avoid the desire for instant gratification. One of the major differences between children and adults is that an adult has learned to delay gratification for a greater goal. This applies to all aspects of our lives. Godly people know that sexual temptations will come and go. But the short-term pleasure will be eclipsed by a lifetime of regret and broken relationships. In the same way mature people learn that buying stuff on a whim frequently leads to long-term financial agony. Remember, what one does in haste is often repented of in leisure.

As we have already discussed, it's a war out there. Advertisers, retailers, and creditors all want your money. Your job is to take control of your money and learn to say no a lot more often than you say yes.

2. Realize that we are only stewards of the money we possess. As we discussed in chapter 2, someday God will expect an accounting of what we did with what we had.

3. Learn to recognize what motivates you to buy. What's going on between your ears? Why are you about to spend money? Is it something you really need or want? Or is there a baser motive at work? Before I make a questionable purchase, some questions that have helped me sharpen my focus include: Is it something that will tickle my vanity? Am I simply trying to impress others with my ability to outspend them? Do I hope that buying something else will fill an emptiness within, rebuild my self-esteem? Am I trying to fill the hole in my heart with more stuff? Maybe I need to examine that hole more carefully. If I look closely, I may see that the hole is shaped like Jesus, and nothing else will ever really fill it.

4. Understand the concept of accountability. Many people have found that one of the best ways to control their money is by having an accountability partner. Two people can be wiser than the sum of their individual parts. King Solomon talks about the strength of two in Ecclesiastes 4:9–12:

> *Two are better than one,*
> *because they have a good return for their work:*
> *If one falls down,*
> *his friend can help him up.*
> *But pity the man who falls*
> *and has no one to help him up!*
> *Also, if two lie down together, they will keep warm.*
> *But how can one keep warm alone?*
> *Though one may be overpowered,*
> *two can defend themselves.*
> *A cord of three strands is not quickly broken.*

Finding the right accountability partner is critical. And, no, that person isn't necessarily going to be your best bowling buddy or your shopping pal. We're not looking for a codependent stuff-a-holic with whom to spend more money. This needs to be a person who really has your best interest at heart—and a little bit of maturity to go with it. Hopefully, if you're married, this will be your spouse. But if both of you are fighting the same budgeting battles, it may be simply a case of the blind leading the blind. Don't let pride or embarrassment get in the way of finding the right someone who can give you the needed counsel. Remember, the embarrassment associated with getting some help is nothing compared to the humiliation of crashing and burning in bankruptcy court!

Understanding the Difference Between Need Money and Seed Money

If you hope to control your money, a good starting point is to know the difference between *need* money and *seed* money. When I first heard this phrase, it made perfect sense to me. The first money we all deal with is need money. This is the money we need to live and function on each month. As we discussed in chapter 4, this includes the dollars we spend on housing, giving, clothing, food, recreation, transportation, debt service, and insurance. The second category is our seed money. These are the dollars we save and invest for the future. It is the seed we plant anticipating growth and future abundance. This is the money in our Murphy Account (I'll explain this a little later), retirement accounts, and college savings.

The Wolf Barrier

In chapter 4 we focused on ways to allocate our need money properly, as I discussed household budgeting. Now I want to give you some ideas on how to plan and prioritize your seed money. Before I go further, remember that this is just like everything else I am sharing with you in this book. These are only ideas for your consideration—thought starters, if you will. My hope is to inspire you and help you catch a vision. I'm not suggesting that any given idea is going to be right for everyone. We all have different circumstances, priorities, temperaments, and philosophies. Feel free to read and ponder these concepts. Then accept, modify, or reject them as you see fit.

When it comes to allocating our seed money, a planned attack is just as important here as it was when we designed a budget for our need money in the previous chapter. I like to refer to my seed-money plan as the Wolf Barrier. I get that name from the expression that was so prevalent with the depression era generation about "keeping the wolf from the door." I like to think of building a wall (the barrier) to keep the wolf from the door. The barrier I use is based on a ten-step hierarchy with the ground-level block being the starting point. Gradually, by stacking one block on top of another as we build the barrier, we go from those seed money expenditures that are vital to those that are more discretionary. The progression that works for me may work for you, too. As you review the way I prioritize my list, decide if it makes sense to you. Would you do well with the same priorities? What would you change or modify? Would a different progression work better for you?

Reviewing the Ten Stones of the Wolf Barrier

Let's spend a few minutes discussing each of the ten stones that make up the Wolf Barrier:

Stone 1: *Establish a crisis cash fund.* I hope this first step isn't necessary in your case. But a lot of folks literally don't have two nickels to rub together. They are living so close to the edge that tomorrow's lunch money isn't even certain. They don't have enough cash to get a tetanus shot at the public clinic for one of the kids. This is a horribly stressful way to live. For peace of mind and a sense of personal dignity, every family should have a little "crisis cash" handy. I suggest at least $75 to $100.

Stone 2: *Start the Murphy Fund.* We've all heard people joke about Murphy's Law. It's the famous adage that says, "If something can go wrong, it will go wrong." Over the years I have become convinced that Murphy's Law must have been written with financial issues in mind. I know of no other sphere where this little proverb is more appropriate. Just about the time you have all the bills paid—

© Joshua Diggs

BOOM! That's when the washing machine floods the floor. Or the transmission gives up the ghost. Or one of the kids breaks an arm. Suddenly you're hit with an unexpected emergency that is going to cost you money. And there you are smack in the middle of a budget-busting mess! Now you have essentially three choices: Leave the problem unfixed, borrow money (usually on high-interest credit cards), or dip into your Murphy Fund.

In my mind the second stone of your Wolf Barrier needs to be a Murphy Fund. I would encourage you to put at least $1,500 to $3,000 into this account as quickly as possible. (My personal rule of thumb: Try to build up an amount equal to about 5 percent of your "true income.") This will give you the luxury of being able to tackle many unexpected problems without those problems tackling you.

Let me leave you with two suggestions regarding your Murphy Fund. First, never use your Murphy Fund for anything that isn't a real emergency. This money isn't there to pay for a vacation or a new computer. Second, put your Murphy Fund money into a separate account. This will help you avoid accidentally mixing it with your need money. Also it'll make it a little harder to get your hands on it. Some people put their Murphy Fund in a money market account with a mutual fund company or a savings account at a bank or credit union that pays interest and allows check-writing privileges on the account.

Stone 3: *Consider funding your insurance.* Insurance is a matter of philosophy. In my judgment it makes sense to fund a term life insurance policy before we go further in the process. Like the commercials say, life insurance isn't for the living—it's for those left behind. I'll have more to say about this in chapter 7, but for now, keep in mind that future planning is one of the most loving things you can do for your family. Of course, in saying this I am assuming that you have already addressed your health insurance, possibly through group coverage where you work, and auto insurance (see the Personal Financial Freedom Budget Plan in chapter 4). Depending on your circumstances, you may need other insurance like disability, home owners, umbrella, renters, etc.

Stone 4: *Accelerate payments on short-term debt.* I hate debt, so I like to encourage other people to consider speeding up their short-term debt repayment schedules. This includes school loans, credit cards, department stores, home equity, and debt consolidation loans. (I'll address mortgages in Stone 9.) Many of these are relatively high interest loans. I would rather pay off a loan that is costing me 12 percent than to put the same money into a mutual fund. Why? Because lots of mutual funds don't average a 12 percent return, and I know of none that guarantee it. Also I hate bondage. And as I have mentioned before, I really believe the Book when it says, "The rich rule over the poor, *and the borrower is servant to the lender*" (Prov. 22:7, author's emphasis). I want freedom in my life. I don't want to go on vacation and worry about a mailbox full of bills when I get home. That's why Bonnie and I decided over twenty years ago to get rid of short-term debt in our lives. I'm still convinced it was one of the best decisions we ever made.

Stone 5: *Begin an "I don't need this job" fund.* Wouldn't you like to go to work because you find it challenging, enjoyable, fun? Wouldn't you like to know that if circumstances change where you work you could simply resign and take your time looking for another position? Also, wouldn't it be great not to be concerned about lay-offs, mergers, or downsizing? Well, the good news is it's possible, and lots of people have done it! Stone 5 is where I encourage people to build up what I call the "I don't need this job" fund. Ideally, this should be an account with six (even tweve) months of living expenses. One reason I encourage you to build such a cushion is so that in the event of a disability, hopefully you would have living expenses until your long-term disability insurance kicks in.

Yeah, I can hear the collective groan now: "That's pie in the sky! I'll never save that much." But, au contraire, my dear friends. Three things will help as you consider this goal: First, with Stone 4 (paying off short-term debt) behind you, there's now more money available for purposes like this one. Second, remember not to confuse six months of living expenses with six months of income. Usually your living expenses are significantly less than your gross income since they won't include the money that goes to taxes, Social Security, retirement plans, etc. Third, remember that determination is a great thing. Once you make up your mind that funding an "I don't need this job" fund is a top priority, you'll be less tempted to spend the money for other things.

Stone 6: *Consider tax-advantaged retirement funding.* The next allocation that makes sense for many people is to fund their qualified retirement plans. By this I am referring to investment vehicles that have tax advantages associated with them like 401(k) plans, 403(b) plans, SEPs, IRAs, etc. I'll talk more about this type of retirement planning in chapter 18, but for now, believe me when I say that I have never met anyone who felt that he or she started retirement planning too early or set aside too much.

Stone 7: *Save for college.* This is the best time to begin saving money for college. Sometimes people ask, "Doesn't it seem selfish to begin my retirement planning before I set aside money for my kids to go to college?" I don't think so, and here are some reasons: First, remember, I am primarily referring to tax-advantaged retirement programs like the ones mentioned in Stone 6. Many of these offer incentives that, especially in the case of employer matches, can catapult your account growth faster than almost any other way. Second, although most parents want to help with their children's education, there certainly is no disgrace in not doing so. A young person can always apply for scholarships, work his way through school, or get college loans (although I don't encourage this form of borrowing).

But as his parent, you are not going to find any retirement scholarships or loans. So I come back to this simple question: Which is the more loving thing to do: let your kids arrange for their own education, or you pay for college only to become a ward of your own kids in your retirement years?

Stone 8: *Continue retirement planning.* Now is a good time to reassess your retirement funding needs. Will the tax-advantaged investments we talked about in Stone 6 be adequate? If not, you may want to consider using annuities, regular mutual funds, or other investments to make up the shortfall.

Stone 9: *Pay off your mortgage.* If you are like Bonnie and me, you hate all forms of debt. So, with Stones 1–8 already taken care of, why not get rid of that pesky monthly mortgage? Remember two things: First, with all of your other debts and expenses under control, this won't be terribly difficult. Second, the odds are high that this stone won't occur until a number of years into your Wolf Barrier Plan. By that time your mortgage should be well along the way to being paid off.

Stone 10: *Begin your legacy building process.* With all of your other financial needs addressed, this is when you can begin to change the world. This is that golden opportunity that most people never experience but always dream of doing. This is when you can establish foundations and charitable plans that will allow your life to count for good long past the time you spend on earth.

Over the years I have been blessed to know several people who reached this stage of life financially and spiritually. I think of one godly man whose business formed a foundation that set as its goal to be Christ's hands on earth. Although this good brother is old and in poor health today, he has left a legacy of good works through his foundation. Another Christian couple of means is spending their senior years empowering a Christian university here in Nashville with its continued mission to train young people about Jesus. And

I could write another book about my mentor, Alton Howard. This Louisiana businessman has used his blessings to reach people around the world with the good news!

I never encourage anyone to pray for personal wealth. But what goal could be higher or nobler than the goal of having the financial resources to bless others and bring the news of Jesus to the world! Maybe this is the time in your life to begin talking to the Father about this.

The Best Way

Another old saying has become one of my mantras: There is only one best way to do anything. Once you figure it out, keep doing it that way.

I apply this philosophy to the way I approach money management issues. There is only one best way to accomplish anything financial. As one listens to different teachers, it isn't long before some of the same tried-and-true principles begin recurring. Why? Because common sense and human experience show that these principles work. Accordingly, please understand that the ten Wolf Barrier Stones I have shared with you are a compilation of my own ideas as well as derivations of those taught by other authors like Larry Burkett, Dave Ramsey, Ron Blue, and others. While we don't always agree on all of the finer points, I strongly suggest that you acquaint yourself with these teachers. You may find Dave Ramsey's book, *Financial Peace*, helpful as you work through the maze of money issues. He is a man committed to helping people get free from the bondage of financial pain.

I am a big believer in reading and listening broadly. Just last week I attended yet another retirement planning seminar. I didn't go expecting to hear life-changing information. As a matter of fact, just as I expected, there was little that I hadn't heard before. But the seminar was worthwhile because it presented some of the things I already knew in a different light; and it clarified some points that had previously confused me.

Commit to being a lifelong learner. Read, listen, and ask questions.

Part III

Catching Up,

Getting Ahead,
and Dealing with Life

In the first five chapters I tried to lay a spiritual foundation for our financial thinking. In Part III, we will look at financial issues from a more practical level. Our focus will shift from the eternal to the temporal nature of money and its usage. In this part of the book, I'll show you practical ways to stretch your money, buy what you need, and maintain some sanity in the process.

Chapter 6

The Fine Art of Buying a Car (or How Not to Become a Victim of the Walking Man's Friend)

IN THE EARLY 70s I had an afternoon radio show on a Nashville station. Being a poor college kid, eating out was a luxury I couldn't afford. So it was always a challenge when I got off the air, at 6:00 P.M., to rush back to the school cafeteria in time to get supper before they closed the line. Usually when I arrived, some of my friends were still there, and we would hold court at a long table that we considered to be our turf. I had begun noticing the cutest little brunette sitting at the end of the table with a girlfriend. They seemed to show up at the same time every evening. She was one of the brightest, happiest girls I had ever seen. As you can guess, one thing led to another, and it wasn't long before we were a serious item on campus. It wasn't until some time after we had been dating that Bonnie finally confessed and told me that I had simply fallen into her cunningly laid trap. She told me she listened to the show until I went off the air each day, then freshened up and headed over to the dining hall, arriving only minutes before I did.

I have always been so grateful that she took the proverbial bull by the horns and reached out to me. I can tell you after twenty-six years of marriage that, next to my salvation, Bonnie is the sweetest blessing I have ever been given.

But I'm getting ahead of myself. Before we finally got married in August 1976, there were a number of hurdles to overcome, not the least of which was my own selfishness and immaturity. Despite my profession of true love, I was plagued with a terrible case of cold feet. As months turned to years and college gave way to jobs, I still had not gotten the courage to ask Bonnie to take a trip down the aisle with me. Finally, with a noncommittal boyfriend and pressing family needs back home, Bonnie left Nashville and returned to Pennsylvania.

My heart hit the floor. She had left me, and it was my own fault! By this time we had been out of school for nearly two years. I had a successful real estate business going in Nashville. I knew what my options were. I could either stay in Nashville, become a real estate tycoon, and lose Bonnie forever, or I could swallow my pride, close up the business, move to Pennsylvania, and help Bonnie care for an aged family member. Then maybe I could rewin her heart, and she would marry me.

Well, thankfully, I did the right thing! I moved to Erie, Pennsylvania, in the spring of 1976 to rebuild my relationship with Bonnie. Things went great with the two of us. We were married within six months. But the job situation was another matter. It soon became evident that my work options were pretty limited. As a matter of fact, the only job I could find was selling cars. Actually, it has crossed my mind that maybe God figured this was the best way to take me down a few notches.

Ugh! I thought, *Not cars. Anything but selling cars!* I had heard all the jokes about these guys. I knew they were the last people firemen pull out of burning buildings! (Old joke: What's the difference between a lab rat and a car salesman? Answer: There are some things you can't get a lab rat to do.)

Over the next six months I learned a lot. I saw just how dishonest people could be. I heard buyers lied to and taken advantage of. My manager told me not to do my friends any favors because my enemies wouldn't buy from me anyway. I saw business conducted with little sense of morality and practically no concern for putting others' needs first. Although I did pretty well selling cars, I hated every minute and was thrilled the day I left!

Let the Buyer Beware

Am I saying that all car salesmen are evil? No. As a matter of fact, I have friends in the car sales business who are honest and trustworthy. One of these, David Chadwick, is a deacon in our church. David has been in the car business for over twenty years. I have bought from him and sent friends to him. He is a dedicated Christian who is willing to tell the truth to his own hurt. Over the years he has built a career based on trust and confidence.

But unfortunately not all salesmen are like David. They work in a high-pressure business and are usually paid a commission based on their sales. The competition is tough. Taking moral shortcuts can be easily rationalized and is sometimes encouraged by management. Atmospheres like this are breeding grounds for deceitfulness and greed.

Smart Money says, according to the Better Business Bureau, franchised car dealers receive vastly more complaints than other businesses. In a recent year there were more than seventeen thousand auto dealer complaints.[1]

A Word of Advice from Jesus

I don't want to overspiritualize what I have to say about car buying. However, a comment from Jesus comes to mind as I write this.

As he prepared his apostles to go out into the world, one of the Master's admonitions was, "Behold, I send you as sheep in the midst of wolves; so be shrewd as serpents and innocent as doves" (Matt. 10:16 NASB).

This short comment of Jesus has served me well for much of my business life. It reminds me that not everyone can be trusted. I need to keep my guard up and not believe everything I'm told. Sometimes a little skepticism is a good thing. Christians should not be ignorant and gullible people. We need to ask hard questions and drive fair deals. But, as Jesus also reminds us, we must be as "innocent as doves." I know there is the temptation to "fight fire with fire." But, as Christians, we need to avoid the urge to become cynical and dishonest ourselves. As a believer, my goal is to deal honestly, yet at the same time remain a good steward of my money.

Tricks and Tips of the Car Business

In the following pages, I want to share some insights that I have learned about car buying based on my own sales and purchasing experiences, as well as those of others.

Show up near the end of the month. Car dealers are like most other businesses. There is often a mad dash in the last few days of the month to make the numbers. You may find that the dealer will bend a little further in the closing days of a month to put another sale on the books. Remember, the best time to buy a car is when the salesman wants to sell it more than you want to buy it!

It is hard to know what a car really cost the dealer. Don't be too trusting when a salesman vows that he's giving it to you at cost. To begin with, his idea of *cost* and yours may not be the same. When you hear *cost,* you probably think of the amount the dealer paid to buy the car. On the other hand, the salesman actually may be referring to what he paid for the car, plus other "little incidentals" like shipping, undercoating, dealership overhead, profits, and commission.

And even if the dealer is willing to discuss his invoice price, there may be more here than meets the eye. Despite some helpful tip books and Internet sites that disclose dealer costs on cars, it's still not always easy to get to the bottom line. One reason has to do with a thing called "holdbacks." This is a practice that allows some dealers to get an additional 1–3 percent discount from the factory, taken off the invoice price they may show you. Being aware of this may help you negotiate a better deal.

Don't let your emotions take over. Nothing toughens a salesman's pricing resolve more than a customer who is drooling on the hood of one of his cars! These guys are pros. Just as a dog can sense fear, a car salesman can tell when you have car fever. Be cool. Be nonchalant.

Learn the negotiating game. Just like football and basketball, the game of car selling has its own set of rules. The better acquainted you are with these rules, the better your car-buying experience will be.

Frequently, it goes something like this: You come onto the lot. Based on a rotating system between the sales staff, you are assigned to the next salesman. With a happy smile and a firm handshake, the game begins. When you become interested in a particular car, the salesman will invite you into his office. Once you're seated, usually with your back to the door, he has your full attention. Now it is his job to get you to make an offer, preferably in writing, that he can "take to the manager." If you fall for this, you will be in a position of weakness. By making the first offer, you show your level of interest and your financial starting point. Now all the salesman has to do is "present your offer to the manager." Momentarily, he comes back telling how his manager, who may not even be involved, is crying and saying it would bankrupt the dealership to sell you the car at that price. But glory be, his manager has agreed to sell the car at a price that's only a couple of thousand dollars higher, which is curiously close to the original sticker price! From here it often is just a waiting game to see who blinks first. Their job is to keep you on the lot until you buy the car. By the way, if you have made the mistake of handing them the keys to the car you're trading, you may have a long wait while the used-car manager appraises your car.

My approach is different. When I come on a lot, I move fast. I like to see how many cars I can look at before the sales guy gets to me. When he arrives, I'm friendly but noncommittal. He doesn't really know what I want or how bad I want it. If I find a car that interests me, I ask him for the price. If it's too high, and it usually is, I tell him so. Then despite his protests I refuse to go to his office. I simply pull out one of my business cards and jot my cell phone number on it, as I'm walking back to my car. I hand him the card and say something like, "Look, I know you're going to have to get with management on this because I'm not willing to pay anything close to your sticker. I'm going to be visiting some other car lots in the area. Why don't you guys figure your best price and give me a call in a few minutes? If you're in the ballpark, maybe I can drive back over and we'll talk."

By doing it this way, I have reframed the transaction. The ball is in their court. They know I'm serious and that if they don't deal I'll probably find someone else who will. So the pressure is on them to perform.

Does this always work? Of course not. Often they don't call back. But if they really want to deal with me, they're the ones who have to come up with a starting price. Then I can negotiate from a position of greater strength.

Beware of add-ons. Car dealers love add-ons. They can be big revenue generators for the dealership, but they are not always so good for the buyer. I know one luxury car dealer that puts expensive, non-factory tires on its new showroom cars. Why? Because if a buyer either likes the special tires or is too inhibited to tell the dealer to pull them off and replace them with the original factory tires, the dealer makes an instant $800 extra on the sale!

While that may be a more creative type of add-on than some dealers come up with, add-ons are by no means a new idea. Beware of these budget busters when you buy a car. Little things like extended warranties, rust proofing, credit life insurance, and dealer-added accessories should be bought with caution and a full awareness of what they do to the total price.

Learn how trade-ins work. There are different strategies about trade-ins, but my experience selling cars taught me that trade-in pricing is often used to flatter and confuse prospective buyers. Here's what I mean: Suppose you are interested in buying a car with a $20,000 sticker price. The dealer might offer you $6,000 trade allowance on your old car, leaving a trade difference of $14,000. Feeling pretty good, you say to yourself, *Wow, $6,000 for that old junker. That's more than anyone else will ever give me! I'd better take this deal while it's still on the table!* But in the rush of the moment, you forget that you're basing the trade-in value against the full, nondiscounted price of $20,000.

If you really want to know what your old car is worth to the dealer, there's a better strategy. Start your negotiation by telling the salesman not to factor your old car into the trade yet. Instead, ask for a price based on a straight sale without a trade-in. Then, when you finally hammer out a price of $18,000, say, "If I wanted to trade my old car in on the deal, how much would you give me for it?" Now he's stuck and has to tell the truth that the bottom line is still $14,000, and that they're really only allowing another $4,000 for your old car.

It may hurt your feelings a little, but it will help you make a more informed decision. You may decide to sell your own car at a price closer to what the dealer would turn around and charge for it.

NO DEBT, NO SWEAT!

Bait and switch is not a forgotten art. Have you ever seen a car dealer billboard or newspaper ad promoting a vehicle at an unbelievable price? Don't be surprised if you arrive at the dealership only to find that "we sold the last one of those just last night, but I have something else that you're going to like better." Then you find out that the "something else" is not only better; it's also a lot more expensive.

Lowballing and bait-and-switch games are still around. Don't let new car fever short-circuit your common sense.

Don't put too much trust in "book value." I am not convinced that a book value always has much relationship to what a car is truly worth in the real world. A car's value is what a motivated and informed buyer is willing to pay for it. Book values can be based on wholesale value (what a dealer might pay to buy a car before he adds his retail markup). This number may not help if you want to know what your car may be worth to a retail buyer.

Some experts suggest that the best way to determine the actual value of your car is to do your own research. Check car magazines and newspaper classifieds in your area to see what similar cars are selling for.

Dealers don't arrange loans just to be nice. Financing has become a big part of the car business. It is not unusual for a dealer to make more money on a car's financing than on the actual sale of that car! That's often why a salesman may push his financing plans even after you have told him that you're going to pay with cash.

"No haggle pricing" is another way of saying, "It's our way or the highway!" In the last several years there has been a trend by dealers to promote what they euphemistically call "no haggle pricing." Well, duh! That's the way it's always been. As long as you were willing to walk in and pay the full sticker price, there never was any haggling. The only kind of "no haggle" policy that would interest me is if a dealer will let me come in and announce *my own price* with no

haggling. So far, I'm unaware of any dealers who take that approach. So until they do, I want the right to haggle!

Research the dealership. Chances are, you will bring your car back to the same dealer you bought it from for repair, maintenance, and warranty work. Ask around about the company's reputation. Check with the Better Business Bureau or other reporting organizations. Beware of the dealer's claims of great service or customer satisfaction awards. Some of these may be self-awarded or given by the manufacturer who sells cars to the dealership—hardly an unbiased source. (Do you remember the old story about the fox guarding the henhouse?)

The Good, the Bad, and the Ugly: Three Ways to Buy a Car

New cars are expensive. In a ten-year period, while inflation grew about 40 percent (based on the Consumer Price Index), new car prices rose more than 70 percent.[2] According to *Consumer Reports*, the average new car price has risen to $24,857![3] Any way you cut it, that's a lot of money. Since we as Americans have been sold on the idea that it is our birthright to get another vehicle with that "new car smell" every couple of years, paying for our cars has become a major financial issue in many of our homes.

Although I say this with tongue in cheek, there are three ways to buy a car—and, in my opinion, they are not all equally good. I call them the Good, the Bad, and the Ugly. Let's take a quick, snapshot overview of these three options in ascending order:

The Ugly: Leasing. As car prices went higher and higher, people held onto their cars longer (from three or four years up to seven or eight years). Something had to be done to get people back into new car showrooms. The answer was leasing. The promise of lower payments, less hassle, and a new car more often was compelling to many buyers.

My personal belief, however, is that car leasing is the least attractive way for most people to buy a car. Yes, I've heard all the benefits of leasing. At least theoretically, there can be business tax savings, reduced down payments, lower monthly costs, extra insurance coverage, reduced trade-in inconvenience, and other reasons that make leasing appealing. But since there is so much proleasing advertising (roughly 30 percent of all new cars today are leased),[4] I'm not going to take the space here to make the case for leasing.

I am, however, going to bring some balance to the discourse by sharing some concerns about leasing. To begin, no matter what you may have been told, a typical car lease is really a long-term rental agreement that may or may not have a purchase option at the end. A car lease is not the same as a car loan! And in a lease, unlike an outright purchase, unless you exercise your option and buy the car, you end up with no ownership or equity. A car loan payment may cost you more per month, but at least you are buying ownership in the car.

Many people believe that dealers prefer leasing because it maximizes their profits. This probably occurs for several reasons including higher fees, lower discounts, and the fact that lease contracts are confusing to many buyers. Add to that the horror stories of high turn-in costs for extra mileage, or what the dealer claims are excessive wear and tear, and you have more reason for pause.

The Bad: Car Loans. As you know, I have a bias against borrowed money. Every debt in a person's life is just that much more bondage he or she is under. It is my goal to be as debt-free as possible—including with my cars. Do I think it's wrong to borrow money to buy a car? No. As a matter of fact, there are some occasions when it may be the best option. But that is the exception, not the rule. Most car loans are made because of wants, not true needs.

If you feel that a car loan is the only possible way to go, here are some things to consider. Many people who negotiate great deals when buying their cars lose all their gains when it comes time to arrange the financing. Today some dealers make more money handling car financing than they do actually selling cars! Dealers frequently bring in consultants and hire specialists to run their F & I (finance and insurance) departments. These guys are smart, and they tend to know how to maximize the profit potential on the back end of the deal.

The key to a good car loan lies in this little phrase: *Borrow as little as you can, for as short a time as you can, for as low as you can!*

Borrow as little as you can. The more you borrow, the harder it's going to be to pay it back. There are two ways to lessen the amount you borrow: buy a less expensive car, and put down a big down payment. Not easy. Not great for the ego. But, boy, does it make for peace of mind!

For as short a time as you can. I'm old enough to remember when most car loans were for thirty-six months or less. Today some car loans resemble home mortgages. Many people get "upside down" (a phrase meaning that one owes more than the car could sell for) because of loans that last four, five, or six years—and even longer! People, this is crazy! I don't like any loan repayment schedule that lasts longer than about 50 or 60 percent of the car's reasonable life expectancy.

The longer the loan repayment schedule lasts, the more interest you pay. For instance, if you make a $20,000 car loan at 9 percent for three years, the total cost will be $22,896 (including interest of $2,896).[5] But if you finance that same $20,000 car at 9 percent over a six-year period, the total cost will be $25,963 (including interest of $5,963). That's $3,067 more in interest payments!

For as low as you can. A third factor that can make or break your car loan is the interest rate. The time to arrange your loan is *before* you negotiate with the salesman. Dealers are notorious for charging higher rates. Many experts suggest first arranging your loan with a friendly bank or credit union, then start dealing. And, remember, everything is open to negotiation. Don't hesitate to push for the lowest possible interest rate.

Of course, there are those too-good-to-be-true factory loan deals that come along occasionally. If you run across one of these, go cautiously. Make sure you are clear about the rate and that it applies to the car you're thinking of buying. Be sure all finance rates are quoted at the annual percentage rate (APR) instead of an add-on rate that may appear to be lower. Never sign a contract until it has all the blanks filled in, including the total dollar cost and finance charges. Other details should include the monthly payments and the length (or term) of the repayment schedule.

The Good: Paying with Cash. Wow! What a cool feeling! There is nothing else like it. You pick out the car you want, and because you developed a plan and stuck to it, you drive off the lot with a car that belongs to you! Not some lease company, bank, or credit union. It belongs to you!

Believe it or not, 22 percent of cars and trucks are sold for cash.[6] Who are these people who can buy a vehicle and pay cash for it? For the most part they're people just like you and me who have made up their minds to get control of their lives. Instead of living like the masses, these are people who got fed up with business as usual. They decided that eating out all the time and buying designer clothes they couldn't afford was crazy. They realized that getting ahead was something that only happens when you get really tired of being broke all the time. They finally got tired of living on the edge, so they changed things.

The good news is, you can do it, too. Don't believe the lie that only rich people buy cars with cash. It isn't true. Lots of people on their way to becoming financially free are buying vehicles and paying cash for them. Besides, how do you think those rich folks got rich? They didn't do it by making interest payments to someone else!

How Never to Have Another Car Loan

There's a way never to have another car payment—EVER! (And, no, I'm not talking about taking the bus!) This little idea has reduced financial pain for a lot of people. Here's how it works:

Step 1: Forget your ego. Believe me, this is the toughest part. As I discussed earlier in the book, egos are expensive to maintain. It's especially hard for people to forget their ego when it comes to the car they drive. For Americans, cars are an extension of our personalities. We show the world who we are by the cars we drive. Even Christians fall into this trap. But if you ever want to pay cash for a car, the first thing you must agree to is never drive a car you can't afford to buy with cash. Curiously, by making this determination, many people have gradually stepped up to some of the nicest cars on the market.

Step 2: Save $3,000 to $4,000 quickly and buy a safe, affordable car. Get focused on saving that $3,000 to $4,000. Do whatever it takes: Brown bag your lunches, skip a vacation, work overtime, get a second job. See how quickly you can make this happen. This is enough money in many areas to buy a decent, *safe* car. (Note: I didn't say fancy or prestigious.) Obviously, you may pay a little more or a little less.

Step 3: Now, start making monthly car payments to yourself. With your car in the driveway, it's time to start making car payments. But instead of making them to a bank, pay yourself instead. Here's where you have to be tough and intellectually honest with yourself. Don't ever cheat. Just as surely as you would have to send monthly payments to the bank, set aside a monthly payment to yourself. Since the average car payment in America is over $350 per month, I would encourage you to set aside something in that range. Do this for a couple of years. By that time you will have $6,000 to $9,000 in your Paid-for Wheels account. Sell your old car. Suppose you get $1,000 to $2,000 for it. Now, you have around $7,000 to $10,000 for a much nicer car.

Just yesterday I put more money into our Paid-for Wheels account. It really felt good! Give it a try.

Step 4: Repeat the process. Now all you have to do is repeat this little strategy until you are driving the car of your dreams—still never making a payment to the bank!

Buying New Versus Buying Used

Unlike some of today's financial advisers, I am not opposed to new cars. Buying a new car is a personal decision that revolves around issues like your individual financial strength, your motives, and even your walk before Jesus. In this section I simply want to share some of the pros and cons of both new and used car buying. Ultimately the decision is yours.

Advantages of New Cars. Let's start with the advantages of buying a new car. Experts point to at least three reasons new cars can make sense. First, a new car means you don't have to worry about someone else's abuse and neglect. New cars usually have fewer problems and repair costs. Usually new cars come with great warranties that protect the buyer for a number of years. Second, new cars frequently are safer cars. The latest models generally have the most advanced airbags, integrated child seating, etc. Third, if you're into technical goodies, a new car is likely to have the latest bells and whistles. Every year there are advancements in braking and suspension systems, night vision, mapping systems, and the like.

Disadvantages of New Cars. But there are two huge disadvantages to buying a new car: *cost* and *depreciation.* As I mentioned earlier, the price of a new car today averages around $25,000. You can usually buy a wonderful used car for 30 to 60 percent of that amount. And, wow, the depreciation is unbelievable! Some experts believe that a new car can lose as much as 30 percent of its value the minute it rolls off the dealer's lot. So we come back to the fundamental question:

Can you afford that amount of front-end loss? In my judgment, the only person who should ever consider buying a new car is the one who can pay cash and feel no significant financial impact.

Advantages of Buying Used. It doesn't take the sharpest knife in the drawer to realize that the number one advantage of buying a used car is affordability. Frequently a two-year-old used car will cost as little as 50 to 60 percent of the original retail price. Some financial planners have calculated that, in addition to the lower purchase price, a used car can save its owner thousands of dollars more over the years in lower sales taxes, insurance premiums, and finance charges. Also, when you buy a used car, there normally isn't a charge for dealer prep or shipping.

Another good reason to think used is that some of the old arguments against buying these cars carry less weight today than they once did. For instance, the concern about quality is not as valid as it once was. For a number of years now, cars have been better built. Features like advanced engine designs and greater corrosion-resistant materials in the body parts increase dependability and road life. I regularly get over 150,000 miles out of my personal cars.

Also, the fear that a used car is nothing more than a breakdown looking for a place to happen is less of a worry today than it used to be. Some of the manufacturers now offer dealer-sponsored used-car certification programs on many of their vehicles. And with the popularity of auto leasing, there is a constant stream of late-model lease cars coming onto the market. Most lease contracts require that the lessees maintain the cars in good condition or pay a penalty.

If you are planning to finance a used car, you may find better news on this front as well. In many places used-car loans are less expensive today—frequently something in the range of 1 percent over new car loan rates.

Disadvantages of Used Cars. By shopping carefully, you may not find many downsides to buying a used car. Obviously, a used car will tend to be less dependable than a new car. You may have more frequent repair costs. And used cars often don't have all the technical and safety features available on their new counterparts.

Now, armed with knowledge and strategy, I challenge you to go forth and buy wheels that really are great deals!

7

Buying Insurance (Protecting Yourself and Those You Love)

IN RESEARCHING THIS CHAPTER I ran across a copy of a letter in my files dated October 1991. Although it's been more than ten years, it is still one of the most impassioned letters I have ever written. I sent it to one of my closest associates pleading with him to pay attention to his health insurance needs. At the time Jeff (not his real name) had just dodged a bullet that could have cost him his life. His father had died of cancer a few years earlier, and it had appeared that the son also might have the disease. Thankfully, Jeff got good news. But through the ordeal it became obvious that he did not have adequate health coverage.

Because of the closeness of our families, I decided to write to Jeff urging him to get the insurance as soon as possible. He needed the protection not only for himself but also for his wife and three children. As one who has battled heart disease, I was convinced that having proper health coverage was one of the most important acts of love Jeff could show his family. I had personal experience with the high cost of medical care and the difficulty of getting good coverage after an illness is diagnosed. Thankfully, Jeff decided to buy the insurance he needed.

I say thankfully because earlier this month his wife was diagnosed with a serious form of cancer. None of us know what the next year will bring. But at least we can plan well so there will be money available to pay for good quality medical care.

The Philosophical Question

If I were writing this book primarily to a secular audience, I probably wouldn't include this section. However, because of the Christian worldview many of us hold, I want to address the issue of buying insurance and its relationship to trusting God to provide.

I remember a Christian radio program I heard a number of years ago. On this particular day the host was visiting with an evangelist who traveled the country preaching the good news of Jesus. While I admired much of what he had to say, I was really disappointed by part of his presentation. At one point in the conversation, he began to brag about the fact that he carried no health insurance and that he simply trusted God to provide. With that he told a story about some health expenses his family had incurred and then gleefully told about how other Christians had paid their bills.

Boy, that fried me! Didn't this good man know about the biblical mandate to care for one's own family? Also, what about his witness to the outside world? What does this say about a Christian's sense of duty and responsibility?

I realize that there are those who differ with me on this point. Some people feel that it is more spiritual simply to trust God to provide rather than to depend on the "devices of man." But I find it curious that these same people are often willing to accept the devices of other men when they can't afford to pay their own bills. It is also interesting to me that some of these same people are willing to use selectively other "devices of men" like locks on their doors, seat belts, and so forth.

I wonder if what presents itself as a form of superspirituality isn't sometimes something else. At best it may simply be a misunderstanding of faith. At worst, it is an irresponsible refusal to accept the appropriate—and, even God-ordained—responsibility that comes with the headship of a home.

Our Goal

In this chapter we are going to look at some of the basic types of insurance: life, health, home owners, and auto. My goal is to give you a broad overview of these primary insurance products. Of course, other types of insurance may be appropriate and necessary for you. For instance, most employed people should consider disability coverage. You may need additional coverage in the form of an umbrella policy. And, as we reach middle age and beyond, long-term care insurance may be a viable consideration.

When it comes to insurance, there is no one-size-fits-all approach that's right for everyone. My goal in this chapter is to open your eyes to the benefits of insurance so you will be encouraged to learn more. Knowledge is power. The more you know about insurance and your coverage options the better you will be able to protect your family from unforeseen loss. Like the insurance people say, insurance isn't just for the living; it's also for those who are left behind.

Life Insurance

Experts tell us that most people don't have nearly enough life insurance protection. In America only 45 percent of all adults have individual life insurance, and of those who do, over 65 percent are woefully underinsured.[1] A lot of this has to do with confusion about what life insurance does and what it costs. In many cases the folks who sell life insurance are a big part of the problem. Most of us would rather take a bullet to the head than to be locked in a room with an insurance salesman. But a little bit of education can go a long way here.

To begin, you need to understand that life insurance falls into two broad categories: whole and term. For as long as they have both been around, there has been a debate over which is the best. Let's take a snapshot of both types of coverage:

Whole-life insurance, also known as permanent insurance, is designed to give an individual coverage throughout life, assuming premium payments are made properly and other provisions are followed. When an individual buys a whole-life policy, he pays a regular premium and gets the promise of a certain amount of money payable upon his death. Whole life costs more than term for a comparable amount of coverage because the premium you pay for whole life covers two expenses—the actual insurance protection as well as a separate cash account that is expected to grow over time. Some of the earnings that an insurance company makes (over those needed to pay the death benefit) are put into the policy's cash value account, which the policy holder can borrow from, use to pay the premiums, withdraw, or allow to accumulate for retirement or other purposes.[2]

Much debate revolves around the actual value of this cash account. Some experts argue that whole life makes better sense only if one plans to keep the policy for more than twenty years.[3] They explain that high front-end costs and commissions make whole life expensive unless the cash value is given time to grow and increase in value. Other experts in the field make the case that whole-life cash-value growth is often paltry compared to many other investment options and may not make good financial sense. However, some advocates of whole-life insurance point out that, in many cases, you can keep coverage even if your health deteriorates in future years.

There are a number of variations on the whole-life theme. One of them is known as universal life insurance. Universal life became popular in the 1970s when interest rates shot up and people began looking closer at the returns they were getting from their traditional whole-life policies. One of the goals was to rewin consumers' hearts by allowing more flexibility and paying higher rates of return. But experts at InsWeb explain that people soon learned that fluctuating interest rates could work against them with these policies, and in the worst cases their coverage could lapse.[4]

Term-life insurance is the other broad category of life insurance. Frequently referred to as "pure insurance protection," term insurance doesn't include the cash value feature that distinguishes whole life. Accordingly, term is usually significantly less expensive than the same amount of whole-life coverage. This form of insurance covers you for a specified period of time (often ten, twenty, or thirty years), and then it expires. If you are still alive, you get no money.

In recent years there have been a number of changes (better term-life products, a generally more astute public, and a greater assortment of investing options) that have diminished the appeal of traditional whole-life insurance for many people. In my judgment, term insurance is the way to go for many people. To me the purpose of life insurance is just that—to insure a person's life, nothing more and nothing less. I prefer to do my investing separately. I see life insurance as most appropriate until an individual either builds adequate assets to self-insure effectively or until he has no more need for the coverage. The old adage, "buy term and invest the rest," may prove good advice. Granted, it requires greater discipline to send a second check to a mutual fund or other investment. But many people feel that the rewards outweigh the extra effort.

There are at least three important things to look for in a term-life insurance policy:

1. I'm big on stability, so I prefer policies that have a guaranteed level premium for the term of the policy. Annual renewable term policies can raise the premium every year until the policy is surrendered. If you are only going to keep the policy for a short while, annual renewable term may be cheaper, but experts warn that in the long run it will probably be more costly.

2. I prefer term insurance that guarantees level term benefits. This means that if you buy a twenty-year, $100,000 policy, your beneficiary will get the full $100,000 whether you die in year two, ten, eighteen, or whenever. Decreasing term is another type of policy that will pay a lower benefit the closer it is to the end of the term. Sometimes sold by banks as mortgage protection, decreasing-term benefit coverage is a big profit maker for banks, but many experts don't believe it's good for consumers.

3. Guaranteed renewable can help safeguard an uncertain future. Of course, the goal is to get to the point where you don't need insurance coverage at some point. And, besides, if you still do need coverage at the end of your term, you can just buy some more insurance at that time, right? Not necessarily. It's possible that you may still need insurance at the end of your term, and it's also possible that health conditions could make it impossible to get decent coverage. What to do? You might wish to consider buying the original policy with the guaranteed renewal option. This may make it possible to get more coverage at a later date. However, be aware that future rates can be prohibitively expensive, especially if your health declines. Get detailed future-rate information before you buy.

What About Insurance for Mama?

In families where the mother stays at home to raise and nurture the children, sometimes you hear a thoughtless husband say, "Oh, we don't need life insurance on her because we don't depend on her income."

Rather than argue the point, I think the best thing to do is to ask the question, "What does mama do around here?" After he has listed everything from counseling to car pooling, shopping to studying, bookkeeping to baking, correcting to cleaning, then you might ask, "What would it cost to hire a professional to come in and do all of those jobs?" Finally, with an amount agreed on, multiply that times the number of years of childhood still ahead, and there you have a ballpark figure of the amount of insurance you need to replace mama!

Health Insurance

Every day new discoveries are being made on the health-care front. New medications, treatments, therapies, and procedures are being reported in the popular press. But along with these advances the cost of health care has skyrocketed. The old joke about the guy who complained that he went to his doctor and all the doc did was take his temperature and his $5 has given way to modern-day horror stories. Earlier this week Bonnie took our twelve-year-old daughter, Mary, to the pediatrician because of a rash and a sore throat. It cost $117 to find out that she has a virus!

As you are beginning to see, I'm a *big* believer in health insurance. A leading cause for bankruptcy in America today is medical bills. Without proper health insurance, your home and assets could evaporate after one serious illness. People who haven't had a medical crisis in recent years are sometimes shocked to find that a relatively short hospital stay can cost $20,000 or more.

Whether you get it through your employer, your spouse's employer, individually, or otherwise, health insurance needs to be near the top of your must-do list.

QuickQuote divides health insurance into four basic plan types. The first falls under the category heading of traditional coverage, while the last three are all forms of managed care. Following is a brief overview of these four plan types:[5]

Traditional indemnity plans (sometimes known as fee-for-service). Some people prefer the freedom and flexibility offered by fee-for-service plans although they tend to require greater out-of-pocket expenses, more paperwork, and higher premiums.

Preferred Provider Organizations (PPOs). Similar to the other types of programs listed below, PPOs typically involve an agreement between a group of selected health-care providers and the insurance company. Often the insured individual receives financial incentives to select health-care professionals from the network and is allowed to refer himself to a specialist without getting special approval from the insurance company.

Point-of-Service Plans (POSs) are much the same as PPOs but introduce the primary care physician into the mix. Prior to going to a specialist, you will usually be expected to go through your PCP for a referral. Some POSs cover more preventive care and health improvement services.

Health Maintenance Organizations (HMOs) (often close-panel HMOs) are usually less costly and less flexible than many other forms of coverage. Frequently they require that you see their doctors and get a referral before seeing a specialist.

There is no best option here. Different people prefer different types of coverage. Buying health insurance can be confusing, but it is time well spent to learn all you can about the available options. Be aware that, due to competition in the insurance business, distinctions between plans may become blurred. The information I have presented here is only a broad-brush overview. Be sure to read your contract carefully and ask all the questions necessary to understand fully what you are getting. It's much better to know what you have before you need it than to be surprised when you enter the hospital!

Home Owners' Insurance

The Insurance Information Institute tells us that the main purposes of insuring your home are twofold: to protect the structure of your house and to protect your personal belongings.[6] Many homeowner policies in the United States include coverage for direct losses due to lightning, fire, tornadoes, hail, explosions, smoke, theft, and vandalism. Generally covered are losses from liability claims, such as someone coming onto your property who slips and falls. However, you need to be aware of limits and exceptions. Additionally, be aware that most basic policies do not cover loss from flood damage or earthquakes.

Pertaining to the structure, the Insurance Information Institute explains the three main types of coverage available:

Replacement cost coverage usually pays the insured the cost of replacing the destroyed or damaged property, without reducing the sum for depreciation, up to an agreed-upon maximum amount.

Extended replacement cost coverage is designed to pay for losses up to a certain percentage over the limit.

Actual cash value coverage usually permits the insured to get payment for the damaged or destroyed property in the amount that equals the replacement value minus an allowance for depreciation. Beware! Unless your policy says that your assets have replacement-value coverage, the coverage is probably just for actual cash value!

My personal preference, if you can get it at a reasonable price, is replacement cost coverage. This way, if the worst happens, you should have enough insurance to take care of most of the losses. I also believe in the inflation guard feature that is designed to raise coverage automatically (and its cost) periodically to keep pace with current building costs.

Preparing for the Worst

I encourage people to do a few basic things to reduce their risk of loss—or at least minimize the havoc it causes:

1. Keep a detailed, accurate, and current inventory of all assets. I remember taking several days to prepare an exhaustive list of all our possessions. When I was through, I had two notebooks full of information. I went through every room of the house and inventoried each item. I included a photograph of each significant piece along with pertinent information: price, place and date of purchase, identifying data (serial number, model, etc.), and current value. In the cases of more expensive items, I included appraisals. Then I went through the house and videotaped everything. I took the videos and catalogs off the premises. Talk about a real bummer; could you imagine having your house burn and losing your inventory lists in the same fire!

2. Read and review your policy and your inventory at least every year. Stay familiar with its provisions and exclusions.

3. Call your agent occasionally—maintain good contact. It's helpful to have a personal and friendly relationship if you ever have to file a claim.

4. Stay generally aware of rebuilding costs in your area. Also check the latest building codes. Be sure that your coverage is adequate to rebuild your home to current code requirements.

5. Your mortgage company may only require you to carry enough home-owners insurance to cover the outstanding mortgage. Be sure that it is enough to cover the cost of rebuilding, too.

6. Check your policy limits on things like jewelry and computers. You may need to add some extra coverage for such items.

A Word to Renters

If you're a renter, two really bad things can happen to you: First, you can come home one evening to find that someone has broken in to your place and ripped off all of your stuff—your TV, workout equipment, furniture, bike, even your computer. That's bad. But what comes next makes it even worse. That happens when you go to your landlord for help, and all he does is shrug his shoulders and say, "Sorry." That's right, the guy doesn't have coverage for your loss, and he isn't going to give you a dime! That's when you finally sit down and read the lease contract—that boring-looking document you should have read when you first moved in. And, sure enough, he's right!

Within the agreed-upon limits, renters insurance can protect you from losses caused by lightning, vandalism, theft, fire, etc. It can also give you liability coverage for other people injured at your home.

My advice: Get it! Of course, as with any other types of coverage, renters' policies vary. Shop for the coverage and prices that fit you best. Read your policy thoroughly.

Auto Insurance

For over twenty years I owned a business that was located on Nashville's famous Music Row. What a place to work! It's a great area of town. Everywhere you go there are creative people working with the various record labels and creative shops. I love almost everything about the Row except the driving. Since this is where the country music stars work, it's also where the tourists come. They're everywhere. (Some of the locals call Music Row the Plaid Shorts District.) As much as we appreciate the tourist business in Nashville, driving can be a real problem. Especially when you throw in the homegrown folks who make their share of driving gaffes, too. Over the years I have had a couple of fender benders in the area when someone wasn't paying enough attention. Through these regrettable experiences I've grown to appreciate the value of good car insurance.

One thing I have learned is the essential nature of car insurance coverage. I've learned the hard way that, even if I do everything right, I can still be faced with thousands of dollars of repair bills. And if I ever should make a major mistake on the road, my insurance may be the only thing standing between me and bankruptcy! So with this as my introduction to the subject, let's talk about what car insurance covers and a little about how it works.

Six Basic Parts of an Auto Policy

A typical car insurance policy may include all, or some, of the following six types of coverage. Usually, each coverage is priced individually. They include:

Bodily injury liability is designed to help protect the policyholder from claims and defense costs if he kills or injures someone.

Property damage liability helps cover damage the policyholder may do to someone else's property. However, this coverage does not cover the policyholder's own property or car.

Medical payments or personal injury protection pays on the medical expenses for injuries to the driver and passengers of the insured's car. It may also pay if the insured is injured while riding in someone else's car or while walking.

Collision is designed to cover costs for damage to the policyholder's car if it is in a collision with another vehicle or some other object.

Comprehensive physical damage is for damage to the insured's car resulting from theft, vandalism, fire, hail, etc.

Uninsured or underinsured motorist coverage is for cost related to property damage and injury to the insured by an uninsured or underinsured motorist. This is frequently the coverage that comes into play after a hit-and-run accident.

Read your policy and ask questions, as these are only broad explanations and will vary from policy to policy.

A Few Money-Saving Pointers

No matter how I prune and fertilize them, the trees in my backyard simply will not grow money. Without such a "cash crop," saving money has become important in my life. Following are some money-saving tips from experts in the field, as well as some of my personal experiences:

Check the competition. Lots of companies sell insurance. Check around. Compare the prices from four or five companies. You'll find that rates and prices vary a lot. But not all companies are equally good. As is the case with any form of insurance, the cheapest price isn't always the best buy. Ask your friends about the experiences they have had with their companies and check the rating services.

Drive like you know you should. One thing that will raise your car insurance costs the fastest is a bad driving record. This is something you can control, so do it!

Arrange for higher deductibles. A deductible is the money you have to pay before the insurance company fulfills your claim. You can reduce the cost of your insurance drastically by raising the deductible—the amount you're responsible for—on collision and comprehensive coverages. Once you have your Murphy Fund (see chapter 5) in place you'll have extra money for such emergencies.

You may not need comprehensive and/or collision coverage if you drive an old car. Assuming your agent is trustworthy, this might be worth discussing.

Inform your agent if you're a low-mileage driver. Some companies determine their rates based on the amount of annual driving a policyholder does.

Tell your agent about any safety features and antitheft systems on your car. Some companies reduce their costs to people who drive cars with automatic seat belts, air bags, and other safety and theft devices. It's worth asking about.

Pay your premium in one lump sum. Some companies charge less if you pay your premiums annually or semiannually. This can avoid some of the service charges associated with monthly payments.

Check to see if your insurer discounts car coverage when you buy other insurance from him. Some insurers give price reductions to clients who buy their home owners, umbrella, and other coverages from them.

A Little Grief Saver

Recently I have been reevaluating my own insurance coverage. Of course, every agent I talk with presents a convincing case for his product and the companies he represents. So how can people like us really know which company does the best job settling claims? Do we simply have to buy the coverage on blind faith and wait until we have an accident to find out?

Let me tell you what I did a couple of days ago. I collected the names of all the companies I was considering and went to visit the manager of the body shop that I would take my car to. I said, "Stewart, here are the companies I'm looking at. What kind of results have you had working with these outfits?"

It took about five minutes for Stewart to illuminate me. I left with a much better picture of the real world of car insurance companies as seen through the eyes of a guy who works with them every day.

Not All Insurance Companies Are Created Equal

We all accept the fact that not every restaurant chain is equally well capitalized. For instance, with thousands of locations worldwide, it's obvious that McDonalds has far deeper pockets than the single-location, hometown hamburger stand. When you hire a major, national home builder to construct a new home, it's expected that the company will have greater resources than a guy working out of the back of his pickup.

But things are not so clear and easy to see when it comes to insurance companies. After all, you are buying an intangible product, the description of which is usually reduced to a few pieces of paper. You may or may not know the agent. And you probably have never been to the company's home office, reviewed their books, or studied their claim-paying capabilities. Yet you are about to invest money (maybe a lot) with this company based on its promise that it will be able to pay future claims you make. Wow! That's a lot of trust.

All insurance companies are not equally strong financially. It doesn't happen often, but there have been policyholders who couldn't collect on their claims. This is why it behooves anyone buying insurance to research the company.

Fortunately, there are some ways to get helpful insights into an insurance company's financial strength and ability to pay claims:

1. Contact your state department of insurance. Often these governmental agencies can be helpful in assessing a company's operations within your state.

2. For more information there are several insurance research and rating organizations. Some of the better known are: Standard & Poor's (800–556–9393); Fitch Ratings, Inc. (212–908–0200); Moody's Investor Service (212–553–0300); and A. M. Best (908-439-2200).

3. Don't forget about your friends. There's a lot to be said for word-of-mouth advertising. Ask around about their experiences with the companies you're considering.

4. Check out consumer-oriented publications and Internet sites. Notice that I said *consumer-oriented*. There are sales-based Internet sites that present themselves as unbiased authorities. Beware.

Look Before You Leap

That's always good advice but especially with insurance. Before you make any major coverage change, consider the implications of your decision. Never cancel one policy before you are certain that you have another policy to take its place.

As I've told you, I believe in term-life insurance. I think it makes the best sense in most cases. However, I bought whole life coverage more than fifteen years ago—before I had developed a serious heart problem. Today, if I wanted to drop my whole-life coverage and buy term, it might not be possible. Because of my health, term-life insurance probably isn't an option. Can you imagine the problems I would have if I had dropped my whole-life coverage before checking the availability of term? Always be sure your new coverage (whether it's life, health, auto, home owners, or whatever) is in place *before* you drop what you already have.

Other Options

When it comes to insurance, there are a million types. The urpose of this chapter has not been to assess all the options in the marketplace. Instead, I have shared a few thoughts regarding some of the most universally needed types of insurance. Most people in our society should at least consider life, health, home-owners/rental, and auto protection.

Your lifestyle and individual circumstances will determine your particular insurance needs. For instance, I recommend disability and umbrella coverage for many people. These types of insurance are designed to protect you from inability to work and from lawsuits that exceed the limits on some of your other coverages. Many experts recommend long-term care insurance to provide for future nursing home, or similar, care. Obviously, if you own a business, there will be other insurance needs to consider.

The options are endless. Don't forget, insurance companies are in the business of marketing their products. Some coverages have broad appeal, and others have more specialized applications. Still others seemingly make no sense at all to me. For instance, I doubt many people really need pet insurance. And, with proper life coverage, I'm convinced that credit life (insurance that pays off a debt at your death) almost never makes good sense.

My advice is threefold:

First, become an informed consumer. Read and study. Learn about insurance—because it will be a lifelong issue.

Second, read your policy and ask all the questions necessary to understand fully what it covers and what it doesn't cover. I have learned from hard experience that, while insurance companies are great at collecting premiums, sometimes it isn't as easy to get claims paid.

Third, find someone in the business you can trust—someone who is more missionary minded than marketing minded. Then build a relationship of trust and good communication. What I've shared with you here are only broad, general principles that may or may not prove correct in your experience. Find a true "friend in the business." Someday you'll be glad you did.

8

How to Buy a Home (and Some Hints on How Not to Buy One)

WITH APOLOGIES to Charlie Dickens, I remember the summer of 1974 as the best of times and the worst of times. There I was, a twenty-two-year-old college senior about to graduate, and I didn't have a clue what I was going to do with the rest of my life. This was before the time when major corporations did a lot of heavy-duty, on-campus career recruiting. In those days you pretty much left college with a diploma, a pat on the back, and a solicitation request from the alumni fund.

My hopes for a career in the entertainment business had ended abruptly a couple of years earlier when my record label realized that I was drastically lacking in the talent department. And I sure didn't want to be a disc jockey for the rest of my life. The little ad agency I had started in my dorm room was fun, but at that point I didn't know how to turn it into a career. I had been excited a few weeks earlier when the college had asked if I would be interested in a job in the recruiting department. But after two trips to the barbershop to get my hair to regulation length, they finally decided that I didn't suitably represent the school. So there I was. No job. No future.

Enter Dave Floyd

About this time a friend of mine at church had some of us over to his home for a party. Dave Floyd was a successful businessman in Nashville who owned a vibrant, young real estate company that was really doing well. I liked and admired him and was thrilled to be invited to his home. Little did I know how that evening was going to change my life.

During the party Dave asked if the two of us could visit for a few minutes. It didn't take him long to get to the point, "Steve, have you ever considered a career in real estate?"

Wow! What an idea! I had sold lots of things. Before college I had sold books for the Southwestern Company. As a matter of fact, I had been one of the top sales guys in the nation. I'd also sold radio production, advertising, and lots of other things. But real estate? This was serious stuff. I didn't know if I could do it. But Dave had faith in me, and, besides, I needed a job. So we shook hands, and I had a career!

I learned a lot during the time I worked for Dave. I sold and listed my share of homes. By the time I moved on, I was among the top 5 percent of real estate people in the mid-state area. But the most valuable thing I left with was an abiding love for real estate. I had seen what home ownership means to people. I had learned the financial benefits of buying a home. I really believed in the product!

Over the years I have always kept my fingers in real estate. From the first one-bathroom home that Bonnie and I bought, through a fistful of residential and commercial investment properties, real estate has been a big part of our lives. I have made money and lost money in real estate. I have left my warm home to settle arguments with renters in the middle of the night. I have had great tenants and others that I would have paid to leave. But I can tell you from first-hand experience, there is nothing like owning real estate.

In this chapter I want to share some of the things I have learned over the years. My hope is to help you decide when to buy, how to buy, and, hopefully, how to come out unscathed in the process.

Home Ownership in America—the State of the Art

Today home ownership in America is at an all-time high. According to the Heritage Foundation, prior to World War II less than 50 percent of Americans owned the homes they lived in. But by 1950, the postwar boom saw home ownership catapult to a record 55 percent. By 1960, the numbers had risen to 60 percent. Finally, by late 2000, 68 percent of all Americans owned their homes.

Compared to the population as a whole, home owners have far greater financial security. A survey found that while the median net worth of renters was only $4,200, the median net worth of home owners (counting both their homes and other assets) was an unbelievable $132,100.[1]

People in America aren't shy about moving either. According to the National Association of Realtors, most home owners sell their first home within five years. Second-time buyers usually stay put a little longer—usually seven to eleven years. And, in the course of a lifetime, many of us will own four different homes.[2]

To Buy or Not to Buy? That Is the Question

The simple fact is: No matter how great home ownership is, it isn't for everyone. Even most real estate agents will admit this in their more lucid, honest moments. There are all sorts of good reasons to buy a home, but there are some equally good reasons to wait. Home ownership is a huge decision, and it shouldn't be taken lightly. Jesus warned that prudent people "count the cost." Although he was talking about discipleship, that's pretty good advice for home buying too.

Renting (or even living with family) is sometimes the best option. There are at least six times when renting may make good sense:

When your future is uncertain and there is a likelihood that you will move within a couple of years. Granted, some homes appreciate in value quickly, and there are cases where people have sold homes shortly after buying them and made a profit. But that is the exception, not the rule. When you factor in loan and closing costs, moving expenses, and other outlays, it usually takes at least two to three years before a home can be resold at a profit.

When you are in a sellers' market. Real estate is like most other investments; there are better times than others to buy. Occasionally, people find themselves dealing with market conditions that make home buying dangerous, especially if they hope to resell their home at a profit in the near future.

This is what happened in the late 1990s in the Silicon Valley area. Because of the unusual growth in the high-tech world, homes in that area of California became so pricey that average folks simply could not afford them. There were reports of little two-bedroom cracker boxes fetching over $500,000. But many of those tech-savvy folks proved to have less savoir faire when it came to financial matters. Some of them jumped headlong and purchased these overpriced houses. And then the bust of spring 2000 hit! Suddenly all those promises of unbridled stock-value growth in many of the high-tech firms began to crumble. Housing prices fell, and people found themselves stuck with houses they couldn't even sell at break-even prices.

For the first year or so of marriage. I like to see newlyweds take their time making major decisions regarding family and housing. No, I'm not saying that a newly married couple shouldn't have a baby or buy a house. But I do believe it usually makes sense to go slowly with life-forming decisions. The first months of marriage are a time of celebration and getting to know each other. Although you may have dated and been engaged for a considerable period of time, there's still a lot of learning to do. Both partners learn that their spouse has likes and dislikes they never knew about. This usually isn't the best time to add the frustration of home buying to the mix.

Here's a Tip: To get a rough idea of how long a newly married couple might choose to wait before buying their first home, subtract their age from eighty. Then wait a week for each year. For instance, if you are married at age twenty-five, subtract twenty-five from eighty. You might consider waiting about fifty-five weeks, around a year, before buying that first home.

When cost is a major consideration. Frequently, you can expect that owning a house will cost more that renting—especially in the first few years. Even if your mortgage payment is no more than the rent, there are other costs to consider like home-owners insurance, property tax, yard mowing, landscaping, and maintenance.

If you hate doing maintenance. Remember, when a lightbulb burns out in your new home, there won't be a maintenance man to come and replace it. Jobs like mowing the yard, shoveling the snow, fixing a leaky roof, repairing a broken dishwasher, and cleaning the gutters are all responsibilities that come with home ownership.

When there is excessive debt. Since I hate debt so much, it probably won't surprise you that I like to see young couples delay home buying until excessive consumer debt is paid off or at least under control. Believe me, the joy of home ownership can evaporate quickly when bill collectors are ringing the doorbell every evening!

My Bad Advice

I've always regretted some bad advice I gave one of my employees. Shortly after Tom came to work for me, I encouraged him to buy a house that he had to stretch to afford. At that point in my life, I bought into the traditional logic that says, even though it may be tough, it still makes sense to buy a house as early as possible.

But this house was too expensive for Tom and his wife. It strained them financially, and even worse, it put pressure on them emotionally. It added stress to their marriage and sapped their personal peace. Fortunately, Tom had good enough sense to forget my advice and sell the house, which the Lord helped him do. They moved into a more affordable rental home that was perfect for their needs. It gave them the financial breather they needed to regroup, pay off some debt, and begin saving to buy another home. Eventually, with their financial house in order, Tom and his wife bought a lovely home that fit their needs and financial abilities.

When the Time Is Right to Buy a Home

All right, now that I've been a real killjoy, let's look at the flip side of the coin. There are some right motives—and times—to buy a home. Without question home ownership is a cornerstone of the American dream. Today, there are more than seventy million home owners in America, and most are happy with their decision.[3] Each year about five million homes are purchased, and of those buyers over 40 percent are doing it for the first time![4] So, if this is your first time into the home-buying market, relax. It can be a lot of fun. Following are some of the reasons that could make home ownership a good consideration for you:

"Oh, Toto, there's no place like home." With that one short statement, Dorothy summed it all up. There really is nothing like getting up in the morning and putting your feet down on your own floor.

Most families long for a place to call their own. While home owner-ship can become a source of inappropriate pride, there is a healthy sense of security that comes with owning a home. Of course, many happy, successful families never own a home. But most people will agree that home ownership enhances a child's sense of permanence and well-being. It has a stabilizing effect on most families.

Appreciation of value. For many people their greatest financial asset is their home. Historically, home ownership has been one of the most dependable and conservative ways available for the average Joe or Jane to build their net worth.

Home ownership allows you to build equity in two ways: First, since you are no longer making payments to a landlord, the mort-gage payments you make on your home serve as a type of savings plan. As you pay down the price of the house, you build equity (an ownership interest). Conversely, a renter's monthly payment goes to the landlord and doesn't allow the opportunity to build equity. Second, over time most (but certainly not all) home owners see the original value of their homes increase. We have all known of people, maybe our own parents, who bought a home decades earlier for $30,000 or $50,000 only to sell it at retirement for many times their original investment.

More privacy and greater lifestyle flexibility. Just a few weeks ago Matt, one of our youth ministers, and his wife Elizabeth, bought their first home. About a week after closing, I asked Elizabeth how they were enjoying their new house. "Wow, I can't believe how quiet it is," she said. Then she went on to tell me how it was the first time in their married lives when they didn't have to put up with other apartment renters' stereos.

When you own your own home, you set the rules. If you want it quiet at 10:00, just turn off the lights and shut the door. If you want a garden, plant one. If you don't want to listen to the CD player at 2:00 in the morning, don't turn it on. It's great!

Price stability. Unlike renters, who usually have to contend with annual lease increases, most home owners enjoy greater price stability. Most fixed-rate mortgage loans are structured so that the principal and interest portion of the monthly payments stay about the same for the full term of the repayment period. Historically, this has been a great advantage because, due to the effects of inflation, you repay the mortgage with "cheaper" dollars.

Tax advantages. Although I don't usually advise investment decisions be driven solely by tax considerations, tax benefits can be a great way to ice the cake. This is especially true with home ownership. In most cases the interest paid on your home loan is tax deductible. Additionally, there may be other tax benefits available to home owners that renters don't get. Of course, as is the case with anything else, consult a competent advisor before making any investment or tax-related decision.

How Much Home Payment Can You Handle?

According to the National Association of Realtors, an old rule of thumb says that most home buyers can afford a house that costs about two to two-and-a-half times their annual gross income. (This is total earnings before taxes and other withholdings are deducted.) But as the NAR so correctly points out, this is only a rough rule of thumb.[5]

People's situations vary. Job stability in some areas of the country is not what it is in other areas. Your present debt load may be more, or less, than the average. How about your other financial planning? How long is it until retirement? What arrangements are you making for your kids to go to college? Do you have your financial house in order? These are all considerations that will have an impact on what you can comfortably afford to spend on a house—and, more specifically, your monthly payment.

RealEstate.com reports another rule of thumb saying that lenders feel comfortable with people spending between 28 percent and 33 percent of their gross monthly income on housing.[6]

But don't forget, lenders are in the business of loaning money. If they don't make loans, they go out of business. And the bigger the loans they make, the better. Although a good lender will not make a loan that doesn't fit what his models say you can repay, he may not be overly co cerned about how tough it will be for you to make those payments. Ultimately, it is your job to decide what is affordable for you. How much can you pay back every single month for the next fifteen or thirty years—without sacrificing your emotional and spiritual peace?

In chapter 4, I discussed the concept of "true" income. I use this phrase when referring to the money that a family brings home *after* all taxes and withholdings have been factored out. This is also reasonably predictable income that is not dependent on unreliable bonuses, wishful thinking, and the like. I like to encourage young, first-time home buyers to work from this "true" income amount. Then, if at all possible, my advice is to keep total housing costs, including your monthly payment (which typically includes principal, interest, taxes, and insurance) plus maintenance and upkeep, at no more than 25 to 33 percent of that amount. I realize that this is less than some commercial lenders may allow, but my job isn't to make loans. My job is to encourage you to buy no more than you can afford without adding undue stress to your life.

Fifteen-Year Versus Thirty-Year Mortgages[7]

Americans love to defer pain. Pleasure and gratification have become the mantra of our culture. But sometimes it's a question of deciding how best to cut off the dog's tail: Is it better just to whack it all off at once or one inch at a time? Although our squeamish side might prefer the inch-by-inch approach, the poor dog would probably rather get it all over with at once.

When it comes to mortgages, there is a similar question to be answered: Would you rather have more pain for a short period of time; or would you prefer a low-level, nagging, ongoing, dull pain for a much longer period? That is the difference between fifteen- and thirty-year mortgages. The benefit of the thirty-year plan is that the monthly payments will be somewhat less than in a fifteen-year payout. But that also means monthly payments for fifteen more years—that's 180 more checks to the mortgage company! Also, you need to know that often the interest rate on a thirty-year mortgage is higher than it would be on the same house with a fifteen-year mortgage.

For instance: Suppose you decide to borrow $150,000 on a home with a thirty-year mortgage at 7½ percent. Your monthly payment (principal and interest only) would be about $1,049. But if you bought that same home on a fifteen-year mortgage at 7½ percent, your monthly payments would only go up to $1,391—or, $342 more per month.

But here's the real story: By the end of the thirty-year mortgage, you would have made total principal and interest payments of $377,640. If, instead, you had financed the home over fifteen years, the total payout would have been $250,380. That's a savings of $127,260 in interest costs!

And, as I mentioned, frequently the rates on fifteen-year mortgages are around ¼ to ½ percent lower than for comparable thirty-year mortgages. So, if you chose the fifteen-year loan, it would be reasonable to look for a rate of around 7 to 7¼ percent instead of 7½ percent. Based on that, with a fifteen-year mortgage at 7¼ percent, your monthly payment (principal and interest) would be around $1,369—or, only $320 more per month. And your savings over the life of the loan would increase to about $131,220!

Adjustable Rate Mortgages: The Path of Least Resistance

An adjustable-rate mortgage, often referred to as an ARM, is a home loan with an interest rate and monthly payments that are subject to change. Most of the time the payment starts low with a teaser rate. This rate, though, is designed to go up or down depending on what interest rates do. Usually the loan rate is tied to some external interest rate index. Mercifully, there is usually a maximum interest rate.

My advice for someone convinced to roll the dice with one of these loans is twofold: Be sure never to sign anything until you understand all the details of the loan document; and second, make sure you can pay the highest possible rate.

If you can't afford those higher payments today, what makes you think you'll be able to pay them in a couple of years? Yes, I know, your salary will increase, and you may hit it big on a quiz show, but don't bet on it. Do you remember when we discussed Murphy's Law in chapter 5? Well, this is where you'll hit it face first. Just when you think you'll easily be able to absorb those higher monthly payments, an elderly parent will need financial aid, or you'll be downsized at work, or the stork will knock at the door with that sweet, little, unexpected bundle of joy.

Maybe instead of calling these ARMs, it would be kinder to admit the obvious and name them ARM & LEG loans—since that's what they can cost! I'm not enough of a riverboat gambler to appreciate this offering from our friends in the lending business.

Twelve Tips for an Easier Home Purchase

Following are twelve thought starters that I can tell you from personal experience should make for a happier, easier home-buying experience:

1. Make the decision with prayer. Before you decide to buy a home, go before the Father and ask for his guidance and leadership. Ask him to open (and, if necessary, close) the doors in your decision-making process. Be sensitive to his direction.

2. Get wise counsel. Talk to your parents or other older, wiser, more mature people about your plans. Ask questions about their home-buying experiences. Often gray hair hides a lot of wisdom.

3. Get to know the area. This is especially important if you have recently moved into a new area. First impressions are not always correct. You wouldn't be the first person to buy a home in a neighborhood that appears perfect at first blush only to live to regret the decision. Renting for a while and becoming familiar with a new town can pay big, long-term dividends.

4. Learn about real estate. Most of you aren't as jazzed about real estate as I am. But since this may be the biggest investment you will ever make, doesn't it seem wise to do some research? As part of the home-buying process, buy a good book or two on the subject. Begin perusing the "for sale" ads in the paper and realty magazines in your area. Get on the Web and do some reading. Visit some open houses. In a phrase: Get smart about real estate!

5. Get prequalified or preapproved for your mortgage. Before you start house hunting, it's a good idea to meet with several mortgage lenders and discuss rates, options, and various programs for which you may be eligible. Sometimes this is done informally (often referred to as "prequalifying the buyer"). By simply reviewing your credit history and financial situation, a mortgage lender can give you an estimate of what you can qualify for and how much it will cost.

You may prefer to get fully preapproved for your mortgage. After submitting all the required material, the lender will submit the package to underwriting. Then, if you qualify, they can make a firm commitment on your loan.

Another reason I like to see people arrange their financing before they begin house shopping has to do with "negotiating leverage." When a buyer enters the market with a loan already approved, realtors and sellers take him more seriously. When he makes an offer—even at a reduced price, it gets their attention. In the event that two people are bidding on the same house—one with an approved loan and one without, which do you suppose will win?

6. *Decide whether you want an agent's help.* There is not a right or wrong way to do this. Some people like to shop without an agent; others want the help that an agent can bring. A good real estate agent can be worth her weight in gold. If you decide to use an agent, get references from friends, business associates, and people at church. Sometimes mortgage people and bankers can make helpful recommendations.

Get to know the agent before you begin looking at houses. Meet over dinner and discuss his qualifications and your desires. Be clear as to whom your agent's legal and moral allegiance is to. You may be surprised to learn that since the seller is paying the commission, the agent's responsibility may be to the seller. Before you share personal information or discuss strategy, it's best to confirm that the agent is going to be on your side of the fence.

7. *Get good legal representation.* The cavalier way some people handle the legal side of home buying blows my mind. This may well be the biggest investment of your life. Think twice before you go it alone! I prefer to use my own attorney whenever I'm involved in a real estate transaction. He is my eyes and ears in an arena that I don't fully understand. It's his job to advise and protect me. The extra money it costs to hire a good lawyer is nothing compared to the problems you can run into without one.

8. *Don't be afraid to ask lots of questions.* Home buying is no time to be embarrassed to ask questions. Also, if some less-than-

satisfactory answers are given, it may help as you negotiate a final price.

Some of the questions that I might ask are:

- How long has the house been on the market?
- Why are you selling?
- Have there been any problems in the neighborhood? Crime or vandalism? Troublesome neighbors?
- Are there a lot of other homes selling in the neighborhood? If so, why?
- Is there a home owners' association? If so, what does it do? What will it expect from me? How much are the fees? What do they include?
- What are the property taxes? Are they likely to go up in the near future?
- What property easements are there?
- Has there ever been a problem with flooding or other natural disaster?
- If there is a basement, does water get in when it rains?
- How old is the roof? What about the air and heat systems, etc?
- What do the utilities average per month? Don't hesitate to ask for a look at the past year's utility bills. If the seller really wants to sell the house and if he has nothing to hide, this shouldn't be a problem.

9. When you find the right house, don't be afraid to make an offer. For first-time buyers this can be tough. It's a big decision. You don't want to make a mistake. But don't let irrational fear keep you from doing what logically you know is right. If the house fits your predetermined budget, needs, and other criteria, don't let cold feet send you running in the other direction.

Your realty agent (and possibly an appraiser of your choosing) have helped determine a fair price. You are armed with all pertinent information; you are fully educated. Now is the time to step up to the plate. While there is no law that says you have to offer full price, it is important to be realistic. Every real estate agent has a story of a sale that fell through because a prospective buyer went on a last-minute fishing trip to see if he could lowball the seller. The seller, insulted by the unrealistic offer, refused to make a counteroffer, and everybody lost. Be careful to be within the ballpark with your first offer if you really want the house.

10. Don't be a shy negotiator. There is almost always room for negotiation in a deal. The trick is to find a win-win approach. Maybe the seller has an emotional attachment to an old family chandelier in the entry hall that he wants to take when he leaves. My advice is not to argue with him over that chandelier. Instead, why not ask him to replace it with another one?

Look for things in the negotiating process that will sweeten the deal for you without harming the seller. For instance, you might ask that the drapes be included at no extra cost. Home buyers sometimes forget how expensive items like drapes can be, and most sellers won't be able to use their old drapes at a new house.

11. Consider having the house inspected. If you have any questions about the condition of the house or its systems, it might be wise to agree that the sale is contingent on the house receiving (at your expense) an inspection and a satisfactory rating from a qualified home inspector.

12. Tie up lose ends. Just because the contract is signed, that doesn't mean your work is finished. There's still a lot to do. Don't forget to shop for the best deal on home owners insurance. Also, begin planning the actual move. Will you use a moving company, rental truck, or will you simply impose on the good nature of your friends?

Some Things to Think Twice About

There are some things that would concern me about a house. These don't necessarily have to be red lights to your purchase plan, but they should serve, at least, as yellow caution lights.

The biggest, most expensive home in the neighborhood. In most situations a given home's appraised value is somewhat contingent on what other houses in the area are selling for. The most expensive home in the neighborhood may not appreciate as fast as one of the less expensive homes in the same neighborhood.

Homes that are close to property zoned for retail, business, or other nonresidential purposes. Traditionally, most people have been willing to pay more for homes in areas reserved strictly for residential use. However, this is beginning to change in some urban areas today as expensive, planned residential developments are now being built close to office and retail complexes.

Houses with odd or unusual design treatments. I just got off the phone this afternoon with a home-builder friend of mine. He was telling me about an expensive new house he's building for a couple who recently moved to Nashville from Canada. The owners have decided on some pretty unusual treatments, including a metal roof and no interior baseboard trim. I don't know anything about Canadian-style homes, but I do know something about the grits-and-guitars crowd here in Nashville, and it doesn't include metal roofs and walls without moldings! While these good people from the north may enjoy their uniquely designed home, one day they are probably going to have a hard time selling it.

Areas where there is little or no code enforcement. If you see over-grown yards with cars jacked up out front, that's not a good sign. Also check to see that most of the homes in the neighborhood are generally comparable in value.

High-density areas. I like to encourage people to drive by the home they are considering during the peak traffic hours (usually between 7:00 and 9:00 A.M. and 4:00 and 6:00 P.M.) to see if they will be happy with the noise and congestion. Will it be easy getting in and out of your driveway during those times?

Lifestyle concerns. Are you in the airport's flight line? Will car headlights be flashing in your windows every evening?

Areas that are prone to flooding.

Houses that are functionally obsolete. This can take many forms. For instance, a four-bedroom home with only one bathroom is going to be tougher to resell. Is there adequate ceiling height in the basement? Is the garage actually big enough to allow you to open your car doors? Are there central air-conditioning and heating?

When Does It Make Sense to Refinance Your Present Mortgage?[8]

Most of my comments so far have been directed at first-time homebuyers. But let's suppose you bought a home several years ago when rates were higher than they are today. You have heard mortgage company advertisements for refinancing. But refinancing sounds confusing. Yet you have a sick feeling in the pit of your stomach that with every monthly payment you are spending more than you should. So what to do? Follow the line of least resistance, or look into refinancing?

Contrary to popular belief (and fear), there really isn't anything conceptually complicated about refinancing your home. Granted, you might want to contact your tax advisor since the IRS may treat some of your refinancing expenses differently for tax purposes. This, however, is usually not a major issue for most people. The main difference in the original purchase mortgage you made on your house and a refinance is that with the first loan you were moving into a new home, and with the second you're going to stay put. This time there won't be any long good-byes or moving vans involved.

It's possible that a lot has changed since you first bought your home. You may find that it's much quicker and easier today to get a home loan than it was several years ago. Also think about the savings. What if I told you that this simple exercise could put an extra $2,500 (pretax) a year into your pocket—then would you be interested? Well, it can. Look at this hypothetical example: Suppose, at present, you have a $150,000 mortgage loan at 8¾ percent with a monthly payment (principal and interest only) of about $1,180. By refinancing it at 2 percent less (6¾ percent), your monthly payments would drop by more than $200 per month to around $973. That's almost $2,500 a year in savings.

Obviously, this is just an illustration. Refinancing your loan can be a time-consuming and expensive process. There are often a number of costs involved like origination fees, title insurance, appraisal fees, tax implications, etc. All of these things will have an effect on whether a refinance is appropriate for you. Also, it is wise to review your present mortgage agreement for prepayment penalty clauses before you go too far in the process. Mortgage experts say it all boils down to this: Do you plan to keep the home long enough to recapture the expenses involved in getting a new mortgage? You can determine this by figuring how much you will be saving each month at the new rate, then divide the refinancing and other costs by that monthly savings to see how many months it will take to recapture those expenses.

For instance, suppose your new monthly payment is $300 less than the old one, and the refinance expenses total $4,500. First, since the $300 is a pretax figure, you will want to know what the "true" net savings are. If, for instance, you are in the 31 percent tax bracket, your monthly savings would net down to $207 ($300 x 0.69=$207). Then divide the $4,500 of refinance costs by the $207 you are saving each month, and you will see that it will take about twenty-two months for you to break even.[9]

If It's Too Good to Be True . . .[10]

It's a competitive world out there. Because of competition many lenders will reduce or even waive some of the fees. Don't be afraid to ask. But, on the other hand, beware of deals that look too good to be true; they may well be. For instance, don't be fooled into buying a mortgage just because the company promises fewer closing points. (Often, as a one-time rate enhancer, a lender charges points on a loan at closing. One point is equal to 1 percent of the principal amount of the loan.) For instance, suppose you were talking with two lenders about a fifteen-year, $200,000 mortgage. Lender A offers you the loan at 7½ percent with three points (or, $6,000). Lender B pitches you the same $200,000 mortgage at 8 percent with only two and a half points (or $5,000). Which is the better deal?

Here's how to figure it: Begin by comparing the monthly payments on the principal and interest of each loan. You'll see that Lender A's 7½ percent loan will carry monthly payments of about $1,854, and that Lender B's 8 percent mortgage will cost about $1,911 monthly. That's a difference of $57 per month. Now, by dividing that $57 (of monthly payment difference) into the $1,000 (of extra point cost from Lender A), you see that in about eighteen months the cost of the extra half point from Lender A is recaptured. If you are planning to stay in the house for much more than 18 months, it may make better sense to pay the extra half point to Lender A and take the 7½ percent loan.[11] Of course, other costs and tax implications may affect the numbers somewhat, but the general principle holds.

Three Reasons to Consider Refinancing

Experts in the field frequently mention the following three reasons to consider a refinance. I consider only the first two reasons to be valid. In my opinion, the third reason is almost always a mistake.

NO DEBT, NO SWEAT!

To cut your monthly costs. Home mortgage rates fluctuate tremendously. When I came into the real estate business in the mid-70s, rates ranged from the high 8 percent range to over 9 percent. Since then, the numbers have been all over the board. In the early 1980s rates went over 15 percent. At this writing some are under 6 percent. A wise home owner pays attention to rates, and when the time is right, he springs into action. As the earlier illustration shows, sometimes refinancing can save a family tens of thousands of dollars in interest over the life of the loan.

To improve the terms or conditions of your present loan. Some people find themselves stuck with an adjustable rate mortgage (ARM) that begins to escalate shortly after they move into their home. As I have already said, I don't think this is generally the best way to buy a home. Often the only way out of such a loan is with a new fixed-rate mortgage. Also some people get into a short-term mortgage that has a huge balloon payment due. More often than not, they have a tough time paying the full amount when it comes due, and refinancing their mortgage can make sense.

To get money out of the equity in your home. This is the worst reason to refinance a home. However, some people can't resist the pitch to refinance their homes with larger mortgages that allow them to take "spending cash" away from the closing. Please don't do this! Why jeopardize your family's security and your own peace of mind by going deeper in debt on your home to buy a new car or stereo? Your goal should be to pay your home off as quickly as possible—not to go deeper in the hole!

What About the 2 Percent Rule?

Some people in the field suggest that the time to refinance is whenever loan rates have dropped by 1½ to 2 percent, or more. While this is probably not a bad generalization, it doesn't hold in every situation. There are times when rates have dropped by 2 percent, or even more, and it still may be unwise to refinance. Such could be the case if the lender's costs and other expenses are excessively high, or if you are planning to move in the near future, before you can recoup the refinancing expenses.

Conversely, there are times when refinancing can serve a home owner well even when rates are down by less than 2 percent. Frequently, a home owner can enjoy real savings with even a lesser rate reduction if he watches his expenses and doesn't plan to move in the near future.

Five Considerations About Refinancing Your Home

According to my friend Mike Hardwick with Churchill Mortgage Corporation, there are five things to consider before you refinance your home:

1. How much will the new mortgage reduce your interest rate?
2. How much will your monthly payment be reduced?
3. Check to see if there are any prepayment penalties on your present mortgage.
4. What will the expenses be for things like closing costs, points, loan origination fees, application charges, appraisals, inspections, title insurance, mortgage insurance, etc.? (I would also add possible tax implications to this list.)
5. How many years do you plan to stay in this home?[12]

9

Kids, Cash, and Character

I WAS TOLD of a news report about a dumb criminal in Fort Worth, Texas. Apparently, the guy rode his bicycle up to a taco restaurant carry-out window, pulled a gun, and ordered the clerk to give him their money. That's dumb, but hold on; it gets worse.

He ordered a meal while he was waiting for the money. Well, the money came out before his meal was ready. And, believe it or not, this Einstein hung around waiting for his food. In the meantime one of the employees called the police. Since our biker hoodlum had also forgotten to wear a mask, they recognized him as an ex-employee of the restaurant and gave his name to the police. The law arrived before his meal did, and they arrested him right there at the drive-up window! To make matters worse, he proceeded to aim his gun at the police who pulled their weapons and shot him twice. (Fortunately, the wounds weren't life threatening.) On closer examination it turned out that he was carrying a toy pistol.

As I thought about this incident, one phrase seemed to sum this guy up: dumb but fearless.

Is There a Similar Situation in Your Home?

If you're a parent, that phrase may have occurred to you several times over the years. I know it pretty well describes some of the experiences we have had with our kids. I remember the time when our son Joshua was peeved with me because I refused to believe that he was mature enough to be trusted with my car. Call me an old fogy, but the kid was just four years old!

Actually, it's part of what makes a kid a kid—more bravado than common sense. By their nature children are immature. They believe themselves to be far more intelligent than the facts would warrant. And to make matters worse, there's that time somewhere between twelve and fourteen when most kids go through a season of omniscience.

That's where parents come in. Unlike animals that desert their young, God gave human parents a greater mandate. For better or worse, it's our dubious job description to stick around for the first eighteen to twenty years. And if we're any good at the job, we'll do more than simply be there. We'll aim higher. Our goal will be to be our children's mentors and key advisors. We're the ones they should come to for their life-skill advice. I know that is a unique idea these days. With all the buffoon parents on TV sitcoms and the disrespect dished out by society in general, it's tough to maintain credibility through the full twenty-year run. But just because it isn't easy doesn't mean it isn't vital.

Many of society's ills can be laid at the feet of parents who have abrogated their responsibilities. That's why I want to challenge you as a parent, especially if your kids are still young, to love them enough to direct and discipline them in all areas of their lives. Stay involved. Don't be shy. Don't be marginalized or intimidated away from your God-ordained responsibility. Just because some other eight-year-old philosopher teases your child about your involvement in his life, don't back off. Insist that your beliefs and ideas be respected, honored, and followed. It is your duty not only to your children but to society as a whole, to teach them about Jesus, basic morality, respect, and the appropriate life skills.

Insulation Versus Isolation in an Age of Affluence

America is the Disneyland of the world. Kids in this country are blessed with a level of affluence that is unknown throughout most of the world. Even those of us who grew up only a generation ago can barely comprehend many of the things today's culture takes for granted. According to the American Express Retail Index, parents and teens spent an average of $550 per child on back-to-school shopping.[1] Teenage Research Unlimited reports that teenagers spend an average of $84 per week of their own and their parents' money.[2] Wealth in America grew exponentially in the 1990s. The Spectrum Group reports that high net-worth households (those with assets of at least $1 million, not counting their primary residence) exploded from $1.8 million in 1990 to $7.2 million by 1999! Today fully 55 percent of all American millionaires are under fifty-five years old, compared with only 26 percent in 1990.[3]

Whether you're a part of this new financially elite segment or not, these data have a direct impact on your family. You don't have to be wealthy to be a victim of the wealth factor. Just as a tide raises all boats, wealthy friends affect what your kids want. When their friends buy the newest brand of shoes or the most popular line of jeans, your kids will want them, too. And even if you run with a decidedly middle-class group, don't underestimate the effect the media and advertising have on your children's wish lists.

A big part of parenting today has to do with helping our kids live within the culture without becoming a part of the culture. It is an issue of *insulating* them from the pressures and temptations around them without *isolating* them from the world at large.

Where We Came From

I suspect that many of you are a lot like me. I grew up in the 1960s. Things were somewhat different in those days. Back then money wasn't openly discussed in many households. There are several reasons for this: First, our parents came from a more genteel era. After all, if they had prospered, talking about money was considered vulgar and tantamount to bragging. If they were struggling, they suffered silently, never admitting their pain. In those days money was a guy thing. Dad handled the dollars in most homes, and Mom and the kids heard little about the family's financial picture except when there was a crisis.

But I suspect the most important factor of all was a general lack of financial education among most of that generation. After all, these were the people who had fought and won World War II. Many of them had sacrificed their own childhoods and dreams of a college education so their kids wouldn't grow up speaking German or Japanese. In many ways this generation abandoned their hopes to give the next generation a future. It's little wonder that they weren't as educated (or as cocky) as their kids have become on monetary issues.

Three Rules for Teaching Kids About Money

Many people think our society has grown fat and lazy. We have luxuries our parents could only have dreamed of. Imagine—two or three cars, color television with more than a couple of fuzzy channels, family arguments over where we're going to vacation this year. Many of us also have greater financial resources and the time to ponder how to invest them. So it behooves today's parents to help their kids understand money and how it works. But before we focus on what we want the little banditos to do, let's spend a minute on what the grownups need to be doing. I believe there are three all-important rules:

The first and most important rule for teaching your children how to manage money is to set the right example yourself. This is one time when the physician had better heal himself first—before he starts dispensing pills. Kids are smart; their hypocrisy meters work over-time. To tell a child to do something that you are unwilling to do not only dilutes the impact of the message, but it also dilutes the respect they have for the messenger. To have credibility and moral authority, a parent has to be willing to go the extra mile and not cut corners simply for short-term gratification.

Does this mean you have to do everything right? What about the past—can a parent regain the moral high ground when the kids know you've made previous mistakes? Yes, but it requires honesty and a willingness to admit the obvious: "There have been times when Mom and Dad have blown it. But we're learning, and we want to help you kids avoid some of the painful mistakes we've made."

Then it's a matter of walking the talk. The kids will be watching. If they see you making the tough decisions and lifestyle changes to get your own financial house in order, it will serve as a powerful motivator and example. But, if you slip back into old habits, that, too, won't go unnoticed.

What parents do with liberty, the kids will do with license. One of the most important things any parent can do is to understand and accept this concept. What you do on a controlled, moderate level as a parent, your kids are likely to take to the extreme. Lots of Christian parents who insisted on their "liberty to drink socially" when they had small children would give anything if they could change things today. Many of them are dealing with grown kids who used their par-ents' liberty as a license to drink or use drugs destructively.

The same holds true for family money issues. Whatever your children see you do will tend to have a geometric effect on their behavior. If your children perceive a lack of self-control and good stewardship in the purchasing and savings decisions you make, don't be surprised if one day you see the same behavior on their part being played out in an extreme, mutated form.

Keep the communication lines open. My friend Mike Root likes to say, "If you don't communicate, you'll speculate." Nothing takes the place of open communications in a family. One of my regular "go to" passages in the Book is Deuteronomy 6:6–9:

> *These words, which I am commanding you today, shall be on your heart. You shall teach them diligently to your sons and shall talk of them when you sit in your house and when you walk by the way and when you lie down and when you rise up. You shall bind them as a sign on your hand and they shall be as frontals on your forehead. You shall write them on the doorposts of your house on your gates (NASB).*

Although God was speaking about the spiritual education parents owe their children, the principle holds even more broadly. As parents we must be good communicators with our children. There have been a lot of times over the years when I was able to parlay a drive to get a Coke, or a fishing trip, or just a walk through the yard into a teaching opportunity. As Christian parents we realize that whatever the surface topic (school, friends, or financial issues), it all goes back to teaching God's principles for how to live this life and prepare for the one to come.

Practical Principles

In the next few pages I want to share some of the ideas and concepts that I have learned about kids and money. Some of these are ideas that Bonnie and I have developed, or at least implemented, with our own kids. Some are good ideas that others have found helpful. My goal here is not to exhaust this subject. Instead I hope to give you a few thought starters that may apply to your situation.

Sometimes people assume that because I teach this stuff I've got it all together in my own life. Ha! As the people who know me the best will readily confirm, the answer to that is an emphatic no! As young parents (and even now as older ones), we have failed more times than it's easy to admit. As they say, hindsight is 20/20. I wish I could say that I'm a perfect man, but I'm not. Nowhere close. And I suppose that you could probably say the same about yourself. But thankfully we have a perfect Savior. Jesus is in the business of fixing broken people like us. He also fixes broken kids. So as you read these ideas, be at peace. These ideas aren't given in an attempt to make you feel guilty or inadequate. I share them in the simple hope that as we each learn better ways to live, we will share that information with those who follow us.

The 10/45/45 Rule

The best place to start anything is at the beginning, so let me tell you where Bonnie and I began our kids' financial education. It's what we call the 10/45/45 Rule. It's not complicated, but it is the cornerstone on which everything else—financially speaking—is built in the Diggs household.

We teach our kids that money can be used for three things: God's purposes, the future (deferred gratification), and the present. To that end, we tell the children that for every dollar they receive 10 percent of it goes to God, 45 percent goes into savings for college (I'll have more to say about this in chapter 10), and the remaining 45 percent is for the present to be spent as they wish.

After more than fifteen years of road testing, this little formula has proven itself to be a winner in our family. It's simple and fair. It helps the kids remember what is really important. They are reminded with every dollar they earn that God comes first. We want them to know that he holds them responsible to help others. As you may remember from chapter 3, while I'm not a legalist about tithing, I do think it's a great way to teach anybody the principles of godly giving. With time and maturity I hope our children will learn to give even beyond the tithe. But for now it seems like a good way to learn an important principle.

The second 45 percent is the component that we hope will help the kids learn the concept of deferred gratification. By having a big goal that is a long distance into the future, we hope they will learn that many of life's greatest joys come only to those who plan ahead. In teaching his own son, the writer of Proverbs said it this way:

> *Go to the ant, O sluggard,*
> *Observe her ways and be wise,*
> *Which, having no chief,*
> *Officer or ruler,*
> *Prepares her food in the summer*
> *And gathers her provision in the harvest.*
> *How long will you lie down, O sluggard?*
> *When will you arise from your sleep?*
> *A little sleep, a little slumber,*
> *"A little folding of the hands to rest"—*
> *Your poverty will come in like a vagabond*
> *And your need like an armed man (6:6–11 NASB).*

We want our kids to be willing to invest their work in things that won't pay off immediately, because someday this same discipline will serve them well as they make hard choices about saving for a home or even retirement.

The final 45 percent is for the present. As Paul reminded Timothy in 1 Timothy 6:17, God gives us gifts to enjoy. It's perfectly OK to have some fun, to enjoy the present. We want our kids to have a balanced view of money. Sometimes too much talk and teaching about saving for the future can backfire. We've all seen articles in the news about misers who died after hoarding fortunes that could have been enjoyed and shared with others during life.

Some Christians, in an attempt to be good stewards, do the same thing. They squirrel away far more than they'll ever need thinking that this is somehow virtuous. To avoid this obsessive-compulsive abuse of money, we encourage our kids to blow some of their money in the here and now.

What About Allowances?

There are about as many opinions on this subject as there are parents. Some parents believe in allowances while others don't. Some parents tie allowances to certain chores the kids are expected to do, while other parents believe allowances should be free gifts. One survey indicated that over 80 percent of sixth graders do some chores for their allowance. Allowance amounts also vary widely. Some allowances are pathetic pittances, while others are big enough to make a down payment on a Florida condominium. The High School Awareness Survey reports that the median allowance is eleven dollars.[4]

Let me share a few broad suggestions on allowances that may simplify your planning:

The parents should decide the amount and purpose of the allowance. I recently ran across the results of a survey conducted by Kids' Money that said the average weekly allowances for twelve-year-olds is $9.58; for sixteen year olds it's $17.84, and for eighteen year olds it's $40.10.[5] I don't know about you, but that's a lot more than we give our twelve-, sixteen-, eighteen-year-old kids!

My point is simply that the amount and purpose of an allowance is a personal matter to be determined by the person who pays that allowance—you. While there certainly is nothing wrong with soliciting the children's input, it's your money! Do with it as you feel is best and right for your family.

Be clear what the allowance is, and isn't, for. If it's a weekly gift, great. But if you tie its payment to certain chores the child is required to do, be clear about your expectations.

Stick to your guns! If you begin by requiring that certain jobs be performed in order to receive the allowance, then respect your child enough to pay the allowance only when the jobs have been completed.

Many parents think that by backing down they're showing love to their children. Unfortunately, kids often see it as softness and weakness. They soon learn that there are no absolutes; with enough pleading they can get their way. If a child doesn't learn about responsibility and boundaries at home, he'll either learn about them the hard way in the real world, or he'll spend his life as a drain on society.

Avoid advances. As long as there have been allowances, there have been kids asking for advances. I would encourage you to avoid this trap. If you really want to raise a child who will see nothing wrong with living on borrowed money and credit cards as an adult, allowance advances are a great way to reinforce this behavior.

Expect children to do some of the household chores without any form of financial payment. Kids need to learn that running a household is a big job. As a part of the family, they should contribute to the welfare of the whole family. In our experience this has helped our kids develop a level of self-respect. They know that the rest of the family depends on them in some way. This has helped us enjoy a wonderful closeness and interdependence as a family unit.

Be consistent. Once you establish a payday, make it a point to have the money ready on time.

Helping Your Kids Earn Money

Invariably, one of the first questions most parents struggle with is whether a child should have a job. Of course, this is another question that will find different answers in different families. The child's age and temperament, where you live, job availability, and your lifestyle as a family all play into this decision.

But I believe wise parents should look for ways to help their kids earn at least part of their money. This can take many forms. Personally, I like jobs that can be done at, or at least close to, home. It's a dangerous world out there. Too much can happen to children without proper supervision. Jobs near the home front can give younger children (those under sixteen) the experience they need without as much risk.

I encourage parents to be involved. Become your children's partner. Make it a game. Look for a job that fits the individual child's temperament and skills. Let your youngster's imagination soar. I am still grateful that my parents rarely told me that I couldn't try out my ideas. I'm sure it embarrassed them the day their six-year-old son struck out into the neighborhood, offering to do carpentry work on their friends' homes. But I still remember the pride and confidence I felt when Mrs. Simons hired me to fix her wooden lawn chair. By the time I quit, it wasn't in much worse shape. But she made me feel like a star and paid me with a pack of gum and six cents to buy a Popsicle. I had other employment ventures that probably made my folks blush. I'm still not sure they ever knew that I tried to start a pottery business by forming little containers from the red clay I dug up in the backyard.

Salesmanship: Society's Great Equalizer

When you factor out those fortunate people who are born to wealth and a few athletic and entertainment superstars, virtually every millionaire in America got there one way: by learning to sell. Salesmanship is the great equalizer of our society. It is the one line of work that is available to virtually everyone. You don't have to have family connections, a big bank account, or a lot of education. All you have to have is some basic product knowledge and an inexhaustible supply of drive and ambition. Sales skills are the best way the average person has to earn a fantastic income. Sure it's tough. If it were easy, everybody would be doing it. Salesmen face lots of rejection. They don't get paid until they sell something. At the end of every day, they know exactly what they are worth because they are paid exactly what they earned—not a penny more, not a penny less.

What a feeling! The knowledge that you are charting your own course is unbeatable. You aren't dependent on the whims of a boss. It's great knowing they can always make a good living.

What Could Be More Important Than a College Education?

If there was one thing I would urge any parent to do to prepare their children for the professional world, it wouldn't be to get lots of technical skills or a college education. *It would be to encourage their children to learn the art and the heart of selling.*

I can trace so much of the business success I have enjoyed in my adult life back to some early decisions I made about selling. I remember being a little embarrassed when people talked about the way I was always trying to sell something as a kid. I did not want to be known as a salesman. But as I got older, I grew to appreciate the choices I had made as a boy. All those school-day afternoons as a little guy knocking on neighbors' doors selling Christmas cards, all-occasion cards, flower seeds, fire extinguishers—whatever. Then, in my teens, instead of working at Burger King, I began to realize that I could make more money and control my life better by selling Swipe miracle cleaner.

When I graduated from high school, most of my friends either took summer jobs or just took the summer off. I decided to leave home and go to the big city of Nashville for a week of intensive sales training by the Southwestern Company. After that, they sent me to South Georgia to sell Bibles and family medical books door-to-door. I soon realized why so many of the guys left after the first few days. One-hundred-degree temperatures were common. For the first part of the summer, we were working out on country back roads where the houses were sometimes a half mile apart. There were plenty of stories about the snakes and wildcats that lived in the swamps near the roads. Since we were expected to work until about 10:00 at night, those stories took on a special impact for me! After all, at that point, I didn't even have a car. It was tough work. When I went for a day or two without a sale—and ran into a bunch of people who truly seemed to enjoy being rude to me—I learned the importance of focusing on the finish line. I learned to set and achieve my goals.

I'll never forget the feeling when the summer of 1970 came to an end. I was beat and worn out. I had lost weight and gotten a tan. I had become a lean, mean selling machine. When I started college that fall, I had enough money to buy a car, a new wardrobe—pretty much whatever I needed. I had won several sales awards. But I had gained more than that. The seventeen-year-old kid who had left home in June had learned how to deal confidently with people and provide for his own needs. I knew, going into college, that I already had the ability to make a good living and get ahead in the world. The next four years were just frosting on the cake.

Those early sales experiences were the building blocks for the radio and television production company I started during college that eventually became the advertising agency that I headed for over twenty-five years. They were the training ground for the real estate work I have found so satisfying and profitable. All in all, I can tell you that the sales skills I learned as a boy have benefited me far more than any formal education ever has.

That's why I'm so excited when I see a kid with an interest in selling or starting his own business. Just last week I passed a brother and sister who were running a lemonade stand in front of their home. As is my practice, I stopped for a drink. What really thrilled me was how enterprising these kids were. They not only were selling lemonade; they also had snacks available. And when I gave them a dollar for the fifty-cent cup of sugar water, the little girl asked, "Do you want any change back?" Those kids are off to a good start!

Mom and Dad, let your kids' imaginations soar, and dream with them. Have brainstorming sessions on ways they can earn money by selling something or starting a small business. A lot of the most successful business people in our society started their business careers as kids. By the time they were fifteen, Bill Gates was developing his software business, and Estee Lauder was doing facials.

If we hope to raise independent kids who will be able to chart their own course in adulthood, it behooves us to help them catch the vision. Frankly, I am concerned as I watch American culture deteriorate. Arguably the world our kids will live their adult lives in will be tougher than the one we've known. Employers may not be as accepting of employees who hold to the Christian ethic. Laws may not continue to protect Christian workers as much as they do now. Teaching our children how to prepare for such a future—facing it confidently and with the know-how to make a living—may prove to be our greatest legacy.

Business Ideas for Kids

Your family is unique. Not every idea will be right in your individual situation. What fits into the culture of one family may be wrong for yours. Obviously, as a parent, you will have to apply common sense and caution as you determine which of these ideas might fit your kids. And depending on where you live, some jobs may require special permits, inspections, etc. But I thought you might like to hear some ideas for how kids can earn money from, or close to, their homes:

- *Walk dogs for the neighbors.* This can be expanded into washing and grooming services as well.
- *Plant a vegetable garden.* Sell the produce to neighbors or a local grocery store. You might even talk to the grocer and ask if there is a specialty item he has a hard time keeping in stock that you could grow. We have a friend who found a grocer who was glad to buy a variety of small salad tomatoes that she grew in her backyard.
- *Make or bake a product to sell.* One family in our church makes bread and bakery products for a number of their friends who are too busy to bake.
- *Baby-sit.* This can take place either at the children's home or in your own home so you can monitor and advise your children.
- *Do yard work and light landscaping.* Of course, this has been the genesis of thousands of profitable lifelong businesses nationwide. By teaching kids to watch the weather reports and schedule their work accordingly, parents can teach valuable lessons about planning and operating a small business.
- *Breed tropical fish.* Years ago my brother-in-law ran a profitable business out of his home, raising various types of fish and selling them to pet stores in the area.
- *Wash and wax cars.* This was another way I made money in my teens. On Saturdays our backyard became a car wash and wax shop. I made good money and controlled my hours. Of course, this is another business that can grow into a full detailing operation with little overhead.
- *Shovel snow.*
- *Teach computer skills.* Today most kids know more about computers than their parents do. Why not offer a course in the basics of computing for a few dollars an hour?

- *Offer product-assembly services.* Kids with a mechanical bent can make money assembling grills, inexpensive boxed furniture, and other items that most adults hate to do. Why not print up some handbills or cards and see if a local office supply or hardware store will let you post them?

Two Words of Caution for Older Kids

As kids get older, things get more complicated. Before I leave this subject, I want to touch on two important topics: after-school jobs and credit.

After-school jobs. There are certainly times when an after-school job is good and appropriate. But before you sign off on the idea for your teenager, you should be aware of the downsides. According to studies, more than half of American twelfth graders average twenty or more hours of work per week. These kids lose family time, miss out on church activities, and fall behind on sleep and relaxation. A report conducted by the Institute of Medicine and the National Research Council found that students who worked even as many as fifteen hours weekly dropped out at higher rates, had lower grades, and were not as likely to go to college.[6]

As a parent, consider both the pluses and the minuses before you OK after-school work. I encourage these jobs only on an as-needed basis to raise money for real needs—not luxuries. Also, whatever the job, be sure that it doesn't cause your child to miss worship or other important events and family time.

Finally, be sure you know what the job involves. Consider visiting the workplace before he or she accepts the job; and then after the job begins, drop by occasionally unannounced. Be sure you are comfortable with the environment. Are the coworkers and managers trustworthy people? Is the workplace safe? The National Consumer League warns about five job situations that are especially dangerous for kids:[7]

- Jobs that involve driving and/or delivery work. This would also include operating or riding motorized equipment like forklifts.
- Working in a cash-based business alone. This would include gas stations, convenience markets, fast-food restaurants, etc.
- Being a part of a young persons' selling crew. This could include selling various types of products in strange neighborhoods, on street corners, in distant cities and other states.
- Jobs where payroll isn't paid on a normal basis where taxes, FICA, and other withholdings are properly made. This could take the form of under-the-table cash payments.
- Building and construction jobs that involve heights, contact with electrical power, etc.

Credit and credit cards. You may expect me to take a hard line on this issue. Financial advisors are all over the board when it comes to kids and credit cards. Some are absolutely opposed under any circumstance, yet others promote the idea. While I'm somewhere between the two extremes, I do have a definite lean toward the opposition side.

I'll have more to say about this in chapter 13 on credit cards and debt, but I do want to share a few thoughts here as they pertain to our children and the credit card industry. First, we have to realize that credit of all sorts—especially credit cards being pushed on young people—is big business. Americans are swamped with debt. As I mentioned in chapter 1, the average credit-card holder is carrying a balance of $4,400.[8] In the ten-year period between 1990 and 2000, average household credit card balances increased from $2,985 to a whooping $7,942![9] And, unfortunately, our kids are following in our footsteps. Today the average college undergraduate is carrying a credit-card balance of about $3,300! Think about that. Just when a young person should be ready to launch into life with optimism and hopefulness, she has to deal with creditors.

The other night I almost crawled through the phone after a tele-marketer who had the gall to invade our home trying to get one of my kids to accept a credit card he was selling! Nothing upsets us more than when someone messes with our kids. Pushing credit—and the bondage that goes with it—onto untrained kids is next to criminal in my book!

But it's not just happening over the phone. I was saddened to hear that a Christian university, with which I'm involved, allows credit-card companies on campus to sell their products. Talk about selling your birthright for a bowl of stew! These marketers set up tables in the student center loaded with T-shirts, coffee mugs, or some other equally valuable treasures and start signing up appli-cants. There's a reason for this. Studies have shown that people tend to have an affinity for their first credit card. They tend to keep that first card much longer than cards they get subsequently. So it's important to target college kids and be the first company to put a card in their hands.

Fortunately, a number of colleges are beginning to wake up to this. Many of them believe that this practice works at cross-purposes with the education and life skills they are trying to teach. There are fully four to five hundred schools nationwide that have either banned, or are set to ban, these marketers from their campuses.[10]

Before You Let "Joe College" Get His First Credit Card

Now that I've told you how I feel about college kids with credit cards, let me admit the obvious: Some of you will simply disagree with my position on this issue. That's OK; they're your kids. No one knows your kids the way you do. If you feel that you can trust your college-bound student with a card, let me share a few suggestions on how to do it more responsibly:

Have a long talk. Discuss how credit cards work. Read the application together and discuss the small print. This is a great time to teach one of the fundamental principles of adulthood: Never sign anything you don't fully understand. Help your son or daughter see what interest and penalty charges can do to a budget. Be fully aware of how many days you have each month to pay the bill without incurring those extra charges.

Place a spending limit on the card. You might be able to tie the amount of available credit to the amount in your child's checking or savings account. In any event you may want to set a $500 or $1,000 spending limit on the card.

Review the billing records. You have a God-ordained mandate to invest yourself in your children's lives. Make clear from the start that you expect regular reports on the card's usage. You might consider requiring that your son or daughter photocopy each month's invoice and send it to you. Does this mean you don't trust them? Sure it does! Think back, when you were their age—how much did you know about these things?

Pay every cent every month. If you do arm your student with plastic, at least make clear that the first month he doesn't pay his bill in full the card gets destroyed! There's a reason for this. If your young person falls into the trap of making minimum payments, she's hung. Bankrate.com computes that if a person makes just the minimum monthly payment on a $1,000 charge on a card that has an 18 percent interest rate, it will take more than twelve years to pay off that debt![11]

Have a clear understanding of what the card may be used for. Establish a written agreement listing what the card can be used for and what it should not be used for.

Only one card. I know of no justifiable reason for a young person to have multiple accounts. It only adds to the confusion and temptation. One study showed that one-fifth of all college students carry four or more credit cards.[12] Folks, this is a disaster looking for a place to happen!

A Sensible Alternative: Consider a Debit Card

Several years ago when Joshua was in his midteens, I arranged with our bank for him to get a debit card. This has been a good experience for us, and it has helped Joshua manage his money.

Debit cards work much like credit cards, with one great advantage: Instead of extending credit, a debit card drafts money straight out of your bank account as soon as you use it. We have found that debit cards are accepted most places that traditional credit cards can be used. While there are some advantages to credit cards, on balance, our family likes the debit card approach best.

Before I leave this, let me warn you that some experts voice concern about debit cards. According to a recent report on Fox News Channel, some banks are not fully disclosing the risks associated with debit cards. Consumers may have a potentially greater liability with debit cards than they do with credit cards. If someone fraudulently uses your debit card, present laws do not give consumers as much protection for speedy recovery as with credit cards. Many banks voluntarily make good on debit card losses; however, it is the consumer's responsibility to understand fully his bank's debit card policy.[13]

Debit cards have some of the inherent weaknesses that credit cards have. For one thing, anytime you buy anything without using cash the pain is less. Whether you use a credit card, a debit card, or a check, somehow it just doesn't feel as bad as pulling out the old billfold and cracking out some greenbacks. Studies show that when people use plastic they spend more money. Of course, merchants and the credit card industry like this.

Five Tips for Helping Kids Understand Money and Work

1. *Be a friend and partner, not a tyrant.* Dealing with money and understanding its relationship to hard work don't come easily for any of us—especially kids. A little gentleness and kindness will go a long way. Times of correction and even discipline will most certainly be needed, but remember how tough all this stuff was for you to learn.

2. *Don't be in a rush to bail the kids out of every financial problem.* Help them process the situations they confront and find solutions. Look for opportunities to teach life lessons.

3. *Help your children learn the difference between short- and long-term goals.* Usually money for short-term goals like birthday gifts, saving for summer camp, or buying a special shirt or top, is best kept in a simple bank or credit union savings account. These accounts make access relatively (but not too) easy, and usually pay a little interest. Long-term goals like college savings or buying a car might be invested differently. If your timeline is at least five to seven years out, you might want to consider putting the money into a mutual fund. (See chapter 17 for more on this.) The real purpose in all of this is to help teach your children about how money and markets work.

4. *Consider giving older kids larger allowances and supplying fewer of their needs.* Teach them to budget their allowance for clothes and other items that you bought for them when they were younger.

5. *Always remember that God is the source of all wealth.* Use money as an opportunity to teach about God's love and provision and the responsibility that it places on us to use it and share it to his glory.

Portable Outhouses—the Road to Riches

Over the years I have seen a troublesome change in the young people coming into the job market. Today there is less willingness on the part of many job entrants to apprentice and learn the ropes. Instead of a job, too many of the young twenty-somethings want a position. Through the nineties, when unemployment was at historic lows, they got away with this. But this skewed picture of the real world is going to catch up with many of them. With the first economic blip, this sense of entitlement will be replaced by the hard facts of real-world economics.

As parents, we owe our children a realistic worldview. We do them no favors by shielding them from reality. It is our job to prepare them for the world as it really is. That's why we have used the portable-outhouse analogy as the teaching paradigm for our four children.

For years I have (only half jokingly) told our kids that they should consider getting into the portable outhouse business. Here's why: If you want to be financially successful, one of the best ways to do it is by finding a business that achieves three things:
1. It needs to be simple and easy to understand—low-tech.
2. It should fill a real and recurring need.
3. It should be something that other people don't want to do. This enhances job security.

Can you think of anything that fills this bill better than portable outhouses? I can't. Our goal has been to teach our kids the principle I discussed in chapter 1 when I said that an out-of-control ego is the most expensive thing we'll ever deal with.

This point came home for our children in a great way in the summer of 1996. We were on a family trip covering the western United States. One Sunday we had stopped to worship at a wonderful church in the Southwest. The people were unusually warm and friendly. But the person I'll always remember was a pleasant cultured brother who went out of his way to be friendly. He was well dressed, obviously a successful individual. After we had talked about other things for a while, I finally asked, "What do you do for a living?"

"Oh, I have a major portable-outhouse business here in this part of the state," he said.

There it was! Living proof of what I'd been telling the kids! This was a man who could drive whatever car he wished, take off time from work when he chose, and in general, do just about whatever he wanted, whenever he wanted to do it. But this man wasn't too proud to be a servant and supply a simple product that other people needed but didn't want to mess with for themselves.

When the Chickens Come Home to Roost

A few weeks ago I got a call from our daughter Megan that brought this little analogy into stark reality.

Megan has felt called to the mission field since she was eight years old. Last spring when she was given an opportunity to spend most of this summer working at a mission in Tanzania, Africa, she jumped at the chance. But there was a problem. Since the work didn't pay a salary, she wouldn't be able to earn the portion of this fall's college expenses that she is responsible for. So it meant that Megan would have to spend fall semester living at home instead of on campus in the dorm.

This left her mom and me with a real moral dilemma. On the one hand, as you'll see in chapter 10, we require the kids to shoulder some of their college cost (the room-and-board part). But on the other hand Megan was wanting to serve God in an unselfish way. We didn't know what to do. Thankfully, the Lord took over and gave Megan the help she needed and gave Dad a lesson he needed.

Maybe you can imagine the joy (and mild shock) we felt when Megan called home shortly before her trip to announce that she had secured a job with the school that would pay for her room and board in the fall. All she had to do was clean the hallway and rest rooms in her dorm!

Gulp! Here I was, the guy who had always preached about not being too proud to be in the portable-outhouse business, and now my daughter wants to clean toilets to live on campus! Well, I don't know what you would have done, but I decided that since I'd preached it, I had better accept it with grace. So I forced my best smile and said, "Congratulations, Sweetheart! I'll bet those will be the cleanest rest rooms on campus."

10

Planning for College (or How to Earn a Mortarboard Without Bankrupting Your Future)

A RECENT FEDERAL STUDY says that it will cost an average of $233,000 to raise a newborn to age seventeen.[1] But, as any parent of a college student will readily tell you, that's just the beginning. Today, one year in a moderately priced private college or university can easily cost $17,000 to $20,000. While state schools will often be less expensive, many of the more elite private universities cost much more. Any way you attack it, college costs are a major challenge for most families.

Despite the doom and gloom, there is a silver lining. College can be affordable for the typical family if they research wisely and start planning early. While the above numbers are accurate, it is also accurate to point out that more than 70 percent of four-year colleges charge less than $8,000 for tuition.[2] And while there are plenty of high-priced exceptions, the College Board reports that, on average, college is attainable for most families. The average cost for an education at a four-year public college or university (including tuition and fees) is only $3,510 per year. The average cost at private schools is higher but, at $16,332 per year, still affordable for many families.[3]

A Family Affair

I encourage parents to start early and make college planning a family affair. Children need to understand the financial gymnastics that are going to be required to get them into college. They need to understand what loving parents do for their children. Not only does this re-enforce their awareness of your love for them, but it also helps equip them to be better parents themselves.

There are other, more immediate benefits to bringing the kids into the college-planning process. For one thing it helps acquaint them with what things really cost in dollars and sacrifice. There are two ways to accomplish this: First, young people need to be engaged in frank conversations about college costs; second, they need to help pay some of those costs themselves. Recently our son, who has just finished his freshman year, told me, with some dismay, how many of his friends aren't studying and doing what they need to do to succeed at school. With no prompting from me, he went on to say that, since most of his friends hadn't had to work to go to college, they simply didn't appreciate it.

Lots of well-meaning parents set their kids up for needless struggles in adulthood by not encouraging them to carry part of this burden. While every parent agrees that it's easy to spoil a child, not every parent recognizes when he or she is doing it. By paying for every cent of a college education, along with all the incidentals like off-campus apartments, all clothes and food, gas money, cell phones, and date money—we may be rewarding a slothful lifestyle. The early years are the best time to teach the principle: Anything that's worth anything will require an extraordinary level of effort. The college years are a great time to begin learning that sometimes you have to do things you hate (i.e., hard physical labor) to achieve a future lifestyle that will be more comfortable.

A college degree alone doesn't necessarily mean that the individual is truly educated. A total education involves other things like character, gratitude, and an appreciation for hard work.

What About College Loans?

As you can see, the focus of this chapter isn't going to be on how to get quick-and-easy college loans. Like so much else in this book, I am not too interested in financial formulas that accountants and planners might suggest based strictly on what makes financial sense. Instead, I hope that we can focus on the spiritual implications of how we use and manage our money.

When I see the stress and heartache many people experience, I am not excited about borrowing money to go to college. Yes, I know just about everybody does it. And, no, I don't think it's wrong to borrow money for school. But I do think there is usually a better option.

I can hear the gasps as you read this. What's wrong with that guy? Doesn't he live in the real world? Who does he think he's talking to, rich people?

Yes, I do live in the real world. That's why I'm so adamant about this stuff! And, no, I don't think I'm talking to a bunch of wealthy folks. The people I'm aiming most of this book at are people who have struggled all their financial lives, and they're sick and tired of it! I may be suggesting some radical ideas, but in the long run they are far less painful than the way you've been doing it so far. There are times when a school loan can make sense, but my suggestion is simply this: If possible, avoid loans; find another way to pay for college. But if you do borrow money, borrow as little as possible.

The most convincing argument against school loans frequently comes from the twenty-two-year-old college graduate who has just landed a job in his chosen field. At the moment when life should be the happiest and the future the brightest, this young adult runs headlong into Real-Life 101. When he adds up all the education loans he's obligated to repay, the total tops $60,000. Suddenly, the new $42,000 salary doesn't look so big. A sizable chunk of the paycheck starts going to pay down his school loans. And since he's already been trained to buy things before he can pay for them, it comes as no surprise that he begins buying cars, furniture, clothes, and even groceries with credit cards. By the time he turns twenty-five, the college degree he bought on credit hasn't produced a job that pays enough to keep up with the debt, and he's in a spiral that destroys his peace and joy. He spends the next twenty years trying to catch up from the mistakes he made starting with college. By the time his own kids are ready to leave for school, there's nothing set aside for them. And now the question is, does he borrow to pay for their education or finally start saving for his own retirement? What a trap!

Eleven Steps to Successful College Funding

In keeping with my philosophy of approaching college financing as a lifelong educational and character-building project in its own right, I believe there are eleven steps to success that should begin early. In our family we have viewed college, education, and character building in a holistic way. College without education means little, and an education without character means even less.

In most cases the following are all things we have either done, or asked our kids to do, in an effort to make college more affordable. You'll notice each of the eleven steps reflects our college-education, character-building philosophy model in at least one of three ways: First, we start early in the child's life. Second, the entire family is involved in the process. And third, ultimately, success or failure rests on the one who stands to benefit most from the college experience—the child.

As you read through these eleven steps, carefully compare each to the culture and lifestyle of your family. You may find that some of them will be a good fit in your situation.

1. Start saving early. Start the college savings discussions early. By the time our kids are eight or ten years old they have already heard us talking about the importance of college and the need to save for it.

We explain early that Mom and Dad believe each child should partner in his or her own education. While this involves much more than money (i.e., doing well in the earlier grades, etc.), saving is certainly part of the formula. Frankly, I don't think that it matters a whole lot how different families choose to handle the details. Some families require a certain percentage of total costs to be paid by the student. Others have other approaches. The most important thing is that the student is involved.

In our family the parents pay for all tuition expenses, and the kids are responsible for room and board. Of course, there are a few safety nets built into our plan. For instance, to encourage the kids to earn scholarship money, we let them apply the first year of any scholarship to their room-and-board expenses. And, since they go to a university here in Nashville, they are always welcome to live at home if their funds run low. Of course, the campus activities and social life make this a less-than-desirable alternative.

In chapter 9, I told you about the 10/45/45 Rule in our family. Without rehashing it fully here, that's the giving/college saving/spending plan that we have asked our children to adopt. By the time our kids reach about ten or twelve years old, they have begun their college savings program.

2. Take the college entrance exams as often as possible. Scores on your children's ACT and SAT tests may have a direct bearing on their eligibility for academic scholarship money. We have learned that it makes sense to take these tests several times during the high school years. Often the first time or two a child takes one of these tests she is unnerved, anxious, not at her best. By taking it several times, generally the scores go up and improve the possibility of getting a better academic scholarship.

3. Be a good student; make good grades. The occupation of a high school student is high school. It behooves that student to make the best possible grades since they will impact scholarship awards.

4. Hunt for scholarships like bears hunt for honey! I have been surprised to learn how many scholarships are available and how many go unclaimed each year! I like to see young people apply for every scholarship they can find. Check with the college, scour the Internet, visit your local bookstore, and talk with your minister about scholarships for religious studies.

5. Take some of the basic college courses early at a local junior college. Some students have found that they can save a lot of money (compared to costs at more expensive private colleges and universities) by taking some of the required courses at hometown junior colleges during their senior year in high school or during the summer after graduation.

6. CLEP out of as many courses as you can. Many colleges allow students to take special tests to see if they understand course work well enough to be credited for, or CLEP out of those classes. By clepping out of one three-hour course in a college that charges $400 per semester hour a student can save $1,200 of tuition costs plus books! Also, this can help a student get out of college a little faster.

7. Consider starting college a year later. This has helped lots of young people save (instead of borrowing) money for their college education. In some situations this is especially helpful in that it gives the young person another year to mature and prepare for the college experience.

8. *Stay at home; save the cash.* You may have heard the old story about the boy who wrote his father from college, "No mon, no fun, your son."

To which his dad wrote back, "Too bad, so sad, your dad."

Sometimes the hard facts of life close in on a young person. This happened with our oldest daughter. Megan saved money for college but not enough. Later, when I asked her why she hadn't planned better, she said, "Well, Daddy, college seemed so far away, I guess I never thought I'd live to be that old."

If you have a son or daughter who lives in the moment like our Megan does, you have a real blessing. But on a practical level there can be problems—like reaching college age without enough cash! There is no disgrace in finding a college nearby so you can sleep in your own bed at night. (In many cases this can save well over $5,000 per year!)

9. *Don't buy the largest meal plan.* Some colleges offer various meal plans with their room-and-board offerings. We have found that kids usually won't eat twenty-one meals a week in the school cafeteria. You may find that you can save some serious dollars by purchasing a smaller meal plan that allows for ten to fifteen meals weekly.

10. *Get a job.* There is no disgrace in working your way through school. I never let school get in the way of the education I got from various jobs during my college years. During those four years, while carrying a full college load, I had some of the most meaningful work experiences of my life. I worked everywhere and did a little bit of everything. Among other things I worked as a disc jockey at two radio stations, booked shows, started a wedding photography business, worked at JCPenney, helped manage the college diner, started a radio jingle production company and an ad agency in my dorm room. All in all I learned about as much (if not more) from my extra jobs as I did at school.

11. *Make schools compete for you.* There are a lot of colleges out there, and their survival is preconditioned on their getting a certain number of freshmen students enrolled each fall. Competition is stiff. If you have made good grades, then lots of good schools will probably want you on their campuses. So why not let them compete to get you?

One young man in our church, Jeff Thweatt, did just that. Jeff had done well in high school. When it came time to head for college, the colleges came looking for Jeff. Suddenly, Jeff found himself in a buyer's market. To make a long story short, Jeff finally ended up at a wonderful Christian college that gave him a great scholarship and eventually agreed to fly or drive him home twice a year for free!

By Way of Review

As we have seen, there are at least four primary ways to come up with the dollars for college:

1. *Scholarships and grants.* This is the gold standard. While grants can be hard to get, and scholarship eligibility varies from school to school, there is no better way to get an education. The single greatest advantage with grants and scholarships is that they generally don't have to be repaid.

2. *Loans.* As we've already said, while loans can be easily gotten, the downside is: Loans simply defer the expenses into the future; someday they have to be repaid! The College Board estimates that, in 1998–1999, approximately 58 percent of all financial aid came in the form of loans. That was up from 47 percent in 1992–1993.[4]

3. *Work while in school.* There are a lot of advantages to this plan as long as the job doesn't interfere with the primary reason for being in school.

4. *Plan ahead.* For most families saving and planning ahead are the keys to success.

Now Down to the Actual Dollars

There is a reason I have postponed this part of our conversation to the end of the chapter. Paying for college has a lot more to do with teaching our kids and steady, long-term saving than it does with the minutiae of the various financial strategies. It's easy to waste time debating which investment plan is the best and never really get around to saving the dollars and preparing the kids for college.

Like everything else in this book, I see college planning as more a matter of attitude than head knowledge. A lot of parents never learned a single thing about UGMAs, zero-coupon munis, or 529 plans who have prepared for college just fine, thank you. These parents may not have been as financially sophisticated as some, but at least they began saving early, and most importantly they got their kids emotionally ready to go to college.

Assuming you are already preparing your kids for college by teaching them to partner with you in the process—whether that involves saving money, earning scholarships, or whatever—then it's time to look at the various ways you have available as a parent to grow the money you will need for those upcoming college bills.

Four Ways to Save for College[5]

Besides the most fundamental points—start early, save as much as you possibly can—there are a number of options for parents who want to maximize the dollars for their kids' college careers. While each of these options has its advantages, each also has disadvantages. One of the smartest things you can do is sit down with a competent advisor and discuss which plan will be best in your particular situation. Be aware that there may be tax implications; still some of these options are beneficial. Tax laws and savings options are constantly changing and evolving. What may have been great a couple of years ago may not make sense today. Be sure to do further research, get all the details, confirm this data, study current provisions, and get further clarification on all options available before you launch out.

Education Savings Accounts (ESAs). This popular savings technique—also known as Coverdale Education Savings Accounts—got better in 2002. As of that year the maximum annual contribution was raised from $500 to $2,000. Unless your income is too high to qualify, which it shouldn't be unless you are well into the six-figure range, you need to check out ESA investing. While $2,000 may seem like a paltry sum, especially if you've waited until your child is a teenager to get started, it can accomplish great good if you start early. One reason that I like Educational Saving Accounts is that they allow for wide investment flexibility. Unlike the 529 Plans, which have tended to have more limited investment options, with an ESA you can self-direct the investments much as you would in a traditional IRA. Please remember that ESAs have numerous other characteristics—some good, some not so good. One caution: An ESA may hinder your financial aid eligibility. Learn before you invest.

529 Plans. At present these are being promoted by many experts in the field as the best college planning option available for many people. As Savingforcollege.com points out, 529 Plans (named for that section of the IRS Code) are generally operated by individual states and are designed to provide the participant with special tax benefits. At present, it appears that all states will be participating in this program.[6]

According to *Smart Money*,[7] there are two distinct types of 529 Plans: prepaid tuition and college savings plans. The prepaid plans aim to pay tomorrow's tuition at today's costs. Such plans may include residency requirements. And, although you may be able to transfer your money out of state if you change your mind, there may be downsides to doing so since these programs are directed at paying for a specific state university system. There are other drawbacks to prepaid plans, including what they can be applied to, and how they affect your financial aid eligibility. Tread lightly here until you fully understand the product.

The college savings plan option is more appealing to some people. Investment options, requirements, contribution maximums (which are usually generous), and state income tax treatments vary. But, while these plans differ from state to state, many are offering wider menus of investment options. These plans offer a lot of flexibility and can generally be used at accredited colleges and universities nationwide. In addition to the tax advantages and flexibility, such 529 Plans offer a number of other benefits. One benefit is that as the donor, you typically remain in control of the account. The named beneficiary usually doesn't have rights to the money. And generally there are no age or income limitations, and you can invest large sums.[8]

Smart Money points out that there are still misconceptions about these college savings plans. Some people believe that all of these plans are limited to the residents of the state that operates them and that a beneficiary must attend a school in that state.[9] However, if your state offers a 529 Plan, special state tax and other advantages may be available for residents and taxpayers.

Because of the complication and fluid nature of 529 Plans, be sure to research them fully before investing. One stop along your educational path on 529 programs might be the Web site www.savingforcollege.com. You may also want to get professional advice to help you understand these investments, including the potential tax implications associated with contributions to and/or distributions from them.

Custodial accounts. Custodials fall under two main headings: Uniform Transfers to Minors Accounts (UTMA) and Uniform Gifts to Minors Accounts (UGMA). These custodial accounts provide a way to make investments on behalf of a minor. Generally, the money in a custodial account is taxed at the child's rate, which is usually lower than the parents' rate. However, since this is the child's money, it can impact the child's eligibility for financial aid.

**Traditional savings/investment account.** I'm far less interested in _how_ you save for college than in _that_ you save for college. For some people the old-fashioned, KISS (keep it simple somehow) approach may work best. Instead of one of the college-funding approaches mentioned above, you may like the simplicity of a traditional credit union, bank, brokerage firm, or mutual fund company account. You may lose some tax benefits, but many parents like what they gain by taking this more conventional route. To begin with, you have total investment flexibility (choose money markets, CDs, individual stocks and bonds, mutual funds, whatever). As the account owner, you control the account and can withdraw from it. A single account can be used for more than one child's education. And, if your darling daughter decides on a Corvette instead of Cambridge, you can keep the money for your own retirement!

Estimated Amount a Family Needs to Save to Have $10,000 When Their Child Hits the Halls of Higher Learning					
If you start saving when your child is	Number of years of saving	Monthly savings	Principal	Interest earned	Total savings
Assuming a 4% Interest Rate					
Newborn	18	$ 32	$6,912	$3,187	$10,099
Age 4	14	45	7,560	2,552	10,112
Age 8	10	68	8,160	1,853	10,013
Age 12	6	124	8,928	1,144	10,072
Age 16	2	401	9,624	378	10,002
Assuming an 8% Interest Rate					
Newborn	18	$ 21	$4,536	$5,546	$10,082
Age 4	14	33	5,544	4,621	10,165
Age 8	10	55	6,660	3,462	10,062
Age 12	6	109	7,848	2,183	10,031
Age 16	2	386	9,264	746	10,010

The Bottom Line: Start Early and Save All You Can

I'll have lots more to say in other parts of the book (especially in chapters 16, 17, and 18) about investment rates of return. However, I ran across a graph at the U.S. Department of Education's Web site (www.ed.gov/pubs/Prepare) that might help illustrate the importance of starting a college savings program early.[10]

A Closing Word to Parents

The primary focus of this chapter has been on how to arrange and pay for college. But before closing, I want to remind you that there is a real difference between wisdom and knowledge. It is possible to get worldly knowledge without ever gaining true, spiritual wisdom. About seven hundred years before Jesus came to earth, the prophet Micah reminded his readers that "it is sound wisdom to fear Your [God's] name" (Mic. 6:9b NASB). And James directs us to the source of true wisdom: "But if any of you lacks wisdom, let him ask of God, who gives to all men generously and without reproach, and it will be given to him" (James 1:5 NASB).

As parents, God wants you to lead and mentor your children— even when they reach college age. Let me encourage you to research carefully the schools your young person is considering. Four of your son's or daughter's most formative years will be spent at college. Today many universities have institutionalized secularism and immorality. Humanism in its worst forms is frequently propagated on college campuses. University teachers often hold God in distain. The radicalism of the 1960s has taken root. Prayerfully consider your options. You may prefer a school that reflects the beliefs and values that you hold dear. Or, if you select a more liberal institution, look for Christian support groups for your son or daughter. Stay close. Be involved. Monitor his or her spiritual growth as closely as you do the grades. You will be eternally grateful.

11

Finding Great Bargains (or How to Pinch a Penny Until Abe Screams!)

 *ALL RIGHT,* it's all fine and good to suggest that moms should try to stay home with the children. But in the real world how does a family do this? I believe it gets back to a simple principle we discussed in chapter 5. You will remember that I said there are generally three ways to get ahead financially:

1. Spend less.
2. Earn more.
3. Invest wisely.

Throughout the pages of this book, I have shared a number of money-saving tips as they have pertained to the various topics we have covered. In this chapter I want to focus on the concept of living better while spending less. I want to give you a number of ways to save money on the things we buy all the time. Some of these ideas will fit your lifestyle; others may not. My goal is simply to encourage you to look for ways to stretch your family budget.

A Two-Step Approach to Frugal Living

Obviously, if a family spends less, it doesn't have to put as much emphasis on earning more money by forcing Mom to leave home to take a job. This goal can be accomplished in two ways:

By living more simply. This will involve learning to be content with less than many of your friends have. You will have to find more joy and satisfaction in relationships and simple pleasures and less in the trappings of what the world tells us we must have. It will mean that there will be less money to spend at restaurants and on costly vacations. Eating out will become more of a treat than a lifestyle. Designer clothes may have to give way to bargains at Wal-Mart. You may find that vacations are spent with relatives or at state parks rather than at expensive resorts and theme parks. *NBC News* recently reported that the average family is now spending $1,172 on a vacation.[1] Believe me, there are lots of ways to reduce this. Minor changes in distance and destination can save major dollars.

But, if you ask families that have made these lifestyle sacrifices so Mom can be at home with the kids, you may be surprised to find how truly happy they are. For these families the sacrifices have turned to blessings. When the kids are grown and gone, they have hearts filled with sweet memories of being together. Their kids go into the world knowing that they were loved enough to come first. What they may have missed in the form of material gains was more than replaced by an inner sense of harmony and security.

Learn to cut costs and stretch your buying power. Less income doesn't have to mean less lifestyle. Many families are finding that they can enjoy comfortable lifestyles by learning to make the money they do have go further. There is no single "best way" to accomplish this. It involves mastering several different disciplines such as learning to conserve resources, improving negotiating skills, and developing a nose for bargains. Contrary to what some people think, this doesn't have to involve living a draconian, Third-World lifestyle. This chapter isn't going to be aimed at helping you improve your dumpster-diving or panhandling skills. Instead, I want to share some specific things you can begin doing today that will save big money, simplify your lifestyle, and, hopefully, reduce some of the stress of modern living.

Check Your Charges

The old Latin saying "caveat emptor" (let the buyer beware) is the place I like to begin. My simple advice is: Never close your eyes when spending money. Always pay attention when someone presents you with a bill. Always read the small print. Always ask questions. It's not that other people are dishonest. It's just that they aren't usually as concerned about your money as you should be. When Jesus warned his followers to "be as shrewd as serpents and innocent as doves" (Matt. 10:16 NASB), he was preparing them for spiritual ministry. But the same advice applies here. Sometimes Christians are too trusting, too gullible. Because we treat other people fairly, we assume they will treat us fairly. It doesn't always work that way. Some of the unhappiest, most disillusioned Christians I have ever met once blindly assumed they could trust other people to keep their word. As good stewards, it's our responsibility to manage our money prudently.

Here are a few points that will save you a lot of money over a lifetime:

Never be hurried into signing a contract. Always read it. If it is complicated or unclear, have your lawyer review it too.

Watch the prices at the grocery store checkout. Scanner prices can be wrong. Always watch the prices as they ring up to be sure they agree with the prices marked on the shelves.

Review your bills. Be a line-item reviewer. Check every charge on your credit card, long distance, cable, and other bills. If something is wrong, dispute it immediately.

Before approving a project, ask for an exact quote (not an estimate) whenever feasible. Remember, an estimate is just that—an estimate. By definition, it means that your final price may vary. And, based on my experience, there's rarely been a case when that final price was less than the estimate. Usually, it's more than the original estimate—sometimes a lot more.

Saving Big Bucks at the Grocery Store

One of the biggest recurring expenses for most families is groceries. It's important to know that grocers are skilled marketers. It is their job to separate you from as many of your dollars as they can. It's a jungle in there. So it's critical to *think before you buy.* Here are some tips that will make the trip to the grocery store less costly:

Never go grocery shopping when you're hungry! The cheapest meal you'll ever eat is the one you eat just before going to the grocery.

Clip coupons like mad. One of the true remaining bargains in the world of marketing is coupons. Manufacturers like them, retailers like them, and you should like them too. Look for stores that give double-value coupon deals.

Go in with a list. Then, once inside, stick to your budget. If you don't start with a plan, you plan to fail.

Bring a calculator. Add your purchases up as you put them in the cart.

Read labels carefully. Bigger isn't always cheaper. The per-ounce cost may be less on the smaller size. Check it out!

Consider buying store brands. Today's store brands are frequently at least as good as their major-brand counterparts. Some stores also give double money-back guarantees on their own brands if you are dissatisfied.

Prepared foods usually cost more. After all, part of the reason we're doing all of this is to help you stay home with the kids—right? Why not use some of that time in the kitchen with the kids, teaching them how to prepare meals from scratch?

Consider starting a buying co-op with some of your friends. Go to discount stores that sell large quantity units at reduced prices. Then divide between the co-op members and pocket the savings.

Go easy at the deli and bakery counters. These are high-profit centers in many grocery stores. Usually, prepacked luncheon meats in the meat counter in the back of the store are cheaper.

Look for true sales. Many grocery sales are more marketing oriented than bargain oriented. But if you pay attention, you can find good deals—especially on perishable products like produce and expiration-dated meats. One note on this: Don't be obsessive. Driving from one store to another to save 10 cents on a sale item doesn't make good financial sense.

Find a bakery outlet in your area. Outlets that sell day-old bread products can save big money.

Don't assume that retail warehouse stores are always the best place to buy. I love the big warehouse stores. They have everything, and usually they have free samples too! But beware! When you go into a big store, you tend to buy more. Also, my experience has been that the big warehouse operations tend to feature name brands that often cost more than their generic counterparts. For instance, last week Bonnie and I went to a warehouse store to buy canned soft drinks for a party we were having at our home. We found cases of name-brand soft drinks substantially less than they might have cost in a regular grocery store. But they were still $1.00 to $1.50 more per case than the generic brand sodas available elsewhere.

Watch every item as it goes through the checkout to be sure that it rings the correct price. Sometimes I mark the prices on the products as I pick them up at the shelves to help me remember.

How to Get Dressed
Without Getting Financially Stressed

Another major expense for most families is clothing. But there are ways to minimize the financial impact of keeping a family clothed. Following are a few suggestions you may find useful.

Think twice about buying designer labels. I remember a convincing report that built the case that designer clothing is often of no better quality than store brands and generic lines. Since then I've compared well-known designer label goods with store brands and no brands. I believe the report was right!

Clothing purchases can give parents a wonderful opportunity to teach their kids some important lessons. Why not go into a store with your children and compare the quality of some designer lines to the store brands? Then ask hard questions like, "Since the quality is comparable, why do you think people pay more for designer goods?" You will have a great chance to discuss issues like: how marketing affects our decision-making processes, how ego and self-image determine what we buy, and so forth. One of the most important things parents can do is to help their children assess their motives for buying.

Don't misunderstand. I'm not opposed to designer wear. What I am opposed to is spending money we don't have to impress other people who, for the most part, could care less.

Check out yard sales, consignment shops, and next-to-new stores. These are especially great places to find clothing for younger kids. The reason is simple. When kids are small, they usually outgrow their clothes before they wear them out. This means that you will find lots of high-quality, barely worn outfits at prices far below what they would cost in retail stores.

Take good care of your clothes. Clothes that are well cared for and maintained last longer. Wash clothes only when they need to be washed. Store clothing properly.

Select clothes that fit properly—on the loose side, not too tight. Years ago I had a wonderful client who taught me an important lesson. Mr. Old was in the retail clothing business. He really knew his stuff. One of the things I learned from Mr. Old was that a garment usually hangs better when it isn't too tight. Generally, clothing looks better and is more slenderizing when it is slightly on the large side. Also, clothing that fits loosely lasts longer. When a person's clothing is too tight, the fabric, seams, and zippers are all under constant stress. This continual pulling wears a garment out faster.

Buy good quality clothing. It is important, especially for grown kids and adults, to buy good quality clothing that will last. Cheaply made garments have to be replaced too quickly. Not only will the workmanship and fabric be better, but you will also get the "little spiffs" that come with better quality goods—like extra buttons. I have rarely regretted buying a quality-made item, but there have been lots of times I've felt like kicking myself for wasting money on shoddy merchandise.

Opt for classic designs and cuts; avoid the fads. In the 60s it was Nehru jackets; in the 70s it was lime-green leisure suits, and more recently it's been plastic clothes and oversized jeans. Classics are just that, and they always look good. Faddish clothes have short lives, and they spend most of their existence in the back of closets.

Plan ahead; think ensembles. Before buying a new garment, review what you already have. Will the new item mix and match well with other clothes you own? Will the new garment expand your wardrobe, or will you be forced to buy even more clothes so you'll have something to coordinate with the new piece?

Avoid impulse buying. Nothing is more seasonal than clothing. Everybody knows that there will be great sales at the end of the season. Why not wait and buy late and save big?

Look for clothes that don't require special attention. If it has a "dry clean only" tag, you've just increased your clothing budget geometrically.

Keeping the Home Fires Burning

Another big expenditure for most of us comes under the heading of home energy and maintenance costs. Following are some tips that will help you keep the home fires burning without spending as much cash:

Watch the thermostat. A little bit of change can make a big difference. Some experts says that, in some locations, it is possible to cut heating and cooling costs by up to 40 percent by setting your heating thermostat four degrees cooler and your air-conditioning thermostat four degrees warmer.

Wear more clothes in the winter. If you're chilly, put a sweater on or curl up under a blanket before going crazy with the heater.

It won't help to turn the heat way up, or the air-conditioning way down. Heaters and air conditioners usually run at only one speed. Set the thermostat at the temperature you want. Setting it much higher, or much lower, won't get you there any quicker.

Use zone heating and air-conditioning. Heat only the rooms you plan to use. (Experts warn that you can damage your system by shutting off too many vents. Read the system instructions or check with an expert.)

Put an overcoat on your home. Put rolled towels at the base of exterior doors in the winter. When you're not using the fireplace, shut the damper. Avoid opening and closing the doors too fre-quently. Consider insulating your water pipes.

Remember the sun. To keep your home cool in the summer, close the shades on the sunny side of the house. Conversely, in the winter, use the sun's heat by opening shades during the sunny hours.

Go where the house is the most comfortable. If you live in a two-story home, use the laws of nature to your advantage. Heat rises, so in the winter plan activities on the second floor. Conversely, in the summer, spend more time downstairs.

Contact your local energy company. Frequently they will have great ideas on how to reduce energy costs in your home. Some utility companies even offer home energy surveys to help customers use their resources more efficiently. These studies can help you deter-mine the amount of savings you can enjoy by adding roof turbines, attic insulation, etc. (In some parts of the country, a properly insulated attic can pay for itself within three to four years.)

When buying new appliances, check to see how energy efficient they are. Data about the energy efficiency of major appliances (air conditioners, water heaters, etc.) is found on the Energy Guide Labels required by federal law.

Use your washer and dryer conservatively. Try washing with cold water; some experts say it can save over 50 percent of the cost of washing. Wash and dry only full loads. Dry consecutive loads. Keep your filters clean.

Save water. Use low-flow showerheads. Some estimates say they can save over $200 per year. Turn down water pressure in the kitchen and bathrooms.

Put up an inside-outside thermometer. It will tell you when to open and shut the doors and windows.

Great Ways to Cut the Cost of Doctors and Medicine

Roughly 14 percent of America's GDP goes to pay medical expenses. Every year insurance costs go up, and coverages seem to go down. Recently one national health insurer announced it will be raising rates by 20 to 30 percent next year. It behooves any family to look for ways to cut the cost of medical care. Following are some ideas you may find helpful:

When your doctor prescribes a new medication, ask if he can give you a free sample. This will give you time to see if the medication is effective while you compare costs at various drug stores and mail-order outlets.

Usually outpatient services are less expensive than inpatient services. Talk with your doctor. If an outpatient service will be equally good, consider opting for it.

If you are taking a prescription long-term, consider ordering from a mail-order pharmacy; it can be cheaper.

Consider buying generic prescription drugs. Usually, brand-name drugs are more expensive than their generic equivalents. Ask your doctor if a generic drug is appropriate in your situation.

Over-the-counter medications also have generic equivalents; check them out. In most pharmacies you will find generic equivalents of many of the popular, nationally advertised, over-the-counter drugs. Ask the pharmacist for advice on these money-saving alternatives to the cough syrups, cold medications, and laxatives.

Dialing for Dollars (or How to Save on Your Phone Bill)

Own your own phone. In the long run it's usually cheaper to buy your phones than to lease them.

Only buy what you use. Review your phone bill to be certain that you aren't paying for features (i.e., call waiting, caller ID, etc.) that you don't need or use.

Sometimes long distance is cheaper on the cell phone. Some cell phone calling plans allow for free long-distance calls. These can be cheaper than using the hardwired phone in your home.

Schedule your long-distance calls. Long distance is almost always cheaper in the evenings and on the weekends. (Ask your phone company what they consider to be evenings and weekends.)

Plan your long-distance calls. You'll save money if you preplan the points you want to discuss prior to calling. Also consider using a timer.

Consider using low-cost phone cards. Sometimes phone cards are actually cheaper to use than traditional long-distance service. Presently our family makes most of its calls on a card that charges only 3.47 cents per minute.

How to Die on the Cheap (Paying for Funerals That Don't Kill You Financially)

Be kind to your family; plan ahead. Why not write out your wishes and discuss them openly with family members? This may help grieved loved ones avoid overspending on your funeral.

Consider asking that donations be made to your favorite charity in lieu of flowers.

Don't be shy about discussing prices with the funeral home. Honorable funeral directors will be glad to discuss options and pricing. Don't fall for the notion that a more expensive funeral is evidence of greater love on the family's part. If you get the sense that a funeral director is playing on your grief or emotions, go somewhere else. Funerals can range from under $3,000 to over $25,000. I hate to see families spend money they don't have for funeral costs.

Other Great Ways to Save Money Around the House

If you're mechanically skilled, do it yourself. If you like to fix things (and even if you don't), consider making minor repairs with the help of how-to books.

Pick your bank carefully. All banks are not alike. Talk with several banks before opening an account. Ask about the rates they pay on savings accounts, whether they have free checking, etc. If you are a high-balance customer, don't be shy about asking for special services and pricing. Your bank might drop or lower its checking charges if you have your paycheck direct deposited. Check it out!

Fix your car with parts from a junkyard. If used appropriately, junkyard or remanufactured auto parts can save lots of money.

Need glasses? Consider buying them on the cheap. Basic single-lens and bifocal reading glasses can be bought in discount and drug stores for $10 and even less. I'm wearing a pair as I write this. I saw some last week in one of the dollar-store chains for, you guessed it, one dollar.

Take your lunch to work. Eating lunch out is more expensive than most people realize. Brown baggers can save over $1,500 per year!

Fluorescent lights are often cheaper to operate. Consider replacing some of the regular lightbulbs in your home with fluorescents.

Grow your own food. Lots of families save money and have a lot of fun together planting a vegetable garden in the spring.

Buy used. Before making a major purchase, why not check out the newspaper classifieds or trader-style magazines for pre-owned bargains?

Reuse your soft drink cup. One of my little luxuries is Diet Coke. I love having a large cup of ice and Diet Coke in the car when I'm driving. For years I would run into a convenience store, grab a thirty-two- or forty-four-ounce cup, fill it with ice and Diet Coke, pay the ninety-nine cents and leave. Finally, it occurred to me one day that I could reuse my cup! I learned that most of the convenience stores in our area charge much less for a refill than for a soft drink in a fresh cup. As a matter of fact, there's a convenience store near our home where I get a forty-four-ounce Diet Coke on my way to the office for only twenty-nine cents! Enjoy!

Pay with cash! Don't fall for the "ninety-day same as cash" pitches. When you go into a store to buy a big-ticket item, try this: Walk in with a roll of $50 bills. Then ask what kind of discount you can get with cash. Will this always save you money? No. But sometimes it will. And, besides, when you pay cash, there's no risk of getting into trouble on the "ninety-day same as cash" deal. (Did you know that over 75 percent of the people who buy this way don't pay the full amount within ninety days? Instead, they get saddled with high-interest monthly payments.)

Saving on Gifts

Many people spend more on gift buying than they can afford. There are probably several reasons for this: First, some folks, who don't have written monthly budgets, simply don't realize how much they're spending for gifts. Second, lots of people would rather spend themselves into the poor house than to let their friends know they have financial limits. Third, a lot of people really don't know how to give gifts without spending money.

We give gifts to people whom we love and who love us back. By definition, these people care more about the giver than the gift. They don't care what you spend. They care about you. For people like this, it really is the thought that counts. Maybe you'll find some good ideas below:

Give gifts that you make yourself. If you have a garden, why not give fruits, vegetables, or flowers? If you cook or bake, why not give something from your kitchen? Personalize your homemade wonders by dressing them up with pretty ribbons and bows. Make a homemade label and hang it from a string. Attach a poem. Give designer jars of cinnamon sugar mix, pasta samplers, or homemade candies. Make it special.

Give your time. Even if you don't make a product or craft, time is one thing you can give to others. The most valuable commodity any of us have is our time. Each one of us has 86,400 seconds in our day. The question is, Whom will we share our time with? One of the best gifts we can give is a gift that represents our time. Why not give a certificate to a young family that can be redeemed for an evening of baby-sitting?

Save money on gift wrapping. One of the costliest parts of giving a gift can be the wrapping. Why not use the Sunday newspaper comic pages? It's a colorful, fun, whimsical way to wrap a present.

Give personal gifts to family members. In our family it's not unusual to get a certificate entitling the recipient to a thirty-minute back massage. You could give chore certificates where the giver promises to wash dishes, make beds, or mow grass for the recipient.

Give talent gifts. My son Joshua is a fabulous artist. In the past he has given his drawings as gifts. If you write poetry, why not a special verse for a friend? If you sing, why not present a special song for the guest of honor at the birthday party?

Romantic gifts for husbands and wives. The great thing about being married is that you can give your lover special gifts that are both personal and romantic. Why not candlelight, beautiful music, and a review of your wedding album—just before bed? Have you ever surprised your spouse with breakfast in bed? If eating out is too costly, why not a late-night cup of coffee in a quiet restaurant? You get the point. Be imaginative.

The Fun of the Hunt

Like so many other things in life, hunting for bargains can be drudgery or a full-blown hoot! For me, it's great fun. Learning to zero in on and snag great bargains is a blast. It's a great way for the family to learn and have fun—all at once. You might enjoy spending a Saturday with your spouse and kids going to flea markets, consignment sales, and garage sales. It offers a beautiful teaching opportunity.

Be careful not to get caught up too much in the thrill of the hunt. When you buy stuff you don't need or want, any price is too high.

A Serious Plan for Holiday Savings

I'm going to suggest something that not many of you will be willing to do. But for that minority of you who try this, the savings may surprise you.

Why not celebrate holidays like Christmas and Valentine's Day a few days late? Think about it. When do the really incredible Christmas sales usually begin? December 26, right? So why not agree to have your family Christmas celebration on New Year's Day? That way you could do your shopping and decorating starting the day *after* Christmas. The Christmas tree lot would probably give you a tree just to avoid having to throw it away. The decorations will be reduced. And gifts in the stores will be on sale. What a deal! Of course, if you can't bear the thought of not celebrating Christmas on December 25, you might consider giving gift certificates that can be redeemed on merchandise after it's on sale.

Now if all of that seems a little too extreme for your taste, maybe you wouldn't mind celebrating a holiday like Valentine's Day a day or two late. (Have you ever noticed how much a heart-shaped box of chocolates goes down in price right after Cupid leaves town?)

Here's an Old Trick

Always buy a year ahead. Buy seasonal merchandise like gift wrapping, decorations, and ornaments immediately after a holiday is over. Frequently stores offer huge discounts simply to avoid having to warehouse their stock for another year.

A Final Warning: Stay Out of Sellers' Markets!

Try never to get in the predicament of being forced to buy something when the price is at its highest. For instance, if you want a convertible car—great. Just remember, everybody wants convertibles in the spring. Consider shopping for your ragtop in the dead of winter. The same holds true for home buying. The best time to buy your first home may be during a housing recession.

If you're going back to college in the fall, you may want a mini-refrigerator for your dorm room. The best time to buy it won't be in the late summer when all of the appliance stores are overpriced or sold out. The best time to get your fridge may be near the end of spring semester. Why not walk down the top floor of the dorm and see if you can find someone who is too lazy to drag his fridge home. Offer $25 and see what happens.

Go Forth and Conquer!

Bargains are everywhere. It's just a matter of learning where to look. With a little extra time and effort—and a little less ego—anybody can become a world-class bargain hunter. Do it as a game. Do it to save money. Do it to teach your kids the principles of sound money management. Whatever your motivation, just get busy and do it!

12

Negotiating Skills That Get You from Where You Are to Where You Want to Be

IT'S BEEN WELL OVER a decade since the Soviet Union imploded. In the intervening years I've had several opportunities to visit ex-Soviet countries. It's always a thrill for me to visit in these peoples' homes, churches, and universities. I've had some unforgettable experiences sharing Jesus and teaching in their schools. These people are eager to know what has made America great. They are intrigued by our marketing and sales techniques. They are fascinated by how Westerners do business.

One common trait among many of these people is how distrusting they are. I suppose that's what happens when you are never sure which neighbors are working for the secret police. Seventy years of Communism didn't inspire much in the way of trust or goodwill. Today lots of great business and economic opportunities are missed because everyone is afraid someone else is trying to take advantage. Former Soviets simply find it hard to believe that anyone else cares about them. They really believe everyone is out to get them.

This point was brought forcefully home to me a couple of years ago during a visit with Peter and Janis. Janis, an American, married her ex-Soviet husband, Peter, over twenty years ago. They have been an effective missionary couple in Peter's homeland for well over a decade. This dynamic duo has built a wonderful church in one of the Eastern bloc's most important regions. Together they have advanced the cause of Christ in a significant way.

But on this particular day, Janis was pouring her heart out. She was sharing a real problem in her husband's life—one she didn't know how to help him with. She explained that because of his past Peter was having a difficult time trusting other people. "He simply doesn't understand that two people can negotiate an agreement in which both come out ahead," she told me. "Peter believes that in every negotiation one person takes advantage of the other person."

As I have reflected on that conversation, it has occurred to me that there was nothing unique about Peter. This certainly isn't a trait exclusive to old Soviets. Most people have a warped idea of what negotiating is all about. Many people hate the thought of negotiating with another person to achieve a desired agreement. When the word *negotiation* comes up, it isn't unusual to hear comments like:

- "I don't like to be confrontational."
- "I'm not a manipulative sort of a guy; after all, I'm a Christian."
- "I don't want to beat anything out of another person."
- "I can't lie with a straight face."

What Negotiating Is Not

If you recoil at the thought of learning to negotiate, or if you relate to some of the above comments, this chapter is for you! I want you to understand four things that good negotiating is not:

1. Good negotiations are not confrontational.

2.   Good negotiations are not manipulative. Successful negotiating sets up a win-win atmosphere where both parties come out ahead. The goal should always be to help everyone involved get what he wants.
3.   Good negotiators tell the truth. There is no place for dishonesty in the negotiating process.
4.   Good negotiations are not emotionally painful. Negotiating should be fun for both parties.

A Simple Definition

Some people have the ability to complicate a crowbar. There are books written about negotiating—complete with long, scholastic definitions. That's all fine and good. But for our purposes, let me share a concise definition of negotiating that you may find helpful. Simply stated, negotiating is the process by which two or more parties get some, or all, of what they want through the process of open, transparent communication with one another.

Opportunities Missed

Most people go through life settling for far less than they want, and could easily have, because of fear and ignorance. Sometimes it's the fear of being rejected or told no that keeps Person A from asking Person B to work together to find a common solution or reach a common goal. Sometimes it's because neither Person A nor Person B knows how to go about doing it.

So what happens? Nothing. Every day there are:

•   Car salesmen who fail to sell cars to people who really want to buy cars.
•   Husbands and wives who go to bed angry with each other.
•   Employers who don't give jobs to people they really want to hire.

Why? Because neither party had the guts or the knowledge to open the necessary dialogue to negotiate a mutually satisfactory solution.

Control or Be Controlled

One thing is for sure: You will either control your circumstances, or you will be controlled by your circumstances. Part of effective money management is realizing that your money will go to whomever wants it the most. If you don't value and appreciate your assets, someone else will get them. One of the most fundamental ways to avoid "asset evaporation" is by controlling spending. This can be done in two ways: You can simply buy less, and you can pay less for what you do buy. In this chapter we are going to focus on ways to achieve the latter.

Just because someone puts a $100 price tag on something he's trying to sell doesn't mean that it's worth $100. Your job as a negotiator is to find the lowest price the seller will happily trade what he has for your cash.

Nineteen Secrets of the Great Negotiators

1. Always tell the truth. Need I say more on this point? There is an old adage: "The first casualty of war is the truth." Unfortunately, this is sometimes true of the negotiating process too. No prize is worth selling out our integrity. As Christians, we must maintain our honor. Jesus said it this way: "For what will it profit a man if he gains the whole world and forfeits his soul?" (Matt. 16:26 NASB).

2. Use time to your advantage. The less of a rush you're in, the better. Car salesmen can tell when you have car fever. Other people know when you are more anxious to buy than they are to sell. Avoid this temptation. Take your time. Be patient.

3. *Figure out what the other guy wants from the deal.* This isn't always obvious. Frequently, the other guy doesn't tell you what he really wants to accomplish. For instance, he might have said, "I'm selling this car because I need $5,000 cash." If you take his comment at face value and don't ask questions, you will probably assume that he has a $5,000 financial need and that he won't sell the car unless he gets that much money. And, since you can only afford to spend $4,000, you shake his hand and leave without either one of you getting what you really wanted.

Maybe the deal didn't have to fall apart. This is where the art of negotiating becomes valuable. With some open conversation and friendly communication, you might have learned that the truth is a little different. He's really selling the car because he doesn't drive it anymore and he's tired of paying insurance on a car that stays parked in his garage. The $5,000 is a figure he would *like to get* but more than he truthfully thinks the car is worth.

4. *Get into the other guy's skin.* Always try to look at the deal from his side of the fence. This will help you craft your comments so they don't offend. Sincerely try to structure a transaction that is as good for him as it is for you.

5. *Always leave the other guy a graceful way of escape.* Most people think that negotiating is the art of winning arguments. Not true! If your negotiation becomes an argument, you've already lost!

One of the best ways to leave the other person a graceful way out is to avoid putting him in a corner in the first place. For instance, *instead of asking* how much he wants, sometimes *I like to tell* him what I want to pay. Here's why: If we begin the negotiation with me asking him, "How much does it cost?" he may give me a higher price than he would be willing to accept—and definitely more than I'm willing to pay. At that point I am left with three unappealing options: I could accept his price; I could pass on the deal; or I could ask him to reduce his price. At first blush the third option (asking him to reduce his

NO DEBT, NO SWEAT!

price) may not seem so bad, but it can be a real deal breaker. The minute I ask for a lower price, I infer that his price is too high. He may feel offended and become defensive. Definitely not the desired response!

Instead, I might tactfully say something like, "I don't know how much this item is worth to you. It's obviously very nice. But I am on a budget. Would it be all right if I make an offer?" Suddenly, the table is turned, and I am the one establishing the price. Of course, he is free to accept or reject my offer, but at least he knows what I feel is the right price.

6. Never be discourteous or condescending about the other guy's stuff. Some people mistakenly think that they can get a better price by pointing out flaws in what the other person is trying to sell. There are rare occasions (for example, where someone is trying to unload defective merchandise) when the prospective buyer has to call the seller's hand, but usually it's bad strategy to criticize the other guy's stuff. Instead of it having the desired effect of convincing him that he should lower his price, it usually makes him mad. Once he gets mad, two bad things happen simultaneously: He begins to build even greater value into his merchandise, and he begins to dislike you.

7. Your best ally: knowledge. Never go into any important negotiation without first doing your homework. I heard about a lawyer who never asked a question in court that he didn't already know the answer to. The same holds true for good negotiators. A little pregame research will pay huge dividends. Learn all you can about the prices of similar products. Study the competition. Be prepared to conduct an informed conversation.

8. Negotiation is a process, not a battle. Go into a negotiation with goodwill and true empathy for the other party. Try first to win a friend.

9. Good negotiators are good verbal communicators. Learn to use words clearly and precisely. Speak loudly enough to be heard. Avoid using technical or professional jargon that may confuse the other party or make him feel patronized. Stay focused. If you are going to make a lengthy presentation, practice it in the mirror first.

10. Get to the decision maker. One of the first things I used to teach young account executives at Steve Diggs & Friends was that no presentation for a new account would be successful unless they were talking with the person who could make a final decision. Nothing was more frustrating than to work for weeks on a major advertising campaign only to realize that the point person we were working with had no authority to "green light" the project.

The same holds true when you are negotiating. Before you start the conversation, ask, "If we reach a mutually agreeable price and term, can you give the final OK?" If he says no, then go up line as far as you must to get to that all-important decision maker. This is especially important when you're buying a big-ticket item like a car. The last thing you want to do is reach what you think is a final price only to have the salesman get up from the table and announce that he has to take it to his manager for approval.

11. Remain focused; don't bring other problems or issues into the negotiation. Forget about other peripheral issues that might cloud the negotiating process. Stay on message.

12. Your body language is important. People "listen" to more than just your words; they also "listen" to your body. When negotiating, use friendly, inviting gestures. Lean forward, smile easily, and be open. Try to be relaxed. Sometimes I lean back in my chair and put my hands behind my head. It's always wise to avoid closed body postures like crossed arms and legs.

Entire books are written on this subject, and there is no way to cover all of the various body language techniques in this chapter. Generally speaking, effective body language is a matter of common sense. Think about the other person. How will she read your body language? Will your gestures be seen as warm and inviting or cold and aloof? As I write this, I think of two preachers I know. They're both wonderful men. They both know the Bible. They both have a passion for lost souls. But they each have a body language problem that hinders their effectiveness. One of these men rarely makes eye contact when he is conversing with another person. His tendency to look off in other directions causes the people he's talking with to wonder whether he is paying attention. The other man was a preacher I knew as a boy. I always dreaded shaking hands with him because he had the classic "wet fish" handshake. You know the one; it's where the other guy sort of limply lays his hand in yours and waits for you to let go. Yuck!

13. Use gentle words. Negotiating isn't a game of one-up-manship. It's a process of linking up personally with another individual in the hopes of reaching a common goal. To achieve your goal choose your words carefully. Avoid using words that sound harsh or gruff. Stay away from words like *never, no way,* and *you must.* Instead, try to use phrases like "maybe this would work," "there's no rush," or "is there a more convenient way for you?"

14. Pay attention to the other person's nonverbal communication. Watch for body language and facial expressions that tell you if the other person is responding favorably or negatively to the negotiation process. Often you can learn as much from the other person's nonverbal signals as you can from her words. Pay attention to smiles, frowns, glances, and the like. For instance, when a person puts his hands in his pockets, that can be an indication of hesitance or resistance.

15. Find out why she wants to do this. It is always wise to know what is motivating the other person. Don't be overly focused on your own desires. Learn what is motivating the other person. Ask questions, look around, be aware of the job market and the economy. When you learn why the other person is motivated to sell or buy, then you will be better able to tailor your own comments.

16. Always remain calm. Ignore personal insults; that's not why you're here. If the other person gets ugly or emotional, be kind in return. A kind, gentle, non-threatening response to even the most vicious comment can save both the deal and your witness.

17. If he reneges on his offer, don't panic or become angry. Sometimes a person will get nervous and try to back out of a deal. Don't respond emotionally. Slow down, take a breath, and be gentle.

One little phrase that has helped me in such cases is simply to look the other person in the eye and kindly ask, "Were you sincere when you offered to sell me your lawn mower at such and such a price?" At that point he must either honor his earlier commitment, clarify a misunderstanding that I may have had, or admit that he isn't going to live up to his word.

18. Always enter a negotiation with at least one or two alternative plans. By doing some prenegotiation thinking, you'll be able to anticipate the most likely objections to your offer. Be prepared. For instance, suppose you are talking with a neighbor about buying his riding lawn mower. It's late August, and through your conversation you learn that he is planning to move into a condominium in September. Common sense tells you that he won't need the mower at his new home, and a quick sale to you will save him from having to hunt for another buyer. Still, you are $100 apart in price. Why not make an alternative offer something like this, "Bob, if you're willing to sell the mower for what I can afford, I'll do two things to sweeten the deal. First, I'll share the mower with you until you move so you won't have to pay someone to cut your grass. Second, on moving day, my son and I will help you load the truck." Assuming he likes your alternative offer, you have a deal. (Now all that's left is a little negotiation with your son.)

19. Be a good listener. I am convinced that most unsuccessful negotiations fall apart because at least one of the parties was too busy talking and not listening. There's a good reason God gave us two ears but only one mouth.

I learned this lesson the hard way some fifteen years ago. Our firm had been asked to make a presentation to a structural engineering firm. We had high hopes of winning the account. But, alas, after weeks of work and a formal presentation, we got the unwelcome news that they would not be hiring us. After the initial shock had worn off, I summoned the courage to ask one of the firm's executives why they had opted not to engage us. He asked, "Do you really want to know?"

I gulped hard and said, "Yes, I think so."

He looked me in the eye and said, "Steve, the reason we didn't hire your firm was because you didn't listen to us."

I would have understood if he had said they didn't like our creative approach or that the budget was too high. But this stunned me. What did he mean we didn't listen?

He went on, "You fellows were so busy talking and telling us what you thought we should do, you didn't take the time to listen to what we had to say."

Wow! That smarted! But he was exactly right. We had been talking when we should have been listening, and it cost us an account. But we learned an important lesson from the experience that caused us to rethink how we dealt with our clients. Today the conference room at Steve Diggs & Friends has a shiny brass plate on the doors that says, "Listening Room."

Do These Tips Really Work?

Check out the author's photo on the cover of this book. Designing a book's cover is always a big job. Publishers and authors work hard to create covers that "speak what the book speaks" and attract "shelf attention." The book you are holding is no exception.

As we planned the cover, one of the first considerations was the author's (that's me) photo. When we decided to add this dubious decoration to an otherwise attractive cover design, the next question was, What would I wear?

One thing was for sure, I wasn't going to wear a suit! That's just not me. After wearing coats and ties almost every day for twenty years, by the mid-1990s I'd had enough! These days you just about have to die to get me into a suit. As a matter of fact, I have come to like bright shirts. These days I wear them everywhere. The brighter, the better. As I write this, I'm on a plane heading to a No Debt, No Sweat! Seminar in Missouri wearing a shirt adorned with colorful Popsicles! I think it makes me look cool. (I know, bad joke.)

So when it came to selecting a shirt for the cover of this book, I was determined to dress as I usually do. But it seemed best for me to wear a long-sleeved shirt. That's where the problem came. I don't have many long-sleeved shirts. But since this was a special book, it deserved a special shirt. A few weeks later in California, I found the right shirt! I loved everything about it—except the price. No, I'm not going to tell you how much it cost except to say that I could have bought a nice sports coat for the same amount. For an old boy with a bunch of $25 shirts in his closet, this was a little too much.

"But," I reasoned, "I've found what I want. Why not try out some of those negotiating skills you teach in the book?"

So I did. I'm happy to report that I bought the shirt on the back of the book for less than 70 percent of the marked price!

Yes, Virginia, these negotiating tips really do work.

13

Debt and Credit Cards (Plastic Prosperity or Plastic Explosives?)

ONE OF THE THINGS I really enjoyed about being in the marketing communication business was how it allowed me to learn about different companies and business models. I enjoyed discovering how various firms made their products and earned their profits. As a young man I was surprised to learn that many well-heeled, highly educated clients made some very human mistakes. On a number of occasions clients have shared their struggles with me. It always honored me when a client trusted me enough to share such deep concerns. In some cases they sought advice, but mostly they just needed a sounding board. I've sat and listened as these clients admitted to making dumb business and financial decisions. Over the years a number of them have shared painful struggles they were facing. Some of these were business-related worries; others were personal. I've learned how true the old adage is about how even the most powerful people among us still put their pants on one leg at a time.

From Bankers to Manufacturers

Many of the struggles my clients have dealt with have been money related. More specifically, they have been problems with debt and borrowing. Following are three short stories that will help build my point. Be assured that all of the names and some of the other details have been changed to ensure their privacy.

Over the years we have worked with scores of bankers throughout the Southeast. One thing I learned very early was that all bankers are not created equal. Some are brilliant financial people who handle their customers' money (as well as their own) with skill and expertise. Others may be skilled bankers, but they aren't very adept at managing their own assets.

I learned about just such a situation during an informal meeting with the president of one of our banks several years ago. President Jones was worried about what to do with Robert, one of his senior vice presidents. Robert was a great guy who appeared to the outside world as a man who really had it all together. He was handsome and talented, respected by his peers and the community, a loving family man; in general, he was a good old soul. But on this particular day, Jones was worried about a personal difficulty that was interfering with Robert's professional responsibilities. He feared this burden might destroy Robert's career. What was Robert's problem? It was too much personal debt. Jones explained that Robert had gotten involved in a number of leveraged real estate deals that had not worked out. Now he was drowning in debt. Jones simply didn't know what to do about the problem. After all, Robert was a banker himself. He understood things like money, debt, and leverage. He knew better than to get into such a predicament, but here he was.

Another situation occurred in the life of one of the most exciting and talented clients with whom I ever worked. John was the president of a cutting-edge publishing company. Due to John's skills the young company had a knack for signing some of the best-known authors in the nation. The company's books were beautifully designed and produced. Their marketing was dead on. But more than most businesses, publishing is a real cash furnace. The cost of running a publishing house is astronomical. This is where John got into trouble. Instead of conserving cash and growing slowly, he depended far too much on borrowed money. Gradually, the debt load destroyed the joy of publishing. John was always under the stress and strain of trying to meet loan obligations. There were lots of touch-and-go days when they literally didn't know if the company would survive. I still remember a conversation with John, one day after a long volley of meetings with his bankers and creditors, when he told me how he felt completely stripped of his dignity. Sadly, the business finally went under as it drowned in a sea of debt.

A third story that comes to mind is that of Harris. Since a young man, Harris had been intrigued by business. Now in his mid-forties, he was the owner of major manufacturing firm. In addition to being one of the biggest employers in the county, Harris's company made several lines of superior products. His goods were used by companies and bought by individuals nationwide. Harris had it all—including a huge amount of borrowed money. Many of our conversations revolved around his debt load. He was constantly grieving and worrying that the bank would cancel his line of credit. Eventually Harris's constant worry damaged his peace and his health.

You're Not Alone

I've shared these stories because I want you to know that debt problems don't just happen to uneducated folks. Bright, suave business tycoons and financiers fall into the debt trap. Borrowing, and the associated problems it can bring, affects people in all walks of life. Today, if you're struggling with debt, you're not alone—not by a long shot. Total household debt in America topped 100 percent of total disposable income for the first time in 2000. At over one trillion dollars per year, we are now buying more with our credit cards than we are with cash! The average credit card holder's balance is $4,400.[1]

If you are in debt now, I'm not here to make you feel worse. I talk to people regularly who are swamped with debt. It hurts. There is nothing fun about it. It destroys a person's dignity and saps the joy out of life. My goal is to give you hope and the vision necessary to achieve a debt-free future. As a matter of fact, in the next chapter, I want to give you some simple, practical steps to getting out of debt and fixing your credit.

If you are unclear about debt and borrowing money, I hope this chapter will give you some useful insights and perspectives.

Is It Wrong to Borrow Money?

This is the first question I want to address because there is a lot of confusion, especially among Christians, about the whole issue of borrowing and debt. Today many Christians believe the Bible teaches that borrowing is a sin. Despite their good intentions and best efforts, I don't think they can prove their point biblically. Some people have turned to a comment that Paul makes in Romans 13:8 to make their case: "Owe nothing to anyone except to love one another." However, a closer reading of this passage makes clear that the apostle is encouraging the Christians in Rome to be good, obedient, honest citizens. Specifically, he is telling them to pay their taxes as they should. He sums up by telling them to pay their taxes honorably and "owe nothing to anyone." I simply disagree with those who would point to this verse as a prohibition against borrowing money. If anything, it seems to support the idea that Christians should always fulfill their debts and live up to their obligations.

The Seven Stages of Debt

Debt, and recovery from it, can be painful. But, just as with any other addict, the debt-oholic must come to grips with the root causes in order to get better. Myvesta.org has developed a seven-step description of what the person in uncontrolled debt goes through. Below, I've combined Myvesta.org's seven steps with some thoughts of my own. See if you identify with any of these steps:

1. *Denial.* These people may realize that the numbers don't add up and that things are out of control. They feel a need for help, but they may not realize that the problem is with debt.

2. *Anger.* This is when blame sets in. "I've been victimized. My creditors ripped me off!" Until a person stops blaming others and accepts responsibility for her own actions, things won't get better. Anger is not a productive emotion at such a time.

3. *Depression.* "I'm in a hopeless situation. There's no way out of this." Panic and depression cause some people to shut down emotionally. This is no time to give up. Seek help from qualified friends or professionals.

4. *Bargaining.* "If someone will make me a debt-consolidation loan, I'll never do this again." As we'll discuss in chapter 14, bill-consolidation loans can make matters worse. It's dangerous to try to get out of debt by borrowing more money.

5. *Acceptance.* "I'm in this mess partially or totally because of my own bad decisions. The only real answer is for me to start making the right decisions. I'm ready to do whatever it takes to get things straightened out."

6. *Resurrection.* "I'm ready to take responsibility and become financially responsible again." This is when a person comes back to reality. It's the feeling of rising from the dead and coming back to life.

7. *Rebirth.* "Finally, I'm ready to enjoy a healthy financial life again." This is when you exit the tunnel and the light at the end of that tunnel gives way to a sunny new day.

Before I leave this topic, let me put a sharper point on my position. Suppose I were to tell you that I decided to invest in a pornography business. Certainly, you would be shocked and disappointed at my decision. Would it change your feelings if I explained that I personally disapproved of the products we made and that I never purchased any of them myself? You would probably still be dismayed at my blindness. You might even ask me, "Steve, how can you invest money and support an industry that you know is wrong? The fact that you don't personally buy the products doesn't change the fact that your investment is making the business possible!"

In a similar way, many Christians who condemn others for borrowing money are guilty of a double standard. Did you know that anyone who has a bank checking or savings account is also an "investor" in the lending industry? The reason a bank wants your checking and savings dollars is so it can lend most of them back out to their loan customers. So it seems a little inconsistent for someone to take advantage of the checking and savings system while criticizing the lending side that makes it all possible.

But, again, all of this should not obscure the most important point: While the Bible may not prohibit all forms of borrowing, there are plenty of peripheral teachings that should cause one to think hard before getting into debt. As I discussed in chapter 1, there are two questions to ask before we borrow:

1. What are my motives? Is it true need, or is it greed? Am I trying to impress someone else by presenting an image that I can't afford? Remember, according to Scripture, the essence of sin revolves around a form of pride that attributes to one's self the honor that belongs to God. Paul said it this way:

> *Do not be conformed to this world. . . . For through*
> *the grace given to me I say to everyone among you not to*
> think more highly of himself than he ought to think;
> *but to think so as to have sound judgment, as God has*

allotted to each a measure of faith (Rom. 12:2a, 3 NASB, author's emphasis).

Sometimes we borrow money when we should seek God's help. As Christians we serve a mighty King who is more than able to supply all of our needs. I have to confess that there have been far too many times in my life when I have tried to solve my problems in my own strength rather than waiting for God to help me. Borrowing money may be a short-term quick-fix to a long-term problem that could best be dealt with through prayer and mentoring from more mature Christians.

2. Can I repay this loan? The most fundamental question any Christian must answer *before* he or she makes a loan is, "How will I repay the money I am borrowing?" The psalmist said, "The wicked borrows and does not pay back" (37:21 NASB). One of the worst black eyes the church gets is from Christians who don't honor their debts.

A Good Rule of Thumb: Don't Borrow on Depreciating Assets

Generally speaking, a good rule of thumb is never to borrow money on a depreciating asset. This means that we should avoid borrowing money to buy cars, vacations, boats, furniture, and other things that will soon be depleted or lower in value. As I explained in chapter 6, I discourage people from borrowing money to buy cars, especially new ones, because of the terrible way they depreciate. There are millions of people all over the country who owe more on their cars than they are worth. In industry parlance this is called being "upside down."

So what does this leave? Well, as you already know, I hate to see people borrow money for almost anything. But there are some times when debt can serve a good purpose. Everyone has to make his or her own decisions in this area, but I like to see borrowing limited to things like home mortgages, necessary medical expenses, and the like.

What About Bankruptcy?

Today we live in a compromised culture driven by situational ethics. Vows are broken, and no one is shocked. Promises go unfulfilled, and the world shrugs its collective shoulders. Couples who have made vows divorce for every imaginable reason. Contracts are broken, and no one is surprised. We live in the golden age of the victim. Everyone vies for victim status. We look for reasons to blame others for our own faults and shortcomings. The era of personal responsibility is only a dim memory for many of us.

It's little wonder that even Christians have bought into the world system that tells us to grab all the lifestyle we can finance. Then when the payments due exceed cash coming in, we simply walk away from our debts and those faceless people who trusted us to repay them.

Today in America bankruptcies have reached epidemic levels. In 1980, there were fewer than 300,000 bankruptcies in the U.S. By 2001, that number had exploded to more than 1,500,000 filings! It hasn't always been this way. It wasn't because people had more money or were more financially astute. It was because most people felt that bankruptcy was wrong, so they made spending decisions that kept them from getting into financial distress. And when things really did go wrong, there was a bedrock willingness to do whatever it took to fulfill the commitments they had made.

That's Not to Say . . .

Although I dislike bankruptcy, that's not to say that I presume to have all the answers. The fact is, sometimes bad things happen to good people. Even recently I have been closely and painfully aware of a heartbreaking bankruptcy. The man involved is a good and decent fellow. He's a loving father, a faithful husband, and a devoted Christian. For more than twenty years I have known him to be one of the most honest and giving men on the planet.

Yes, he probably made mistakes, but don't you? I do.

My point is simple: While we might agree that bankruptcy is bad; it does not follow that only bad people bankrupt. Sometimes the walls close in. Whether it's reality or only perception, sometimes there doesn't appear to be any other answer. While we may individually determine never to walk away from our own debts, maybe we should be less judgmental of those who feel they must. We don't know their hearts. We may not understand their pain. After all, ours is the God of forgiveness and healing. If we expect God to extend grace to us, we must extend it to others.

The Tale of Two Christian Couples

Frankly, my focus in this book isn't on the outside world. It is primarily aimed at those of us who wear the name of Jesus. We are called to a higher standard of truth and honor. As Jesus said, it is hard for us to be salt to the outside world if we have lost our own spiritual potency. Just this week I have been dealing with two very different Christian couples. While one has left me heartbroken, the other has reaffirmed my faith in the power of Jesus.

The first couple—I'll call them Adam and Connie—have gotten into a real financial mess. It has taken years of missteps and bad decisions, but now they are in a first-rate financial tailspin. Thus far they have been unwilling to make the required cuts in expenses and lifestyle. At the request of a Christian who knew about the problem, I began trying to reach them last week. I left a voice mail offering to help the couple process through their situation and develop an action plan to get out of debt and pay their creditors. Adam finally returned my call this past Monday. It didn't take long to see that he wasn't ready to make the necessary hard decisions. Adam wasn't interested in sitting down and exploring how to revamp his lifestyle so they could begin to repay their debts. Instead he told me that they had met with two lawyers who (surprise) had encouraged them to file for bankruptcy. Although he paid lip service to the need to honor his commitments, his unwillingness even to research his options left me discouraged and disappointed.

Unfortunately, Adam and Connie are not alone. Today many Christians have fallen into the world's way of thinking and making excuses. Just because something (in this case, bankruptcy) may be legal doesn't necessarily mean that it is right. While there may be rare occasions when bankruptcy is appropriate, Christians should not be known as people who look for ways to avoid paying their bills. This means that, as Christians, we are responsible for the things we do that may result in later problems. Too often a person will make bad decisions for years, such as overspending and living beyond his means, then when the chickens come home to roost, he files bankruptcy, shrugs his shoulders, and says, "Things were so bad I had no other choice." This is similar to a drunk driver who tries to explain the wreck he's caused by saying, "I couldn't help it because I was drunk." That may be true, but who was responsible for his getting drunk in the first place? Granted, there came a point of no return when he was so drunk that the wreck was unavoidable. But all of this misses the point: The wreck would never have happened if he had not gotten drunk in the first place.

Sometimes even Christians are tempted to abrogate their responsibilities and ignore the causative behavior that brings them to the brink of disaster. Adam and Connie fall into this camp. They appear to be in denial that their money problems are of their own making. So instead of accepting responsibility, working an extra job or two, and cutting out extras, it is simply easier to file bankruptcy.

By contrast, I became aware of another situation in our own church this week that restored a lot of my faith in the power of Jesus to help us live more honorably and responsibly.

Junior and Peggy Grimes are godly people who live and share their faith everywhere they go. In addition to his regular job with a manufacturing company, Junior is one of the elders of our church. He reflects the love and mercy of Jesus in everything he does. His and Peggy's gentle spirits have blessed untold numbers of people over the years.

Several years ago the couple purchased a florist shop that Peggy operated. It seemed like the perfect investment for their retirement years. Yes, it would cost a lot of money, but after all, Peggy knew the business, and Junior could pitch in too. So they sold a rental house they owned and bought the business. The first days were exciting as they moved into a larger space and remodeled the store. Within three years through hard work and dogged determination, their gross billings were up 250 percent. But a number of setbacks and health problems soon began to take their toll. It eventually became obvious that the business was hemorrhaging red ink and would have to be sold.

Despite their best efforts the sale simply would not fetch enough dollars to cover all the bills. Peggy and Junior's advisor suggested that they approach their creditors and ask them to reduce their debts. It sounded good, and it could have saved the couple a lot of money. But Junior reasoned, "I'm not young, but I've never beat anyone out of a dime, and I'm not going to start now. Besides, God has blessed me with good health, a good job, and the ability to work extra hours."

With the decision made, Peggy and Junior got down to the hard task of working off the debt. Before it was over, they had cut out about as much as they could. The couple even sold their home and moved into an apartment to speed up their payment schedule. Eventually every dollar was paid in full.

Today Junior and Peggy have put the $100,000-plus loss behind them. Retirement savings have begun again, and they're buying a beautiful home. But best of all, it's easy for them to look at themselves in the bathroom mirror.

It all boils down to the fundamental teachings of Scripture. As followers, we must be people who keep our word, whether the commitment is to God or our fellowman.

> *Then Moses spoke to the heads of the tribes of the sons of Israel, saying, "This is the word which the LORD has commanded. If a man makes a vow to the LORD, or takes an oath to bind himself with a binding obligation, he shall not violate his word; he shall do according to all that proceeds out of his month (Num. 30:1–2 NASB).*

> *The wicked borrows and does not pay back"*
> *(Ps. 37:21 NASB).*

> *"But let your statement be, 'Yes, yes' or 'No, no'; anything beyond these is of evil" (Matt. 5:37 NASB).*

> *Do not withhold good from those to whom it is due,*
> *When it is in your power to do it.*
> *Do not say to your neighbor, "Go, and come back,*
> *And tomorrow I will give it,"*
> *When you have it with you (Prov. 3:27–28 NASB).*

> *A good name is to be more desired than great wealth,*
> *Favor is better than silver and gold (Prov. 22:1 NASB).*

When the Situation Really Is Hopeless

Admittedly, there are hopeless situations. Some Christians feel that a time can come when filing bankruptcy is the only way out. But before a Christian considers bankruptcy, at least three tough decisions should be made.

1. Approach your decision with prayer and the best spiritual counsel you can find. In the final analysis your decision is between you and God. He who searches the heart knows our motives. We can't fool God. The excuses that we use with others, and ourselves, won't work with him. With God we have no choice but to be painfully honest. Paul reminds followers that we each must "work out your own salvation with fear and trembling" (Phil. 2:12).

2. Every other possible alternative should be exhausted. This may mean that the debtor takes on extra jobs. There are 168 hours in a week. As a guy who has worked plenty of ninety- and one hundred-hour weeks, I can tell you there's nothing that says you can't work more than forty of them. When an individual has borrowed money and agreed to repay that debt, the least he or she can do is be willing to spend less time in front of the TV and more time at work. Second and third jobs are available everywhere. One of my neighbors owns several pizza delivery restaurants. He tells me that a good delivery guy can earn $25,000 a year! That's enough to pay down a lot of debt.

Other drastic efforts may be necessary. Lots of honorable people, like the Grimeses, have sold their homes and lowered their lifestyles to repay debt. Plans for further schooling and vacations may have to be put on hold. Doesn't it seem inappropriate for a Christian to spend money on nonessentials like cable TV, pets, a second car, new clothes, restaurants, and movies when he can't pay his debts?

Something else that can reduce debt quickly is selling stuff you really don't need. Do you have clothes, toys, cookware, tools, lawn furniture, decorations, a car, or even a boat that could be sold for some quick cash?

3. Make a personal commitment eventually to pay what you owe. Granted, if you go into bankruptcy, there may be legal considerations that you will need to honor, but your goal should be to set things right. This means that your lifestyle and spending habits may become sparse and draconian. But isn't your good name, to say nothing of the name of Jesus, worth whatever it costs?

Credit Cards: Plastic Prosperity or Plastic Explosives?

In the same breath that I use the word *bankruptcy*, I'm also tempted to use the words *credit cards*. Thousands of people can trace their financial undoing to the misuse of credit cards and revolving credit lines. According to the Federal Reserve, the typical family who filed for bankruptcy in 1997 owed more than one-and-a-half times its annual income in high-interest, short-term debt. I'm personally convinced that credit card debt is one of the most painful forms of debt. There are at least four reasons credit cards are so dangerous:

1. Credit cards are easy to get.
2. Credit cards are so easy to use and abuse.
3. Most people don't understand how interest, penalties, and payments are computed.
4. Credit card interest is so high.

As I mentioned in chapter 9, credit cards can be useful servants, but they are terrible masters. Today many Americans live under the tyranny of plastic debt. CardWeb reports that the average household that has at least one credit card was carrying a balance of $8,123 as of 2000. That's up from $2,985 in 1990! Another way of looking at this is to say that total credit card debt has been exploding for more than a decade. In 1990, total outstanding credit card debt was $173 billion. By 2002, it had mushroomed to $660 billion. The average household is paying $1,000 per year in interest. Credit card companies write off about $12 billion per year in losses resulting from their customers filing bankruptcy.[2]

The Meal That Takes Twenty Years to Pay For

How would you like to be making payments on a tank of gas or a meal that you bought twenty years ago? Sounds pretty ridiculous, doesn't it? But, if you fall into the trap of paying the minimum monthly payment on your credit card, that's exactly what you're doing.

Here's what the experts at CardWeb.com had to say when they were asked, "How long would it take to pay off a $5,000 debt on a 17 percent interest credit card making only the minimum payment each month?" Believe it or not, it would take more than twenty years!

And, remember, that doesn't allow for many cards that charge more than 17 percent, or membership fees, late charges, etc.

Stephen Brobeck, executive director for the Consumer Federation of America, says, "The low minimum payment, which barely covers interest obligations, convinces many borrowers that they are okay as long as they meet all their minimum payment obligations."[3] The Consumer Federation of America believes that bankruptcies in America might be significantly reduced if credit card companies raised their minimum payment requirements.[4]

Four Tips on How to Use a Credit Card

As I said, I'm not opposed to credit cards. I'm opposed to their misuse. Following are some tips that might help you stay out of credit card debt trouble:

Get only one credit card account. Extra cards are extra temptation and confusion. Usually one credit card account is enough. An exception might be if you own a small business and need a separate credit card account for business-related purchases.

Commit to pay every penny every month. The first month you don't pay it off in full may be the time to close the account.

Preplan how you will use your credit card. Avoid using your plastic prosperity for an impulse purchase. Be sure that what you're buying with the card is already in your budget. Credit cards are for convenience, security, and record-keeping purposes—not to add to your spending capacity.

Don't let your credit card become a source of pride and showiness. Far too many people try to impress others with their buying power. This is a dangerous trap.

Debit Cards: A Sensible Alternative?

Debit cards are one of the most popular financial products to come along in recent memory. While there may be some benefits to traditional credit cards, I am convinced that for many people debit cards are the better choice. They are accepted most everywhere that credit cards are taken.

Debit cards are payment cards attached to a checking or savings account. Basically, debit cards fall into one of two categories: On-line and off-line. An online debit card uses a PIN access and immediately accesses your bank account. An off-line debit card looks much like a standard bankcard and requires your signature. It acts like an electronic check and may take a day or two to clear the bank.[5] Merchants are generally happy to accept debit cards because they usually pay lower fees on debit cards than they do on credit cards.

Before I leave this, let me warn you that some experts voice concern about debit cards. According to a recent report on Fox News Channel, some banks are not fully disclosing the risks associated with debit cards. Consumers may have a potentially greater liability with debit cards than they do with credit cards. If someone fraudulently uses your debit card, present laws may not give consumers as much protection as with credit cards. Many banks voluntarily make good on debit card losses; however it is the consumer's responsibility to understand fully his bank's debit-card policy.[6] Among other questions, find out how much potential liability you could have and how long the bank might take to replenish your account, and then get everything in writing.

Also, remember that debit cards have some of the same inherent weaknesses that credit cards have. For one thing, anytime you buy anything without using cash the pain is less. Whether you use a credit card, a debit card, or a check, somehow it just doesn't feel as bad as pulling out the old billfold and cracking out some greenbacks. Studies show that when people use plastic they tend to spend more money.

How to Get 20 Percent Return on Your Investments

What if I told you there was a surefire, no-risk, guaranteed way to get a full 20 percent return on your investment? Would you be ready to pull some money out of the bank? Maybe sell a car or a boat? Maybe have a big yard sale?

Well, there is a way you can get this kind of return. It doesn't take a lot of education or study. You don't have to know any of the right people. All you have to do is pull out your credit card bill and pay it. Many people are paying interest rates in the range of 20 percent on their cards today. The quicker you pay those accounts down, the quicker you stop paying those high interest rates. It can be like getting a 20 percent return on your money!

In the next chapter we're going to look at some practical ways to repair your credit and get back on the road to self-respect, dignity, and even prosperity.

14

A Do-It-Yourself Credit Repair Kit

 *IT WAS ONE OF THOSE* rare moments of total, unvarnished truth. Ronny and I had known each other since college days. We were close friends and Christian brothers. Over the years we had shared a lot of private struggles. We had con-fessed and prayed together. But this particular conversation was giving me a glimpse into Ronny's soul. After years of financial chaos, Ronny and his wife had hit a brick wall. For more than a year, they had been aggressively paying off debts and getting their financial house in order. Finally, they were beginning to see a light at the end of a long tunnel. Happily, Ronny reported that within another year they would be out from under a mountain of debt to the IRS and a legion of creditors. He told me how hard the struggle had been. It had been as though they were trying to run a footrace in leg irons. They were always so preoccupied trying to meet the monthly bills that there wasn't much time for anything else. And although Ronny knew that God teaches us not to be stressed and worried, he had a tough time living a carefree lifestyle.

That was nearly ten years ago. Today Ronny and his wife are doing fine. They aren't rich, and because of the past problems, they're probably not as far along on retirement planning as they would like to be. But, all in all, the pressure has let up, and life is easier. Old obligations have been met, and they own a nice home. As I share this story, I probably should also tell you that Ronny is a minister. Yes, that's right. You may be thinking: *Don't preachers know better than to make the same financial mistakes the rest of us do?* I suppose that Ronny would agree that, if he didn't know better, at least he *should have known better.* But just because Ronny spends his life sharing the love of Jesus with others doesn't mean he's immune to the problems of this world. Ronny is a product of his upbringing. He had been raised in a Christian home, but it didn't include much teaching about financial matters.

Being Ready to Travel Light

Today Ronny would be the first to tell you that a Christian cannot be at his or her best when overcome with debt. What if Ronny and his wife had been given an opportunity to move to a new mission field while he was so deep in debt? And what if the new position paid only half his present salary? What would he have done? He would have been faced with two bad options: Take the new ministry and go deeper into debt, or pass up the opportunity altogether.

I believe that God wants all of his children to be ready to travel light. He wants us to be ready to hear his call, pull up stakes, and go where he sends. For some of us that may literally involve packing our bags and moving to a new area. In other cases it may mean adopting a simpler lifestyle that allows us to minister more effectively. For others it may mean clearing out some of the obligations that clutter our lives so we can give more of our time to kingdom work.

Unfortunately, many of us aren't in a position to travel at all. We have too many obligations. We have TVs and boats to pay for. We're upside down on our car loans. Our homes have second and third mortgages. We have bought too many things we didn't need with money we didn't have. Now we're stuck. If we ignore our obligations, we can lose our honor and dignity—to say nothing of our witness. How can a person share Jesus with a creditor whom he hasn't paid and is attempting to avoid? But the alternative isn't good either. Because we are left on the shore waving good-bye to the ship of missed opportunities as it leaves port.

In this chapter I want to give you some helpful tips on how to repair your credit. I want to give you hope. And I want you to know that God is big enough and wise enough to help you through the maze.

Not to Be Overly Simplistic, but . . .

In my world things are pretty simple. I don't see as much gray area as some people do. I don't believe many really important things are terribly complex. A child knows when her parent loves her. Usually, we know when we've been unkind to someone. Most young people intuitively know when they have crossed the line between romance and lust.

So maybe it won't come as a big surprise when I tell you that I believe there are four keys to successfully cleaning up a bad credit history:

1. Be truthful to your creditors, your spouse, and especially yourself.

2. Be available. Never run from a creditor. Larry Burkett says, "It's best for debtors to run to creditors, not away from them."[1] Be open, forthright, and cooperative. Remember, you're not in this mess because of your creditor. You're where you are because of bad decisions on your part.

3. Commit to make things right. Need I say more?

4. *Stay before God in prayer.* Commit it all to the Father. Trust him to be your best Friend. One passage that has blessed me over the years comes from Paul's first letter to the Corinthians. He tells us that God's hand is on us, and despite temptations to take shortcuts, there is a better way:

> *No temptation has overtaken you except such as is common to man; but God is faithful, who will not allow you to be tempted beyond what you are able, but with the temptation will also make the way of escape, that you may be able to bear it (1 Cor. 10:13 NKJV).*

Seven Steps to Rebuilding Your Credit

To be truthful with you, this is a tough section for me to write. Because teaching a person how to rebuild his credit without first fixing the root problems that got him into trouble can be like buying a teenager a new car the morning after he wrecks the old one. So my counsel is simply this: Before attempting to rebuild credit, concentrate first on rebuilding self-discipline and character. Commit never to use your credit (or your good name) carelessly again. Larry Burkett said that the first myth about credit is that a person *must* have it. He says you do not. Until a person has a true, legitimate need for credit and knows how to handle it responsibly, he should not establish it.[2] Credit is like so many other things: The less of it you have, the less of it you use.

Mike Hardwick, president of Churchill Mortgage here in Nashville, is an old friend of mine. He has been in mortgage and financial circles for as long as I can remember. Over the years Mike has developed a coherent, understandable procedure for rebuilding your credit. With his permission I want to combine some of his thoughts from his pamphlet, "Do It Yourself Credit Repair Kit," with some of my own on how to get out, and stay out, of debt.

If you are one of the millions of Americans who have had credit problems, don't give up; there's hope! Even with some negative items in your credit file, there are some positive things you can do to rebuild your credit. Following are seven steps that you may find helpful:

1. Develop a written budget and stick to it. Nothing works like a plan, and that's exactly what a budget is. Go back and review chapter 4 on budgeting. Once you have developed a realistic budget, stick to it!

2. If you simply cannot make a workable budget, get help. Seek the advice of someone in your church with credentials in this area, or get a reference from a friend, an attorney, or an accountant. Look for competent, compassionate help. Some people have found help from Consumer Credit Counseling Service. This is a nonprofit organization that offers free or low-cost financial counseling for people who need help with significant financial problems. CCCS says it can assist with budgeting and negotiating with creditors to set up a debt-repayment plan. But some experts warn that working with such agencies can show up negatively on your credit report. Get full information first.

3. Be sure your credit file is accurate. Most credit files are maintained by three major credit bureaus. You may request a copy of your credit report by contacting one of these organizations.

- Equifax Credit Information Services, Inc.
  P.O. Box 70241
  Atlanta, GA 30374
  Phone: 800-685-1111
  Web site: www.equifax.com

- Experian
  Phone: 888–EXPERIAN (397–3742)
  Web site: www.experian.com
- TransUnion LLC
  Consumer Disclosure Center
  P.O. Box 1000
  Chester, PA 19022
  Phone: 800–916–8800
  Web site: www.tuc.com

When your credit report arrives, check it carefully for any inaccuracies involving accounts that are not yours, late payments, etc. Also check for outdated information. If your experience is the same as mine, you will find the credit bureau people to be most helpful in answering any questions you have about your report.

4. Challenge inaccurate data on your report. To do this you will need to write each bureau and request that the inaccurate data be removed from your credit file. The credit bureau should enclose a form for this specific purpose when they send your credit report. There is also an example letter below. The bureau should contact each creditor that reported information you feel is incorrect. If the creditor does not verify the information within thirty days, the credit bureau should remove the information. If the creditor reports that the information is correct and the bureau keeps it in your file, you have the right to issue a Consumer Statement explaining your understanding of the matter.

5. Contact your creditors and ask for their cooperation. Some of the negative remarks on your credit report may not get removed without help from your creditors. Some creditors may be willing to remove or improve their remarks if you have made payments on the account.

Consider writing to each creditor to explain what the circumstances were regarding your account. Be truthful, but appeal to the

(Example Letter)

DATE:

RE: Request to Delete Accounts

I received my credit report and found the following items due to inaccurate reporting. A copy of my credit report is attached with the incorrect items marked.

Under the provisions of the Fair Credit Reporting Act 15USC section 16811, please reinvestigate and delete these disputed items. You will notice that this letter was sent via certified mail, and I will assume that thirty days is a reasonable amount of time in which to complete this investigation, unless I am otherwise notified. It should be understood that if these items are not reinvestigated, this will result in nonverification, and these items must be deleted from my credit file according to section 16811.

According to 15USC section 16811 of the Fair Credit Reporting Act, please notify me when these items have been deleted. A copy of my updated report may be sent to the address listed below.

Sincerely,

_____
Signed

_____
Name (printed)

_____
Address

_____
City, State, Zip

_____
Phone Numbers

creditor's sense of goodwill. Also remind the creditor that you eventually paid the account and that you appreciated the services/ products they provided. You might ask the creditor either to remove the negative remarks or write a statement that the account has been paid.

Then order an updated credit report after thirty days or so. If the creditor has not removed or improved his comments regarding your file, you may want to add a Consumer Statement of your own in accordance with 15USC section 16811 of the Fair Credit Report Act. In a few weeks you will want to check your report to be certain that your statement has been added to your credit file.

If you do not achieve the desired results, don't give up. Be persistent. Touch base with the creditor again in a few months and try again. Always be truthful and courteous.

6. Add positive histories to your file. If your credit report is missing data on accounts that you have paid on a timely basis, send the credit bureaus copies of your account statements and canceled checks showing your payment history. Ask the bureaus to add this information to your file. You might also benefit from calling non-reporting creditors with whom you have a good payment history. When a creditor agrees to give your data to the credit bureaus, follow up on it. Also you might ask the bureaus to contact the creditors and get the information. Nothing is guaranteed here, but some of these procedures may prove successful.

7. Add stability to your file. Send the credit bureaus data that confirms steady employment, a long time at your residence, and other pertinent data.

Six More Things You Can Do to Reduce Debt

If you are sick and tired of being sick and tired of too much debt, maybe you will find some of the following ideas beneficial. These are not for the faint of heart. They are tough, pull-yourself-up-by-your-bootstraps, take-no-prisoners action steps for people who *really want to change* the paradigms of their lives. Remember, if you are in debt, you didn't get that way overnight; and you won't get out of debt overnight either.

Following are some practical steps you may find helpful in reducing your debt load and getting life back to normal:

1. Try to get overtime work at your present job. For many people this is the most natural and convenient way to boost their income. Frequently employers will stretch to find extra work for a loyal employee.

2. Get a second job. There is nothing wrong with working more than a forty-hour week when the goal is to settle debts, regain dignity, and put your financial life in order. All sorts of second jobs are available. Usually it's best to find a job that will begin generating income quickly. Often work in a fast-food restaurant, at a loading dock, as a motel bellhop, a janitor, or in a retail store fits the bill. At this point *you're not looking for a position; you're looking for a job!* Don't let your ego take over here. The dishonor from not paying your debts is far worse than being seen flipping hamburgers by someone you know.

While I love sales-oriented work, I generally don't recommend that a person take such a job to pay off debts. These jobs usually require the development of contacts and marketing skills. It's tough to develop sales skills in an atmosphere of panic. The better sales jobs generally have a long start-up period. This means that it can take weeks, or even months, before the checks start rolling in; and when they do, they can be pretty unpredictable.

In this same vein, be wary of classified ads that make income promises that are too good to be true. Many of these are sales jobs that make pie-in-the-sky promises most people never achieve. A number of years ago, a friend of mine named Dave made just such a mistake. In desperate need of a job, he found what looked like the perfect solution in the classifieds. Without doing enough research on the company, he took the job selling security alarm systems. He ended up working long hours only to have the company go out of business owing him commissions.

Remember, this is no time to go for the brass ring. Instead, look for something dependable with a sufficient and immediate income stream.

3. *Start a business.* For some people this can be a great solution. But this is best only for people who are true self-starters. If you can avoid the temptation of spending start-up money and buying into the old adage, "you've got to spend money to make money," this might be right for you.

I'm not suggesting a major enterprise here. Look for something that you already know how to do and have the necessary equipment to perform. Be sure that it is a product or service that will begin earning cash immediately. To increase the odds of success, be sure to keep your overhead low.

I know one woman who supplements her regular income by doing ironing at home in the evenings. This allows her to be at home with her daughter, and the only equipment required is an iron, an ironing board, and a car to make her deliveries. Other people have made great money using their mowers to cut other people's grass. Light yard work, landscaping, and leaf raking can be super sources for extra dollars. Some teachers earn extra cash by doing private tutoring. Consider baby-sitting. Start a car wash-and-wax business. Use your imagination!

4. *Sell things.* Have a garage sale. Run cheap (or free) classified ads. Put "For Sale" ads on bulletin boards at laundromats and in other public places. Scour the house and garage for anything you don't need. How about selling an extra car? (An extra car is any car that doesn't bring a benefit that is greater than the pain that the debt load causes.)

One word of caution here: You may want to avoid selling your property to pawn shops. Since these are businesses that have to make a profit to exist, they often won't pay as much as an individual could get by handling his own sale.

5. Mom takes a part-time job. I really discourage this when there are dependent children at home, but sometimes it's the only solution available. In such cases I urge mothers to arrange their work schedules so they disrupt domestic security and tranquility as little as possible. There are at least three things to remember:

- Try to find work that can be done at, or close to, home.
- Remember, this isn't a career move. It's a necessary evil. Try to get back to the most important job as soon as possible.
- Ideally the job should require Mom to work only while the kids are in school or are being cared for by Dad.

I know of two mothers who started a housecleaning business. It allowed them to bring their kids with them or leave their children with each other on alternating days. Another friend made money doing in-home word processing. Still another mother in our church had a parcel-delivery service that allowed her to bring her kids along. Boy, do those kids have a great sense of direction today!

6. Cut down on spending. Curtail all the extras: eating out, entertainment, all the stuff that is optional. Avoid unnecessary driving, and buy the cheapest grade of gas your car will run well on. Make only one trip to the grocery each week; this helps cut down on impulse buying. Consider moving into a less expensive house or apartment, cancel the cable TV, and suspend unnecessary cell phone usage.

What About Credit Repair Companies?

As I've said before, if it sounds too good to be true, it probably is. In my experience there are no shortcuts to cleaning up bad credit. Just because a company promises to erase your past credit misdeeds and get you a new credit identity legally—all for a big fee—doesn't mean it's always true. Fixing a bad credit history is a function of time, hard work, and a workable debt repayment plan.[3]

I am unaware of much that a credit repair company can do for you that you can't do for yourself. The folks at CardWeb.com point out that there is nothing anyone can do legally to remove accurate and timely negative data from your credit report. Although some of these companies promise to help you establish a new credit identity, you can be held responsible, charged, and prosecuted for mail or wire fraud if you use the mail or telephone dishonestly to apply for credit. CardWeb.com also points out that it is a federal crime to misrepresent your Social Security number, obtain an Employer Identification Number from the IRS under false pretenses, or to make false statements on a loan application. Being in debt is painful but not nearly as painful as committing sin to get out of debt.

Some states have laws that strictly regulate credit repair companies. If you have lost money to one of these firms, or you know of fraudulent activities, you can contact the consumer affairs office in your area, your state's attorney general, or the Federal Trade Commission. The National Fraud Information Center also accepts consumer complaints at 800–876–7060.[4]

Are Bill Consolidation Loans a Good Idea?

Like they say, one or two bugs on the windshield don't cause a wreck. But, left alone, they will eventually cover the whole windshield until you can't see where you're going. The same is true with debt. Typically, one or two loans don't cause a financial wreck; but allowed to grow unchecked, they can send you over a cliff. It was because people allowed themselves to become gradually swallowed by debt that bill consolidation loans became so popular. A number of years ago, I remember hearing someone say, only half jokingly, that a bill consolidation loan is the process of taking all of those nagging little monthly bills and combining them all into one, simple, backbreaking payment.

While I will admit that these loans are like playing with a beautiful candle in a roomful of dynamite, I respectfully differ with those who teach that bill-consolidation loans are always wrong. In some rare cases I believe they make sense. Recently I encouraged a friend in another state to make just such a loan to stabilize his financial world so his family could regain its financial equilibrium. However, this man's situation was unique. To begin with, much of the debt he was dealing with had occurred because of his wife's illness. Second, he was totally committed to getting out, and staying out, of debt in the future. Third, he had a viable plan to make this a reality. And, finally, he is a mature Christian totally committed to honoring all of his debts.

Unfortunately, many people who make bill-consolidation loans don't fit this profile. Too often these loans allow people who are already in financial trouble to get more deeply into debt. They treat the symptoms without healing the disease. By borrowing money to repay existing debts with lower monthly payments, many people get a false sense of security. Before long they are running up new debts and getting even further behind.

Three Steps to Take
Before Getting a Bill Consolidation Loan

Before applying for a bill-consolidation loan, here are three things you may want to do:

1. Borrow as little as possible. Don't borrow any more than absolutely necessary to give you the needed breathing room. Some people who are already in financial trouble end up being convinced to borrow even more on a bill-consolidation loan than they already owe on other debts. Watch out for this trap!

2. Be sure that the new loan, in fact, really helps your situation. If you don't gain ground, a bill-consolidation loan is even a bigger mistake. Remember, these are profitable loans for lenders to make. Don't be talked into anything you don't fully understand. Make certain that you are getting the lowest interest rate possible. Think through the implications and conditions of the loan. Can you live with the terms?

3. Most importantly, repent of the life choices that have brought you to this place. Commit before God to change the lifestyle you have lived. Seek his face and ask him to open your eyes to any greed, ego, or trust issues that may have been driving your spending and borrowing. Get help and counseling from someone qualified in these areas. Change the behaviors that got you to this point.

Ultimately, so much of the solution is in our willingness to refocus on the eternal. This world is not our home; we're just passing through. The fewer treasures we lay up here, the fewer monthly payments we have to deal with!

Part IV

The Future: Saving, Investing, and Getting Ready for Retirement

CERTAIN THINGS IN LIFE are pretty predictable. Unless God intervenes, the sun will probably rise tomorrow. Guys will try to get girls' attention. The Republicans will disagree with the Democrats. And you'll probably have a flat tire coming into work the day after the boss gives that speech about being on time.

Another thing that has become fairly predictable when I speak on money management is that someone will say, "Where were you thirty years ago when I needed you?" Of course, the truth is a little embarrassing. I was nowhere to be found. As a matter of fact, the real question is, Where was I thirty years ago when *I* needed me?

Well, the truth is, like most of my generation, thirty years ago (or even fifteen or twenty years ago) I was AWOL when it came to things pertaining to money management and investing. I was generally fat, happy, and oblivious. It never occurred to me to plan ahead.

I remember all sorts of dumb things I did. I confused credit cards with cash plenty of times. As long as I had some "plastic prosperity" in my pockets, I was good to go. As a young college grad, I took off pretty fast in the real estate business. Soon I had more money than good sense. The only thing I did better than make money was spend it. And as for investing, what was that? I could still kick myself for blowing an incredible opportunity to buy a triplex back in 1976. As a matter of fact, I didn't even have enough good sense to take my own advice and buy a house of my own! Instead, I rented an apartment! And, when it came time to buy a car, I bought a new one with borrowed money.

Later, when I started the ad agency, I did a little better. By then I had learned some basic lessons about overspending, and I was more cautious. But just because I was cautious didn't mean I was smart when it came to investing. As the business grew, we began to have more cash in the checking account. One of my employees used to marvel that I didn't at least put some of the extra cash into CDs at the bank. Believe it or not, I was too lazy and stupid to do even that. It took several years for me to wake up to the fact that I was losing money by letting it sit in a zero-interest checking account!

The Slow Awakening

Gradually I started to wake up. Slowly through the 1980s I began to realize that earning money was only part of the formula. To get ahead, I was going to have to get smarter in the disciplines of saving and investing. By the early 1990s, I was investing more and more time studying and learning how money works.

In the last fifteen years, I've grown and learned a lot. One of the things I've learned is how much more there is to learn. As I share some of my thoughts and ideas on saving, investing, and future planning with you in the next few chapters, remember that you and I are both still learning. I don't claim to have all the answers.

Investing is like looking at a chameleon. The more you ponder your investment options, the more they seem to change before your eyes. There are multitudes of saving and investment strategies. For every good reason there is to purchase an investment, there is another reason to reconsider it. Each individual has different time periods, risk tolerances, and circumstances to consider. What is right for one person in one economic period may not be right for another person in another economic environment. The ideas, concepts, an strategies in the following chapters are not intended to be exhaustive in their content. I am simply going to hit a few of the high points on the topics I discuss. As you read, remember that the responsibility for how you save, invest, and plan for retirement is yours. Read lots of good books, attend reputable investment/ retirement seminars, and consult with qualified professionals. Compare, consider, and pray for wisdom.

15

What I Wish They Had Told Me About Investing (Before I Made Some Stupid Mistakes)

 *PEOPLE SAVE* and invest for a lot of reasons. Some do it for ego gratification. Others do it to be showy and ostentatious. Still others hoard money because they don't trust God to provide for them. I don't know what your motives are. It really isn't any of my business. Ultimately, your motives are between you and God. My goal, throughout this book, has been to encourage both of us to walk before God with spiritual integrity. I believe you want to do just that, or you probably wouldn't have read this far. If money were all that mattered to you, you would have already found another book more focused on money than motives.

As we begin these final chapters, allow me to suggest that there are at least two wonderful reasons for saving and investing for the future:

1. To provide for the needs of your family. The scriptural basis for this is solid. Paul was pointed in his instructions to the church in

Ephesus when he told Timothy, "Prescribe these things as well, so that they may be above reproach. But if anyone does not provide for his own, and especially for those of his household, he has denied the faith, and is worse than an unbeliever" (1 Tim. 5:7–8 NASB).

2. To have assets to share with others in spiritual or physical need. In my Bible study a few mornings ago, I read 2 Corinthians 8. What a beautiful teaching on the early church's giving. Take a moment to read this wonderful chapter. The balance and love within these verses will be a blessing. It seems to me that as Christians living in the most financially blessed country in the history of the world, we should be motivated to invest so we can share and meet the needs of those less fortunate.

As you read these last chapters, feel no pressure to agree with my ideas. I simply present them for your consideration. Some of the suggestions I make may make sense in your situation. If so, great. If not, that's OK too. As with everything else in this book, be sure to assess each idea in light of other material you study, the counsel of your own professional advisor(s), current market and economic conditions, and your own tolerance for risk.

Let me also caution you not to become overly consumed by anything—including investing and planning for the future. Driven to an extreme, even virtue can be turned to vice. Jesus warned against obsessing about the future:

> "Do not worry then, saying, 'What will we eat?' or
> 'What will we drink?' or 'What will we wear?' For the
> Gentiles eagerly seek all these things; for your heavenly
> Father knows that you need all these things. But seek first
> His kingdom and His righteousness, and all these things will
> be added to you. So do not worry about tomorrow; for
> tomorrow will care for itself. Each day has enough trou-
> ble of its own" (Matt. 6:31–34 NASB, author's emphasis).

Approach your investment decisions with prayer. Earnestly seek God's will. Occasionally, you may want to rethink your motives. And as with everything else in our lives, investing is a matter of balance. After all, balance and good stewardship are first cousins.

What Paul Harvey Taught Me About Investing

Paul Harvey is one of my heroes. I have listened to him since I was a boy. In a world that has lost its moral compass, his fundamental decency and bedrock integrity have remained uncompromised. Maybe he's partially responsible for my love of radio and the years I spent in broadcasting. Today Paul Harvey's *News and Comment* and *The Rest of the Story* are broadcast on over twelve hundred stations and four hundred Armed Forces Network stations heard throughout the world. His column appears in three hundred newspapers around the country.

With this as background, let me tell you about the lesson in investing Mr. Harvey taught me. It all began in an ad agency planning meeting with a new client in the early 1980s. This particular client was a young oil exploration company. Their existence depended on finding investors to underwrite their drilling projects. Although our relationship with this company was short-lived, it was a real learning experience for all of us.

During this particular meeting the conversation turned to the company's need for a good video presentation to show prospective investors. As we talked, it became clear that we needed to find "just the right person" to do the on-camera presentation. We needed someone who was well-known for his honesty, someone who was universally admired, someone whom other people respected. Suddenly, like a bolt of lightning, it hit me. Why not Paul Harvey? He, I reasoned, would be perfect. Everybody knew and loved Paul Harvey. He would be a natural!

"Paul Harvey!" I blurted out, "Paul Harvey would be just the guy for this project!"

The clients were as impressed as my employees were mystified. "Wow! That would be great," someone said, "Do you know Paul Harvey?"

"Well, no," I admitted, "but that doesn't matter. I bet I can find him."

Over the next few minutes, we hatched a plan that was borne of equal amounts of sheer gall and adolescent stupidity. The plan was for me to fly to Chicago where Paul Harvey's program originates, locate Mr. Harvey, and simply ask him to help with the project. Well, to make a long story short, that's exactly what we did. I won't give you the details (they're too embarrassing and unbelievable), but I located Paul Harvey. Caught by surprise, he thoughtfully explained that his schedule was too tight to discuss the issue with me at that moment. But when he saw how important this was to me (and how desperate I must have looked), he kindly gave me his phone number and told me to call him a couple of hours later.

Those were long hours. I must have rehearsed what I was going to say a dozen times. Finally, the appointed moment arrived. I mustered my most convincing tone, lifted the receiver, and dialed the number. Suddenly I was on the line with Paul Harvey! After the initial pleasantries I told him about the client and the video project. After graciously listening to everything I had to say, Mr. Harvey's deep baritone voice claimed control of the conversation.

"Steve, I really appreciate the invitation to take part in your video production. I hope it goes well, but you will have to do it without me. I have spent a lot of years earning a reputation of trust. For me, it's not about the money; it's deeper than that. I simply can't do such a project because if the company ever disappointed anyone, it could also reflect negatively on me. I hope you understand."

Wow, did I ever understand—Paul Harvey had turned me down flat! I was out of luck! I had to go back home and tell the client that I had failed. But actually there was a much bigger lesson for me to learn.

Shortly thereafter we disassociated with the client. Things weren't adding up. Something just didn't feel right. A year or two later we heard the news. The company had been caught taking some short-cuts. The business folded. People lost money. And the president of the company went to jail.

Over the years, as I remembered the events of those months, my respect for Paul Harvey grew even greater. He had illustrated one of the foundational points that good investing is built on: There is no place for moral shortcuts for Christian investors.

Wish They Had Told Me #1
Look out for moral shortcuts. Don't let the opportunity to make a short-term gain cloud your long-term perspective.

It would have been easy for him to say, "Sure, kid, I'll do a few hours of studio work in exchange for a nice check." But instead Paul Harvey knew that whatever the short-term financial reward was, it would pale compared to the long-term damage that being associated with a disreputable product would do.

The same is true of investing. No investment return is ever enough reward for taking a moral shortcut. While it isn't original with me, there is a three-point checklist that can be applied to any situation to help us determine whether an investment opportunity is appropriate. By asking these three questions *before* we make an investment decision, we can avoid a lot of heartache. And most important, we will have the comfort of knowing that God is pleased with our actions.

1. Is what I'm about to do lawful? Will my actions break any civil, criminal, or tax law? Will this behavior be consistent with company regulations and policies? Will it conflict with any professional standards?

2. Is what I'm going to do good for everyone involved? Am I helping to build a win-win situation that will allow everyone to gain in the end?

3. Am I treating the other person the way I would like to be treated? Jesus said, "Therefore, whatever you want men to do to you, do also to them, for this is the Law and the Prophets" (Matt. 7:12 NKJV).

Such a simple concept but so tough to obey. However, if you show others the same consideration and fairness you would want, you will be well on your way not only to investing success but also to success in all of your relationships.

Your concern for others will be evidence of the Spirit's fruit in your life, and only with this Spirit fruit ("love, joy, peace, patience, kindness, goodness, faithfulness, gentleness, self-control," Gal. 5:22–23) can godly success be yours.

Nothing Is Certain—Not Even Death and Taxes

I remember the first time I heard the little adage, "Nothing is certain except death and taxes." It was spoken by my shop teacher in junior high. While I thought he was a pretty neat guy, I remember thinking to myself, *That's not necessarily so!* After all, I reasoned, some people cheat on their taxes, and the Bible says some of us will be alive when Jesus comes back.

Maybe it's my contrarian nature that makes this particular point so important to me. But if you miss everything else I say in this chapter, please don't miss this: The truth is, no investment is for sure.

Wish They Had Told Me #2
The truth is, no investment is for sure!

That doesn't mean there aren't lots of generally safe places to put your money, but the fact remains, none of them are 100 percent certain. But you say, what about Treasury bills and bank certificates of deposit with FDIC insurance protection? Aren't they totally safe? Well, to be technically accurate, no they aren't. Even though people may say that Treasury bills are "backed by the full faith and credit of the United States government," what good is that if the government falls? And, by extension, one would assume that the FDIC insurance that protects bank deposits would also be of little use if the government collapsed.

All right, I'll admit it. I'm being a bit ridiculous, but I'm straining a point to make a point. Despite what the so-called experts may say, no one can totally guarantee the future of anything—including invested money.

It took a long time for me to realize this. As a young investor, I assumed that the talking heads on the TV business programs knew what they were saying. When an analyst would come on and confidently explain why the market had gone up or down that day, I assumed he knew what he was talking about. When another analyst said that a given stock would increase in value by 50 percent over the next year, I had confidence in his prediction.

But gradually I began to realize that these guys didn't have all the answers. They seemed to be wrong as often as they were right. And, besides, they hardly ever agreed with one another. One would be explaining how we couldn't avoid a bear market at the same moment another one was promising a 20 percent growth in the economy. I began to agree with Harry Truman's assessment of economists when he said, "If I lined all the economists up in one line, they'd all point in different directions."

No one can accurately predict all the markets all the time. So it behooves each investor to study broadly. Get diverse opinions. Weigh the data. Determine your tolerance for risk. And develop a balanced and consistent investment style.

No One Cares as Much About Your Money as You Do

As I've already said, *you* are responsible for your own financial future. Don't fall into the trap of expecting anyone else to care as much about your investments as you do. Does this mean you should try to do it alone? Of course not! Personally, I believe that "in the abundance of counsel there is victory" (Prov. 11:14b). So I get lots of input. I try to keep up with the business and financial news. I read books and investing articles. I attend occasional seminars. And I use the services of a good attorney, three insurance people, an accountant, and two brokers.

Wish They Had Told Me #3
You are responsible for your own financial future. Take responsibility now because no one else cares as much about your money as you do.

The ultimate responsibility for my investment and retirement planning decisions rests with me. The same is true for you. If you reach retirement age without having saved the needed funds, don't expect anyone to rescue you. Just like the foolish virgins Jesus talks about in Matthew 25:1–13, there will be a day of reckoning. Reports say that fewer than 10 percent of Americans retire with adequate resources. No one should have to hock the gold watch to buy extra cat food, especially when they don't have a cat. Take responsibility now because blaming others won't help then.

Avoid the "One Size Fits All" Approach to Investing

Don't be fooled into thinking that what is right for one of your friend's investment plans is necessarily right for your investment plan. As I said earlier, decisions about how much to invest and what to invest in are personal. Different families have different situations.

Wish They Had Told Me #4
Your situation is unique. Don't fall into a
"one size fits all" mentality.

If you are young and healthy, you can probably save at a more relaxed pace than a person nearing retirement without anything set aside. The traditional wisdom suggests that people with long-term investment horizons (i.e., young couples in their twenties and thirties who are in good health) may want to invest more heavily in stocks and mutual funds than in smaller, more volatile companies. While these investments can have big swings up and down, over a long period they may deliver better returns. On the other hand, when a couple is reaching retirement age, it may make sense to shift their investment mix away from some of the high flyers into a more conservative mix of stock and bond funds.

Since every investor is different, I like to encourage people to think through four points before they begin investing:

1. Communicate with each other. Your husband or wife is your best friend. Spend time discussing your individual preferences, interests, and fears. One study indicated that a far higher percentage of men found investing to be fun than did women. If this is the case in your marriage, slow down. Take time to understand each other's temperaments. Like they say, if you don't communicate, you speculate.

2. *Study your options.* Today there are thousands of mutual funds, annuities, 401(k) plans, and IRA products available. Study, read, learn—become an informed consumer.

3. *Get professional help.* As I've already said, there's nothing like a little advice from a qualified pro. Find someone you trust and can communicate with. Paying for a little advice can sometimes save a lot of long-term regret. Proverbs makes my point: "Without consultation, plans are frustrated, but with many counselors they succeed" (15:22 NASB).

4. *Know yourself.* This one is often overlooked. But I am convinced that a vital part of any investment program is for the investor to know himself or herself. We all have different comfort levels. Our tolerance for risk varies. One person is comfortable with a particular type of investment, while another person wouldn't touch it. One investor would calmly wait out the storm if his mutual fund dropped 50 percent in a single year (as one of mine has this year), while another investor would have a hard time sleeping at night. By knowing your personal comfort level with risk, you will be a better investor. Proverbs 14:15 has this admonition: "The naïve believes everything, but the sensible man considers his steps" (NASB).

Beware of Get-Rich-Quick Schemes

Back in the early 1980s, I thought I'd found my ticket to riches. It all began with a phone call from a stockbroker who wanted my business. Never having invested before, I was at once both intrigued and frightened. "Not to worry," she told me, "I have an investment that will give you a great return." She went on to explain how initial public offerings (IPOs) work. She told me that her brokerage firm had access to shares of stock in a company that was about to go public. Her plan was for me to buy shares in the first hours of trading, wait for other buyers to hop in and bid up the price, then sell at a profit. Well, it sounded OK to me, so I bought one hundred shares at about ten dollars each. By the end of the day, we sold at a price several dollars higher—and voila, I was a few hundred dollars richer.

As any compulsive gambler will tell you, the most dangerous thing for a new gambler is to win the first time he plays. It sets up an "easy win" mentality that can lead to ruin. I suppose that's what happened to me. It wasn't long before the same broker called again with a similar opportunity. And, once again, I played and won. By this time I was telling my friends about the plans I had to make a quick fortune in the stock market.

But it didn't take long for things to go south. For one thing I soon learned that these sweetheart deals my broker was bringing me weren't going to go on forever. I learned that IPO shares are often supplied to brokerage houses in limited quantities for brokers to sell to their favorite clients or, in my broker's case, to someone she wanted to win as a client. But the real awakening began the day she called to tell me about a little energy company that was going public. The firm was in the business of supplying drilling equipment to oil exploration companies. It looked like a sure thing. After all, at that time, American companies were poking holes all over the West trying to hit crude. So I bought one hundred shares the day the company went public for around seventeen dollars per share. Almost immediately the stock went up. If memory serves, I think my broker called me when it went over thirty dollars to see if I wanted to sell. "No," I told her confidently, "let's ride it up a bit higher." By now you've probably already guessed the rest of the story. Almost immediately the stock's price began to fall, and like an idiot I held on all the way to the ground. Today I still have the certificate. And, as the old saying goes, it isn't worth the paper . . .

Wish They Had Told Me #5
Look out for get-rich-quick schemes.

I relive this painful story here simply to illustrate the point that get-rich-quick schemes usually have a lot more to do with greed than with reality. But, alas, such "opportunities" are everywhere. And the thing that makes them work is their believability. After all, in my case, the investment didn't come from some guy selling things out of the trunk of his car. It came from someone who was working with one of the nation's largest brokerage firms.

Again, I repeat, if it looks too good to be true, it probably is. This is why I urge people to get smart before they get invested. Is it wrong to invest in an IPO? Not necessarily. But you need to understand what you're doing and not have unrealistic expectations.

Do you remember March 2000? The stock market was at dizzying heights. The business news was running stories asking if the old rules of investing no longer applied. People were making millions (even billions) on dot.com startup companies. Those rare investors who still insisted on buying only the stock of companies that could show good earnings performance were ridiculed. Some of the new wizards of Wall Street (mostly in their twenties and totally ignorant of market downturns) were openly laughing at the "old guys" and waiting for these dinosaurs of the past to wake up to the future of investing. The NASDAQ index went into the stratosphere and finally broke five thousand! It appeared the old rules had all been broken, and people really could make overnight fortunes in the market.

But then it happened. Reality set in. The collective mind of Wall Street suddenly awoke and said, "This is crazy!" And overnight the markets went into reverse. Businesses failed faster than the owners could lock the doors. Overnight, fortunes were lost. Mutual funds and 401(k) plans headed for the basement. A year later the NASDAQ was still off of its highs by 60 percent. Today a lot of the wizard kids of 2000 wish they'd listened to those old dinosaurs. I'll have more to say about this in chapter 17.

The Greatest Risk Is Taking No Risk at All

Matthew 25 includes the well-known parable of Jesus that tells the story of three servants who were entrusted with their master's wealth. Of course, you probably remember that the master gave one servant five talents, another servant received two talents, and a third servant was given one talent. Since this was a lot of money (a single talent was worth more than a laborer could earn in fifteen years), the master expected great things.

Finally, the master returned to see how his guys had done. The fellow with five talents had doubled his money to ten, which pleased the master greatly. Up next came the servant who had been given two talents. He, too, thrilled his master when he announced that he had grown his two talents to four. But then came the third servant. This poor guy mumbled a few excuses about how the master was a harsh man and then finally admitted that he had done nothing with the money. Let's pick the conversation up there:

> "So I was afraid, and I went and hid your talent in the ground. Here you have what is yours." But his master answered him, "You wicked and slothful servant! You knew that I reap where I have not sowed, and gather where I have not winnowed? Then you ought to have invested my money with the bankers, and on my coming I should have received what was my own with interest. So take the talent from him, and give it to him with the ten talents. For to everyone who has, more will be given, and he will have abundance; but from him who has not, even what he has will be taken away. And

cast the worthless servant into the outer darkness, there men will weep and gnash their teeth" (Matt. 25:25–30 RSV).

While the primary focus of this parable is spiritual, there are some applications to our conversation here, as well. Notice what the third servant didn't do. He didn't spend the money. He didn't embezzle it. He didn't even waste the money. As a matter of fact, he carefully protected it. But from the perspective of his boss, who was obviously a good money manager, the servant had utterly failed!

Wish They Had Told Me #6
Sometimes the riskiest thing a person can do with his money is nothing. Money has value. If it remains uninvested, value is lost.

The Story of Two Mice and a Cat

There once were two mice and a cat. The mice lived in a hole at the bottom of the wall. One day they looked out and noticed that across the room from the cat was a large piece of cheese. After days without food one mouse finally got up the courage to make a run for the cheese. I don't know what happened to him. But I do know what happened to the mouse that stayed in the hole. He starved to death.

The point is: Safety is often just an illusion. Holding back, refusing to invest prudently can kill you financially. While the word *risk* means different things to each of us, it is important to learn about the risks inherent in various investments. Then thoughtfully consider your ability to tolerate the various types and levels of risks. The question is not *if* you're going to take a risk; the question is, Which risk are you most comfortable taking?

Types of Investments

Some of the factors that determine a person's tolerance for risk include: knowledge and education about markets and various investments, the time horizon, and the investor's fundamental makeup. Investors can be divided into three broad categories:

1. Conservative investors. These people want to maintain their initial investment, or principal. In return for somewhat greater certainty that they won't lose their principal, they frequently settle for lower rates of return, especially over the long term.

2. Moderate investors. Usually these people are OK with a mixture of different investments (i.e., individual stocks, bonds, cash, or mutual funds that hold such assets, etc.) with various risk levels. While they don't like market downturns, they are willing to wait them out in the hope that the long-term rewards will be worth it.

3. Aggressive investors. Typically, these are younger investors who hope to have a long time horizon. Much of their money is in higher risk investments (i.e., stocks or stock mutual funds), which will tend to be much more volatile. In exchange for this higher potential of risk to principal and volatility, they hope to achieve greater returns.

The Many Faces of Risk

Some people, in an attempt "not to lose my money," succumb to one of the most pernicious of all forms of risk: *the risk of inflation.* While such people may sleep better with their money in a certificate of deposit or a bank savings account, they may wake up to a real unpleasant surprise. This is because such investments may not pay enough interest to keep up with inflation. For instance, if you invest in a CD that pays 5 percent interest in a period when inflation is running at 4 percent, you may be losing money after you pay taxes. Accepting no market volatility and trying to "play it safe" also means accepting the possibility of lower returns.

Below is a graph developed by The Vanguard Group[1] that illustrates this point further. Notice how inflation has affected returns over the seventy-five-year period from 1926 to 2000. For instance, if you had invested your money in cash instruments during that period with a return of 3.9 percent, it would have been nearly destroyed by inflation that ran at 3.1 percent. But that same 3.1 percent inflation rate would not have been nearly so problematic if your money had been gaining around 11 percent in the stock market during those same years.

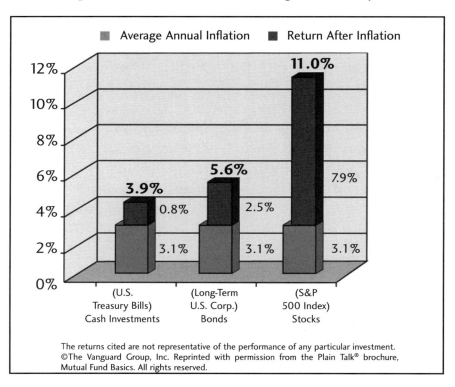

The returns cited are not representative of the performance of any particular investment. ©The Vanguard Group, Inc. Reprinted with permission from the Plain Talk® brochure, Mutual Fund Basics. All rights reserved.

Of course, there are other sorts of risk too. Some of them include:

Market risk. Even when individual companies are doing well, it is possible for their stock prices to go down in the market.

Credit risk. An example of this would be in the case of a company, government, or other organization (n.g., a church) that issues bonds to raise capital. There is always a risk, even though in most cases it may be small, that the issuer could default and be unable to make interest or principal repayments.

Volatility risk. One place where this form of risk can occur is in stock and mutual fund investments. Due to market fluctuations investments can go up and/or down.

Liquidity risk. Some investments are harder to sell (or convert to cash) than others. For instance, if you needed cash in a hurry, you might be better off getting money out of a checking account or another liquid asset, as opposed to having to sell a house or a car. While the house or car might eventually sell for as much as the cash in your checking account, there is a risk that, to raise cash in a hurry, you might have to sell them at a discount.

Risk of losing principal. Some investments lose money. When a person loses the money (principal) she puts into an investment, that is called principal loss.

Interest rate risk. When interest rates go up or down, they can affect the value of some investments. For instance, bond prices usually go up when interest rates go down, and vice versa.

National, international, and political risk. Changes occur in governments and countries. The appointment of new leaders, war, changing political parties, adopting new policies, coups, and a host of other things can have unfavorable economic impact. Such events can affect investments in a lot of ways (e.g., tax law changes, lowering bond and stock ratings, etc.).

Industry risk. Sometimes a specific industry will experience a downturn. Often related companies or industries will also suffer.

Three Golden Questions to Ask

Following are three of the questions you may want to ask your investment advisor:

1. Tell me about the risks. What are they? How could they affect my overall investing plans? Is there anything in particular that I need to know before I invest?
2. Is this investment consistent with the plan I have already established? Will it balance well with other investments presently in my portfolio?
3. What is the worse-case scenario? If the bottom fell out, how much could I lose? Is it possible to lose interest? Principal? Other monies?

Beware of Too Much Cash

Who could have too much cash? Actually, lots of people may have too much cash in their investment portfolios. Cash (this also includes cash equivalents like some Treasuries, money markets, etc.) is usually the foundation of a conservative investment portfolio. I like cash. As a matter of fact, percentage-wise, I hold more cash in my own portfolio than most money managers would advise.

Unquestionably, cash is a safe choice for investors—at least in the short-term. Unlike stocks and bonds that can, and do, lose money, cash generally does not fluctuate in value. But if you are investing with a long time horizon, the returns on cash investments may be critically eroded by inflation.

The table below will give you at least a rough idea of how stocks, bonds, cash, and inflation performed between 1926 and 2000. The research folks at The Vanguard Group have developed the information on the three asset classes in the following table. While different researchers, using different assumptions and indexes, may come up with slightly different numbers, this table makes a strong case for equities (stocks) as part of the mix for most investors. Compare the average annual return of each asset class as it relates to the average annual rate of inflation:

Average Annual Total Returns[2] 1926 to 2000
Stocks. . . . . **11%** (S&P 500 Index)
Bonds . . . . **5.6%** (Long-Term U.S. Corp.)
Cash Investments . . . . **3.9%** (U.S. Treasury Bills)
Inflation (approx.). **3.1%**
Stock and bond investments can fluctuate in value. Unlike stocks and corporate bonds, Treasury securities are guaranteed to pay interest and principal in a timely fashion. Past performance is no guarantee of future results. The returns cited are not representative of the performance of any particular investment. © 2001 The Vanguard Group, Inc. Reprinted with permission from the Plain Talk® brochure, *Mutual Fund Basics.* All rights reserved.

Suggestions on How *Not* to Find an Investment Advisor

Investment advisors are a dime a dozen. Everyone has an angle, an idea, or something to sell. There are certain things to look for in an investment advisor. Some good general pointers would include:

Don't get your investment advice from financial failures! I lead the list with this point because it is so important. Just because your brother-in-law read a great article in the Sunday magazine section about investing, he is not qualified to give you stock tips! I am loath to listen to people tell me how to make money when they are deep in debt. Anyone with a maxed-out credit card, two car loans, and a 120 percent home equity loan doesn't need to waste my time talking investing.

Wish They Had Told Me #7
Don't go to financial failures for investment advice.

Be cautious of advisors and advice on the Internet. There is a lot of great info on the Net, but there's also a lot of trash. We've all heard stories of people who have used the Internet to dupe unsuspecting investors by hyping stocks, driving up prices, and then bailing out.

Late-night infomercials may not be the best place to plan for retirement. I'm not saying that all the money-making pitches on TV are bad or unsafe. But I think it behooves Christian people to walk (and dial) slowly. It might make sense to think the offering through in the morning when you're wide awake. Does it really make good financial sense? Is it legitimate, or does it simply appeal to greed? I always wonder, *If it's such a great opportunity, why is he telling me about it? Why isn't he just doing it himself?* I suspect that, in some cases, the real money is in selling tapes and CDs.

Beware of lines from guys on the line: telephone investment gurus. One thing that really aggravates me is when someone, pretending to be a friend, calls my secretary and says, "Hey, is Steve in? Just need to speak to him for a second." Trying to be nice, she puts the caller through, and BAM! Suddenly, I'm hit with a guy who talks 250 words per minute with gusts up to 400! Nothing I say will get him to shut up. Just like the bunny in the battery commercials, he keeps going and going! And, through it all, he insists that the deal he has for me is the one that will make me rich.

Beware of phone salesmen. Personally, I want to get my financial advice from someone with whom I've built a one-on-one relationship.

Think twice about advisors who try to sell you before they get to know you. Similar to the last point, I want to hire an advisor who has the heart of a mentor, not a marketer. In other words, I want someone who will take the necessary time to get to know me, my family, my goals, risk tolerances, debt levels, and the like. He or she would also be interested in whether I have a will, own my own home, and have proper insurance. To give good advice, a person should know more than just the product; he needs to know his client too.

Be sure he doesn't work out of the trunk of his car. Seriously, it would be wise to have your meetings at the advisor's office. This will give you a chance to see how he operates. You will have a chance to ask about his credentials. Some people suggest hiring an advisor who is a Certified Financial Planner (CFP) or a Chartered Financial Consultant (CFC).

Check the charges. Hire only an advisor who is clear and up-front about his billing. Advisors make their income in at least three ways: commissions, fees, or a combination of these. The age-old argument goes on about whether someone who is on commission, which means he is paid based on how much he gets you to buy, will give unbiased advice. I won't try to resolve that here, but it is important to know where your financial advisor's motivation is coming from. Really great advisors find ways to minimize costs; they aren't always trying to sell something.

Look out for advisors who evaporate in downturns. When the markets head south is no time for your advisor to do the same. Look for an advisor who stays in touch in all economic seasons.

Avoid "Brass Ring" Thinking

We all want to succeed. So it follows that when a person invests, she is doing so in the hopes of getting a greater return. So far, so good. There's nothing wrong with any of this. But something each one of us needs to look out for is greed. I can't determine when you're being greedy, nor can you tell when I am. Greed, like most sins, occurs in the heart. It's dangerous. That's why Jesus said, "Beware, and be on your guard against every form of greed; for not even when one has an abundance does his life consist of his possessions" (Luke 12:15 NASB).

Wish They Had Told Me #8
Grabbing for the brass ring can be financially—
and spiritually—disastrous.

Despite the world's acceptance of greed, it is one of the most destructive of human behaviors. As I write this, the news is reporting the story of a pharmacist who is accused of diluting life-saving cancer drugs to one-third their proper strengths simply to make more money for himself! While this is beyond comprehension for most of us, the virus of greed lurks within all of our hearts. This is why it is so important for Christians to do a "checkup from the neck up" when they enter the investing arena.

It troubles me when I see Christians involving themselves in high-risk investment strategies. There is a place for aggressive investments, but they can make matters worse. I remember a couple who had waited until their late fifties to begin investing for retirement. Then they put everything into a small-cap, ultra-aggressive stock, hoping for a big score. Equally worrisome were all the people in 1999 and 2000 who cashed in their sane investments to become day traders. Today most of them would give anything to have a second chance on that decision! Also troubling are untrained people who invest heavily on the margin or in options.

As Christians, we should do all things in moderation—including investing. In the next chapters I want to share some of the strategies of the truly successful, long-term investors. As you will see, it's not a matter of becoming a riverboat gambler—it's a matter of prudent planning and consistent behavior.

A More Christlike Paradigm

There is an old Wall Street axiom that says all investing is driven by *fear* and *greed*. I've always hated that axiom. It may be true for many investors, but as Christians we should aspire to something higher. Despite what many people say, I don't believe that greed is good. Maybe a healthier, more Christlike paradigm would be for Christians to make their investment decisions based on *discretion* and *hope*.

16

Six Secrets of
the Great Investors

I'VE BEEN TOLD that there are 293 different ways to make change for a dollar. I don't know whether that's true, but I definitely do believe that there are at least that many ways to lose a dollar. Over the years a number of my friends and associates have made disastrous financial decisions. As a matter of fact, I've made a number of my own. It usually happens when our eyes become set on quick riches and we stop using common sense. Could this be the proof that we humans have a lot in common with ostriches whose eyes are larger than their brains?

Following the Lead of Successful People

I was only thirty-nine years old when my doctor broke the news: my heart wasn't doing very well. They told me that if something wasn't done quickly, I might not be around to blow out the candles on my next birthday cake! To make a long story short, God blessed me through five bypasses and a full recovery. It was a radically sobering time in my life.

Believe it or not, those were good days. My faith in God grew exponentially. Trivial things, that only a few weeks earlier had seemed so important, gave way to matters of eternal significance. My prayer life improved. As my physical heart was healing, my spiritual heart became stronger too. I became increasingly focused on knowing God and serving him more completely.

Physically speaking, it was a renaissance too. I determined to get serious about diet and exercise. But for a guy who had always eaten about anything that didn't crawl off his plate first, this was going to require a major lifestyle adjustment! So one of the first things I did was schedule an appointment with a nutritionist. I wanted information and motivation to help me change my lifestyle. I needed an expert to show me how to eat a healthy diet and drop a lot of extra weight. I wanted to learn from someone who led a disciplined culinary life. I longed for someone else to show me, by example, how to get trim and healthy. Boy, was I in for a shock!

The day we came in for the meeting, Bonnie and I nearly swallowed our tongues when the nutritionist came into the room. As she squeezed through the door, we realized that the poor lady was terribly overweight! It would have been funny if it hadn't been so pitiful. Needless to say, we didn't hear a word she said.

We all understand the concept of going to an expert for advice. None of us want spiritual advice from a backslidden Christian. We wouldn't ask a white supremacist for pointers on developing multicultural harmony. And I never went back to my portly nutritionist for advice on weight management. Yet, as I mentioned in chapter 16, far too many of us go to broke people for financial advice. Instead, maybe we should be exploring the techniques that highly successful investors use. In the years that I have been a student of investing, I've seen a pattern among many of these investment all-stars. There are some things that most of these great investors do. Most of their techniques are simple to understand. None of them are patented. They are available to anyone who wants to use them. Let's look at some of them together.

Secret 1: Start Early

They say that today's greatest work-saving device is tomorrow. Maybe that's true for some people. But whether it's a mama bird teaching her baby bird about the best time to catch worms or a financial expert guiding a client, the advice is the same—*start early.*

Running with other procrastinators can be fatal. Putting off until tomorrow what should be done today is a recipe for failure. If you want to succeed, it's best to study what successful people do. One of the greatest financial minds in the Bible was King Solomon. As one of the wealthiest people on earth, this guy knew his way around the financial block. Notice what Solomon had to say about procrastinators:

> *Go to the ant, O sluggard,*
> *Observe her ways and be wise . . .*
> *How long will you lie down, O sluggard?*
> *When will you arise from your sleep?*
> *"A little sleep, a little slumber,*
> *A little folding of the hands to rest"—*
> *Your poverty will come like a vagabond.*
> *And your need like an armed man*
> *(Prov. 6:6, 9–11, NASB).*

The message is clear: The best time to begin an investing program is yesterday. But since yesterday is no longer available, today will have to do. With all the conviction I can muster, I encourage you to begin your investment program as early in life as possible. This may mean putting off some of the extras (expensive vacations, better cars, etc.) for a while longer, but the benefits of becoming a young investor can be staggering.

Nothing makes the case for this any better than hard, cold numbers. So maybe you'll find the table below interesting.[1] Jack and Judy Jumpstart began their investing careers at age twenty by systematically socking away $2,000 annually the first eight years of their married lives totaling: $16,000. Assuming the money compounds at 10 percent annually until the couple hits retirement at age sixty-six, their nest egg may exceed $1,000,000.

Now the question you might ask is: With the same assumptions in place,[2] if three other couples wait until ages thirty, forty, or fifty to start saving, how much would they have to lay aside each year until age sixty-six to achieve the $1,000,000 plus that Jack and Judy's original $16,000 investment may have yielded?

If they begin at age thirty, like Larry and Lisa Loafer, the couple would have to invest $2,800 per year for thirty-seven years, totaling $103,600. If a couple followed in the path of Ollie and Odette Ohno and waited until age forty to start saving for their golden years, the burden would have grown exponentially. Starting at age forty, they would have to set aside $7,600 annually for the next twenty-seven years (a total investment of $205,200). And, if a couple put off retirement planning until age fifty, as Herb and Helen Hurryup did, they would have to sock away $23,000 per year for seventeen years (totaling a whopping $391,000) to try to get their chins over the one-million-dollar bar!

Age	Jack & Judy Jumpstart		Larry & Lisa Loafer	
	Starting @ 20		Starting @ 30	
20	$ 2,000	$ 2,000	$ --	$ --
21	$ 2,000	$ 4,620	$ --	$ --
22	$ 2,000	$ 7,282	$ --	$ --
23	$ 2,000	$ 10,210	$ --	$ --
24	$ 2,000	$ 13,431	$ --	$ --
25	$ 2,000	$ 16,974	$ --	$ --
26	$ 2,000	$ 20,872	$ --	$ --
27	$ 2,000	$ 25,159	$ --	$ --
28	$ --	$ 27,675	$ --	$ --
29	$ --	$ 30,442	$ --	$ --
30	$ --	$ 33,487	$ 2,800	$ 3,080
31	$ --	$ 36,835	$ 2,800	$ 6,468
32	$ --	$ 40,519	$ 2,800	$ 10,195
33	$ --	$ 44,571	$ 2,800	$ 14,294
34	$ --	$ 49,028	$ 2,800	$ 18,804
35	$ --	$ 53,930	$ 2,800	$ 23,764
36	$ --	$ 59,323	$ 2,800	$ 29,220
37	$ --	$ 65,256	$ 2,800	$ 35,223
38	$ --	$ 71,781	$ 2,800	$ 41,825
39	$ --	$ 78,960	$ 2,800	$ 49,087
40	$ --	$ 86,856	$ 2,800	$ 57,076
41	$ --	$ 95,541	$ 2,800	$ 65,864
42	$ --	$ 105,095	$ 2,800	$ 75,530
43	$ --	$ 115,605	$ 2,800	$ 86,163
44	$ --	$ 127,165	$ 2,800	$ 97,856
45	$ --	$ 139,882	$ 2,800	$ 110,725
46	$ --	$ 153,870	$ 2,800	$ 124,878
47	$ --	$ 169,257	$ 2,800	$ 140,445
48	$ --	$ 186,183	$ 2,800	$ 157,570
49	$ --	$ 204,801	$ 2,800	$ 176,407
50	$ --	$ 225,281	$ 2,800	$ 197,182
51	$ --	$ 247,809	$ 2,800	$ 219,920
52	$ --	$ 272,590	$ 2,800	$ 244,993
53	$ --	$ 299,849	$ 2,800	$ 272,572
54	$ --	$ 329,834	$ 2,800	$ 302,909
55	$ --	$ 362,817	$ 2,800	$ 336,280
56	$ --	$ 399,099	$ 2,800	$ 372,988
57	$ --	$ 439,009	$ 2,800	$ 413,367
58	$ --	$ 482,901	$ 2,800	$ 457,783
59	$ --	$ 531,201	$ 2,800	$ 506,642
60	$ --	$ 584,321	$ 2,800	$ 560,386
61	$ --	$ 642,753	$ 2,800	$ 619,504
62	$ --	$ 707,028	$ 2,800	$ 684,535
63	$ --	$ 777,731	$ 2,800	$ 756,068
64	$ --	$ 855,504	$ 2,800	$ 834,755
65	$ --	$ 941,054	$ 2,800	$ 921,311
66	$ --	$ 1,035,160	$ 2,800	$ 1,016,522

Age	Ollie & Odette Oh-No		Herb & Helen Hurry-Up	
	Starting @ 40		Starting @ 50	
20	$ --	$ --	$ --	$ --
21	$ --	$ --	$ --	$ --
22	$ --	$ --	$ --	$ --
23	$ --	$ --	$ --	$ --
24	$ --	$ --	$ --	$ --
25	$ --	$ --	$ --	$ --
26	$ --	$ --	$ --	$ --
27	$ --	$ --	$ --	$ --
28	$ --	$ --	$ --	$ --
29	$ --	$ --	$ --	$ --
30	$ --	$ --	$ --	$ --
31	$ --	$ --	$ --	$ --
32	$ --	$ --	$ --	$ --
33	$ --	$ --	$ --	$ --
34	$ --	$ --	$ --	$ --
35	$ --	$ --	$ --	$ --
36	$ --	$ --	$ --	$ --
37	$ --	$ --	$ --	$ --
38	$ --	$ --	$ --	$ --
39	$ --	$ --	$ --	$ --
40	$ 7,600	$ 8,360	$ --	$ --
41	$ 7,600	$ 17,556	$ --	$ --
42	$ 7,600	$ 37,672	$ --	$ --
43	$ 7,600	$ 38,799	$ --	$ --
44	$ 7,600	$ 51,039	$ --	$ --
45	$ 7,600	$ 64,502	$ --	$ --
46	$ 7,600	$ 79,313	$ --	$ --
47	$ 7,600	$ 95,604	$ --	$ --
48	$ 7,600	$ 113,524	$ --	$ --
49	$ 7,600	$ 133,237	$ --	$ --
50	$ 7,600	$ 154,921	$ 23,000	$ 25,300
51	$ 7,600	$ 178,773	$ 23,000	$ 53,130
52	$ 7,600	$ 205,010	$ 23,000	$ 83,743
53	$ 7,600	$ 233,871	$ 23,000	$ 117,417
54	$ 7,600	$ 265,618	$ 23,000	$ 154,459
55	$ 7,600	$ 300,540	$ 23,000	$ 195,205
56	$ 7,600	$ 338,954	$ 23,000	$ 240,025
57	$ 7,600	$ 381,209	$ 23,000	$ 289,328
58	$ 7,600	$ 427,690	$ 23,000	$ 343,561
59	$ 7,600	$ 478,819	$ 23,000	$ 403,217
60	$ 7,600	$ 535,061	$ 23,000	$ 468,839
61	$ 7,600	$ 596,927	$ 23,000	$ 541,022
62	$ 7,600	$ 664,980	$ 23,000	$ 620,425
63	$ 7,600	$ 739,838	$ 23,000	$ 707,767
64	$ 7,600	$ 822,181	$ 23,000	$ 803,844
65	$ 7,600	$ 912,760	$ 23,000	$ 909,528
66	$ 7,600	$ 1,012,396	$ 23,000	$ 1,025,781

An Incredible Achievement

Now let's put some real-life legs to this. What if you could convince your sixteen-year-old son to trim back a little on the car he is dying to buy—in order to potentially become a millionaire? Here's what I mean: Instead of spending the entire $7,000 he has saved for that super-duper-hippy-dippy-daddy-bopper-car-to-die-for, suppose you could convince him to lower his sights just a little bit—maybe by just a couple of thousand dollars. Then suppose he invested that $2,000 in a mutual fund in an IRA that returned 12 percent. What would you guess that that $2,000 investment might have grown to by age seventy? Would you believe $1,018,641.00![3] Maybe that world-class CD player isn't worth the extra $2,000 after all?

Now, let's look at the first cousin of Starting Early—the concept of compounding.

Secret 2: Compounding (The Great Investment Steroid?)

One night at supper, when I was just a boy, my dad looked at me and said, "Steve, I want to ask you a question. Suppose I told you that I had a job for you to do that would take thirty days to complete. And suppose I offered to pay you in one of two ways; it would be your choice. I could either pay you $1,000 per day for your efforts, or I could pay you one penny on the first day, and then double it each day thereafter for the thirty-day period. Which would you choose?"

Well, duh, I thought. I looked across at my dad and said, "I believe I'll take the $30,000, thank you."

That's when Dad began my education. He explained to me that while the $30,000 would be a great month's salary (especially considering my microscopic job skills), it paled in comparison to what the first day's one penny would have grown to. After 30 days, that pathetic little penny would have exploded to $10,737,417! (Sort of makes the $30,000 sound like chump change, doesn't it?)

Although my dad didn't use the word *compounding*, that was the day my eyes were first opened to the concept.

Simply put, compounding allows an investment to grow larger by generating earnings on reinvested earnings (i.e., interest, dividends, capital gains). In effect, you take money you earn from an investment and reinvest it for the opportunity to make more money. For instance, suppose you invest $10,000 at 8 percent for five years. Without the benefit of compounding, your investment would grow by $800 each year. In five years the total value would be $14,000 ($10,000 principal plus five annual interest payments of $800 each). With annual compounding, at the end of the first year your investment would have grown by the same $800. But beginning the second year, that $800 of interest is added onto the original $10,000 and that year's 8 percent return is then calculated on $10,800 (instead of just the original $10,000). Year by year, as interest is added on top of interest, the growth of the original $10,000 accelerates. By the end of the five-year term, the total has grown to $14,693. While this extra $693 may not seem like a lot, the difference can become enormous over long periods of time, especially with higher rates of return and more frequent compounding. (Many investments compound more often than annually: i.e., monthly, weekly, or daily.)

All of this may have been what inspired Albert Einstein reportedly to declare compounding to be the "eighth wonder of the world." He, too, was amazed at the way interest can earn interest. But to bottom line it, compounding is fundamentally a function of a positive return rate and time.

Although a program of regular investing can't protect against a loss or assure a profit in all situations (especially a declining market), by starting small, many successful investors have seen their portfolios grow with the help of compounding. The following table will illustrate how a hypothetical investment program, begun by a twenty-year-old, might grow if regular contributions of $50 per month are made over a forty-five-year time span. With a total investment of $27,000, notice both how much it can grow and also the radical difference even a couple of percentage points of return can make.

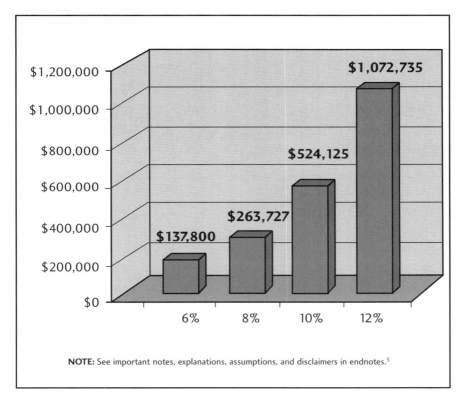

NOTE: See important notes, explanations, assumptions, and disclaimers in endnotes.[5]

But how does compounding work if you don't continue investing for forty-five years? Below is another hypothetical calculation that shows what an IRA contribution of $3,500 (made by investing $500 per year for the seven years from age twelve to age eighteen) might return by retirement at age sixty-five.

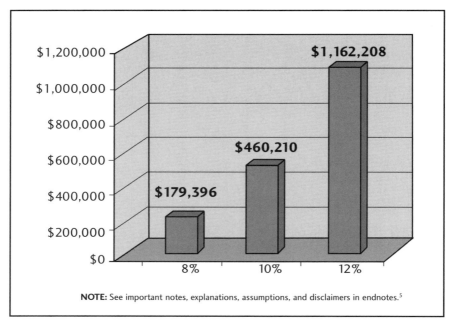

NOTE: See important notes, explanations, assumptions, and disclaimers in endnotes.[5]

Here is the same table with IRA contributions totaling $7,000 ($1,000 per year for seven years from age twelve to age eighteen).

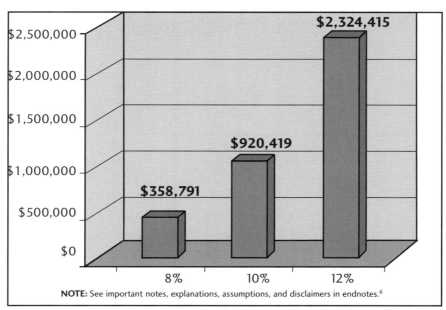

NOTE: See important notes, explanations, assumptions, and disclaimers in endnotes.[6]

Secret 3: Dollar Cost Averaging

The concept of dollar cost averaging (DCA) has been one of the most widely used of all investing techniques. It has been a favorite of many people who are concerned about market ups and downs. The concept is fairly simple: Instead of trying to "time" the market, a person invests a predetermined amount of money at regular intervals (i.e., weekly, monthly, etc.) over a period of time. This works especially well with retirement plans that are often structured to allow regular contributions with every paycheck.

By investing regular chunks of cash, you aren't tempted to try to "time" or outguess the market. DCA allows you to invest both when the market is up and when it is down. This means that you will be buying fewer shares when the market is high and more shares when the market is low. For instance, suppose you decide to invest $1,000 per month in a mutual fund. One month, when the market is down with shares selling at $20 each, your $1,000 will purchase fifty shares (50 shares @ $20 each = $1,000). The next month, when the market may be up, the mutual fund shares could be selling at $30 each. So that month your $1,000 buys only 33⅓ shares. (33⅓ shares @ $30 = $1,000).

Following, are three charts depicting different investment scenarios that were developed by Strong Capital Management (www.Strong.com). Notice how DCA could play out in each investment climate.

Market Scenario 1: A Fluctuating Market[7]

Monthly Investment	Share Price	# Shares Purchased	Cumulative Acct. Value
$50	$13.55	3.69	$ 50.00
$50	$12.20	4.10	$ 95.02
$50	$11.35	4.41	$138.40
$50	$10.90	4.59	$182.91
$50	$10.00	5.00	$217.81
$50	$10.75	4.65	$284.14
$50	$11.65	4.29	$357.93
$50	$11.95	4.18	$417.15
$50	$12.50	4.00	$486.35
$50	$12.95	3.86	$553.86
$50	$13.55	3.69	$629.52
$50	$14.05	3.56	$702.75
Total: $600		50.02	$702.75

Average Cost Per Share: $12.00
Difference: $102.75

Lump Sum Investment Versus Dollar Cost Averaging
An initial lump sum investment of **$600** would purchase **44.28 shares** at the original price of **$13.55**. The ending value of your investment after twelve months would be **$622.14**. If you had invested **$50** a month over the same period, the ending value would be **$702.75** as shown on the chart.

Source: Strong Capital Management. Used with permission.

Market Scenario 2: A Rising Market[8]

Monthly Investment	Share Price	# Shares Purchased	Cumulative Acct. Value
$50	$10.00	5.00	$ 50.00
$50	$10.50	4.76	$102.50
$50	$10.90	4.59	$156.40
$50	$11.20	4.46	$210.71
$50	$11.75	4.26	$271.06
$50	$12.25	4.08	$332.59
$50	$12.85	3.89	$398.88
$50	$13.15	3.80	$458.19
$50	$13.60	3.68	$523.87
$50	$13.95	3.58	$587.36
$50	$14.10	3.55	$643.67
$50	$14.65	3.41	$718.78
Total: $600		49.06	$718.78

Average Cost Per Share: $12.23
Difference: $118.78

Lump Sum Investment vs. Dollar Cost Averaging

An initial lump sum investment of **$600** would purchase **60 shares** at the original price of **$10**. The ending value of your investment after twelve months would be **$879**. If you had invested **$50** a month over the same period, the ending value would be **$718.78** as shown on the chart.

Source: Strong Capital Management. Used with permission.

Market Scenario 3: A Falling Market[9]

Monthly Investment	Share Price	# Shares Purchased	Cumulative Acct. Value
$50	$14.35	3.48	$ 50.00
$50	$13.80	3.62	$ 98.08
$50	$13.45	3.72	$145.60
$50	$12.85	3.89	$189.10
$50	$12.45	4.02	$233.21
$50	$12.10	4.13	$276.66
$50	$11.75	4.26	$318.66
$50	$11.35	4.41	$357.81
$50	$10.90	4.59	$393.62
$50	$10.55	4.74	$430.98
$50	$10.25	4.88	$468.73
$50	$10.00	5.00	$507.29
Total: $600		50.73	$507.29

Average Cost Per Share: $11.83
Difference: $(92.71)

Lump Sum Investment Versus Dollar Cost Averaging
An initial lump sum investment of **$600** would purchase **41.81 shares** at the original price of **$14.35**. The ending value of your investment after twelve months would be **$418.12**. If you had invested **$50** a month over the same period, the ending value would be **$507.29** as shown on the chart.

Source: Strong Capital Management. Used with permission.

Unfortunately, DCA does not assure a lower average cost over the long term. And it doesn't guarantee the highest level of return, but it can have an equalizing, calming effect that many investors like. This type of systematic investing can take the worry out of when to invest since even experts agree that it's tough to predict the market.

Some Drawbacks of Dollar Cost Averaging

Like lots of good ideas, DCA has some downsides that you should know about. Some of them are:

- As is true with lots of the things we buy, purchasing in smaller quantities can lead to higher costs. In the case of certain investments (i.e., individual stocks, etc.), you may end up paying higher commissions or fees by making lots of smaller purchases instead of one large purchase.
- When your investment is going up in price, you may wish you had invested more money faster.
- Some people get scared in down markets and stop their DCA regimen, which could prove to be a mistake.
- DCA can make tax accounting more confusing. This is because the investments were made at a number of different prices and times.

Secret 4: Asset Allocation and Diversification

Jim Taylor, one of my fellow staff members, shared a sad story with me earlier today. He told me about a friend of his who had made a fatal mistake with her investment plan. This lady, in her fifties, had dreamed for years of an early retirement. About a year ago she decided to put all of her 401(k) retirement money into her own company's stock. At the time it seemed logical. After all, her company was doing great. It was one of the most successful high-tech/communications powerhouses in the world. The future looked rosy and secure. Their stock price had skyrocketed to more than $80 per share. The news was filled with reports of people making killings in the market with such investments. *So*, she reasoned to herself, *what better place to put my money for fast growth.*

That was a year ago. And, as we have all learned, a lot can happen in a year. After peaking at more than five thousand points last year, today the NASDAQ stands at less than seventeen hundred. The lady's company stock was hit even harder. After enjoying highs above $80 per share, it closed at less than $6 per share earlier this week. To make matters even worse, the company's financial troubles led to the elimination of her job. So today she is left with no job, a ravaged retirement account, and no prospects for a financially secure retirement anytime in the near future.

This dear lady made two common and dangerous mistakes with her retirement nest egg. Her first mistake was not diversifying her investments. It is never wise to invest all of your money in any single company's stock—whether you work for that company or not. As we will discuss in this section, most seasoned investors build their entire portfolios with an eye on diversification.

Second, she put her retirement money into the same company that she worked for. While lots of people do this, it can be a disastrous decision. Because, just as in this lady's case, if a company gets into trouble, it can result in a double loss for employees who haven't been properly diversified. Not only do they lose their jobs; they also lose their retirement money. What's that thing they say about putting all your eggs in one basket?

The Case for Asset Allocation

According to some researchers, more than 90 percent of long-term investment return may be determined by the way you spread, or allocate, your investments. This diversification approach is known as asset allocation. While assets come in many forms (real estate, collectibles, precious metals, etc.), for the purposes of our conversations throughout most of this book, I will be referring primarily to three major asset classes: stocks, bonds, and cash equivalents. (As I use the terms interchangeably, understand that each of these asset classes can be invested in either directly or through mutual funds.)

One of the keys to successful risk management may be diversifying assets over a variety of asset classes. Although asset allocation may not deliver the highest potential returns, it can reduce the odds of having all your investments clobbered at one time. Many advisors believe it makes sense to spread the risk. Asset allocation may help offset market volatility because different kinds of investments frequently perform differently at the same time. So, hopefully, when one is down, others will be up (or, at least, not down as much).

Of course, there is more to asset allocation than simply putting a certain percentage of your money into stocks, bonds, or cash. There are all sorts of options available within each of these asset classes. An educated investor learns about the different types of stocks, bonds, and cash investments that are available. There are also decisions to be made about buying the stocks and bonds of individual companies versus mutual funds that pool the securities of dozens of companies into one investment. In the next chapter I'll have more to say about mutual funds and how they work.

Different Strokes for Different Folks

A given individual's asset allocation is a personal decision. What is right for me may not be right for you. A host of issues should be taken into consideration as you develop your portfolio's allocation. Some of them might include:

Your age. Typically, younger investors (who hope to have longer time horizons) tend to be more aggressive by putting a larger percentage of their money in stocks, etc. As an individual nears retirement, he usually becomes more conservative and begins to weight his portfolio with more bonds and cash equivalents.

Your health. Illness and disease can affect the level of volatility and other forms of risks an investor is willing to accept.

Your overall financial situation. Refer back to "Part 2: The ABCs of Christian Money Management."

Your tolerance for risk. In chapter 16, I had some comments you may find helpful in understanding the various types of risks. Also, below is a little personal quiz that you may find insightful.

What's Your R.T. (Risk Tolerance)?[10]

Know yourself. That's pretty good advice in any situation—including investing. TIAA-CREF, a major financial services organization, has prepared a little quiz that you may find helpful. I like it because it causes people to think about their risk tolerance through a series of real-world questions.[11] Your answers may give you a sense of what your attitude is toward risk.

1. "Protecting the principal of my investment is more important than achieving significant growth." Do you . . .

❑ A. Strongly Agree
❑ B. Agree
❑ C. Disagree
❑ D. Strongly Disagree

2. Which of the following three investment strategies best suits you?

❑ Strategy A is one that seeks to avoid loss.
❑ Strategy B is one that has potential for both moderate gain and moderate loss.
❑ Strategy C is one that maximizes potential gain regardless of the potential loss.

3. Let's assume you own a stock fund. Over the last year that fund has lost 15 percent of its value, despite previous years of solid performance. The loss is consistent with the performance of similar funds during the past year.

At this time would you . . .
❑ A. Sell all of your shares?
❑ B. Sell some but not all of your shares?
❑ C. Continue to hold all of your fund shares?
❑ D. Buy more shares to increase your investment in the fund?

4. Inflation can greatly reduce the real rate of return on your investments over time. Which of the following best describes how you feel about investment risk with respect to inflation?

I am willing to accept:
❑ A. Significant potential for loss and high volatility in trying to greatly exceed the rate of inflation.
❑ B. Moderate potential for loss and lower volatility in trying to exceed the rate of inflation.
❑ C. Minimal potential for loss, although my investment may, or may not, only keep pace with inflation.

5. Which of the following three descriptions of hypothetical investment portfolio returns over a one-year period are you most comfortable with?

❑ A. A likely return of 6 percent and a slight chance of losing value.
❑ B. A likely return of 10 percent and a moderate chance of losing value.
❑ C. A likely return of 14 percent and a significant chance of losing value.

6. Which of the following hypothetical portfolio average annual returns over a three-year period are you most comfortable with? A portfolio with average annual returns that is likely to fall between:

❑ A. 0 and 10 percent
❑ B. –5 and 18 percent
❑ C. –10 and 26 percent

7. Including foreign securities in a diversified portfolio may reduce the overall risk, or volatility, of that portfolio.

Would you like to include foreign securities in your portfolio?
❑ Yes
❑ No
❑ No opinion

Some Sample Asset Allocation Approaches[12]

My friend Paul Winkler, president of Retirement and Investment Strategies, Inc., has developed the following asset allocation pie charts that may help you visualize what we've been talking about.[13] Understand that these are shown only for illustrative purposes, and they may, or may not, be suitable for you.

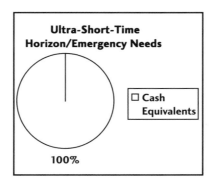

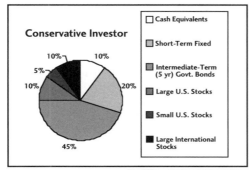

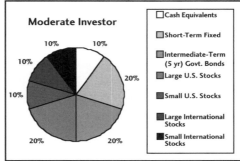

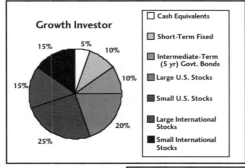

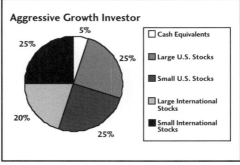

© 2002 Retirement & Investment Strategies, Inc. Used with permission.

The folks at American Funds have developed five different asset allocations that may help you to visualize what we've been talking about.[14] Understand that these are shown only for illustrative purposes, and they may, or may not, be suitable for you. As with all financial decisions, be sure to get competent professional advice based on your unique set of circumstances.

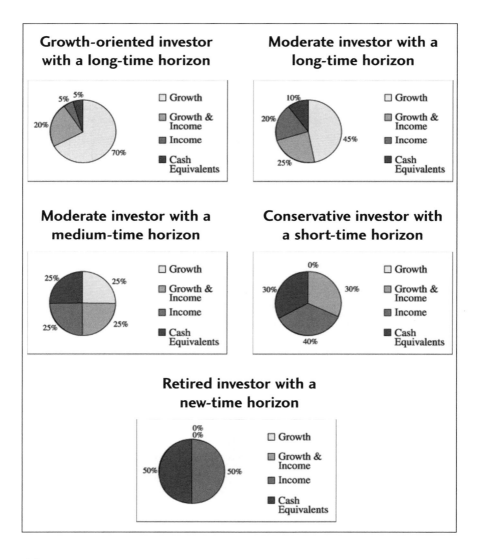

Following is another asset allocation approach developed by the good folks at The Vanguard Group. I especially like it because it includes some wonderful data regarding average annual returns, worst performance years, and the number of years that the various strategies have lost money in the 1926 to 2000 period. Vanguard points out that these are sample portfolio allocations only. Depending on your tolerance for risk or your individual circumstances, you may wish to choose a more conservative or a more aggressive allocation plan than either of the tables shown. Remember that these allocations are for longer-term financial goals. You may well choose to hold cash and/or cash equivalents for shorter-term goals and emergencies.

Vanguard also points out that the return data includes the reinvestment of income dividend and capital gains distributions. They don't include the effects of investment expenses and taxes, nor do they represent the performance of any particular investment.

Suggested Allocation*	Average Annual Return (1926–2000)	Worst Annual Loss (1926–2000)	Number of Years with a Loss (1926–2000)
100%	11.0%	-43.1%	21 of 75
20% / 80%	10.3%	-34.9%	20 of 75
40% / 60%	9.3%	-26.6%	18 of 75
50% / 50%	8.8%	-22.5%	16 of 75
40% / 60%	8.2%	-18.4%	16 of 75
20% / 80%	7.0%	-10.1%	13 of 75
10% / 10% / 80%	6.2%	-6.7%	10 of 75

*Cash investments are represented by U.S. Treasury bills, bonds by long-term U.S. cor-
porate bonds, and stocks by the S&P 500 Index. (The Vanguard Group, Inc. Reprinted
with permission from the Plain Talk® brochure, *Mutual Fund Basics.* All rights reserved.)

Stocks   Bonds   Cash

By Way of Reminder

No matter how smart you are or how good your asset allocation, there are no guarantees on most investments. People can, and do, lose money. Dreamers are often driven by the false belief that they can get something for nothing. But the fact is, potential reward and risk go hand in glove. The great thing about asset allocation (or diversification) is that it allows you to hedge your investments. The goal is to reduce some of the risk of investing. In the real world, there are no "for sure" investments. If you're looking for someone to protect you from all risk of loss, it is not going to happen. The key is to find competent professional advice, become an educated investor, learn what the risks are, and then make informed decisions.

As with all financial decisions, be sure to get competent professional advice based on your unique set of circumstances. By way of disclaimer, as always, be sure to read the referenced endnotes. Understand that these charts are simplified and do not represent all the allocations you may want to consider.

Secret 5: The Rule of 72

Every successful investor I've ever known keeps his eye on the ball. By that I mean serious investors seem to develop a sixth sense about their assets. They know what's going on in the markets, how different asset classes are performing, and generally how their own investments are faring. Many investors seem to be able to figure quickly what an investment, at a given rate of return, will earn.

One little trick that every investment pro uses is the Rule of 72. This simple formula has helped me to estimate quickly investment returns and performances hundreds of times. By learning to use it, you will be better able to size up various investment opportunities in a heartbeat.

The Rule of 72 will help you quickly determine how long it will take for an investment to double in value. Here's how it works: Divide 72 by the annual rate of return that you expect to receive. The quotient of the two numbers (72 and the rate) is the *approximate* number of years that it will take for your investment to double in value. For instance, if your investment is paying 4 percent, it will take about eighteen years to double. A 6 percent rate will double your investment in around twelve years. At 8 percent it will double about every nine years. Ten percent doubles in about 7.2 years. And, if you can get 12 percent, the timeline reduces to only six years.

It's a neat little trick; use it to your investing health.

Secret 6: Smart Investors Are Wary of Highly Speculative Investments and Market Frenzies

I can still remember the gold panic of the early 1980s. It was a time of fear. The investment markets were uncertain, and nationally we were frightened by what the Soviets might do. As is often the case in such times, the "gold bugs" came out. Everywhere you turned, someone was touting gold as the ultimate asset to own. Naturally, the price of the yellow metal began to go up. Eventually, when I could stand it no longer, I too ran out and bought gold—at more than $800 per ounce!

Ever since then I have jokingly told my friends that I was the guy who single-handedly turned the gold market around. Within days gold sales flattened, and prices began to plummet. For much of the last twenty years, the price of gold has been well under $300 per ounce. It's the same feeling you get when it rains ten minutes after you have washed the car. Yuck!

Market hype and investment frenzies are nothing new. In hindsight they often seem like pretty nutty schemes. But in the heat of the moment, even otherwise sensible people get caught up in the whirlwind. In the 1600s "tulip mania" swept through Europe. Tulip bulbs became the preferred medium of exchange. The prized bulbs fetched higher and higher prices. As the days passed, anyone without some of the cherished plants felt foolish and out of the loop. As more and more people decided they had to have tulip bulbs at any cost, the prices soared even higher. At the zenith of the craze, a single bulb was reported to sell for more than the price of a house! Well, you guessed it. One day the bubble burst, and thousands of people were left broke, though they probably had great-looking gardens.

Riverboat gamblers usually don't make good long-term investors. There will always be speculators, day traders, and market timers. But from what I have seen, few, if any, consistently beat the market averages. Sooner or later the bottom falls out, and that fall can be a real bone crusher.

Satan's Investment Approach

As I've already said, good investing is a combination of several disciplines—not the least of which is self-control. Consistently doing the right things, over and over again, in up and down markets, is the best way I know to get ahead as an investor. Trying to make a killing in the market is a sucker's game. Christians need to remember that greed kills—both temporally and eternally. As they say, pigs get fat and hogs get slaughtered! Unbridled lust for more and more gain is not consistent with the heart of Jesus. As with all the other activities of our lives, our investing should be approached with a heart of prayer, trust, and temperance. So many of the pains that afflict humanity come because we ignore our Father's instructions. As Christians we believe, at least intellectually, that God's teachings are for our good—not just to suck all of the fun out of life. Yet so often we ignore his teachings in exchange for the sparkling, tantalizing joys of the moment. We do this at all levels—including financial.

I've spent a lot of my life marveling at this aspect of humanity. Why do we—especially those of us who are Christian—blindly follow paths that eventually lead to our own destruction? While I don't claim to have it all figured out, I have come to the belief that there are at least two things at work here:

1. Our human nature is to want what we want! This drive for instant gratification fuels many of our bad decisions. Instead of paying the price for long-term joy and success, we often opt for whatever feels good at the moment.

As we've seen, this short-term thinking is what has led so many of us into a multitude of hurtful areas ranging from marital unfaithfulness to uncontrolled debt and financial heartache.

2. Our struggles in these areas have to do with a fundamental misunderstanding of what Satan has to work with. Satan really doesn't create anything. All he can do is take the goods things that God has created, pervert them, and then try to sell them back to us. Think about it—everything out there (in its pure, original state) is good. Sex is good. Competition is good. Money is good. So for the devil to succeed at his task of destroying mankind, he has to take the good things that God has made and pervert (or twist) them just a little off center. I use the phrase "just a little" because Satan is smart enough to know that most Christians won't buy into his lies unless he can first convince them that there's "really nothing wrong with doing it this way."

So the net result is that Christians, in unguarded moments, buy into the devil's line. The husband who begins having "innocent" lunches with his secretary never dreams that his marriage will eventually be destroyed by his adultery. And, in the same way, many people who begin investing for all the right reasons gradually lose their focus. Over the years what was once a commendable effort to provide for the family becomes an obsession to beat the other guy and score big in the market. Corners are cut. Chances are taken. The dream of a quick (and undeserved) gain clouds rational thought processes. As I discussed in the last chapter, hope and prudence are replaced with fear and greed. Virtue becomes vice.

> *He who loves money will not be satisfied with money, nor he who loves abundance with its income. This too is vanity (Eccles. 5:10 NASB).*

> *For the love of money is the root of all sorts of evil, and some by longing for it have wandered away from the faith, and pierced themselves with many griefs (1 Tim. 6:10 NASB).*

> *Set your mind on the things above, not on the things that are on earth. For you have died and your life is hidden with Christ in God (Col. 3:2, 3 NASB).*

Don't Forget . . .

As with all financial decisions, be sure to get competent professional advice based on your unique set of circumstances. By way of disclaimer, as always, be sure to read the endnotes. Also understand that these charts are simplified and do not represent all the allocations you may want to consider.

17

Mutual Funds, Motorcycles, and Sushi

THIS HAS BEEN A tough chapter for me to get my arms around. I so badly wanted to explain how mutual funds work, but to be honest, I was confused as to how to go about doing it. I've learned that when I get too technical about mutual funds, peoples' eyes glaze over. Then they lose interest. And when that happens, they deprive themselves of learning about what I believe is the average person's greatest investment tool. Mutual funds aren't perfect investments. As a matter of fact, I don't know of a perfect investment. (No investment always has high returns with low risks.) But mutual funds often allow the small investor to enjoy many of the benefits that would otherwise only be available to the richest investors.

Although they date back at least to the 1920s, mutual funds have really hit their stride in the last twenty years or so. As of 2000, there were about eighty-two hundred mutual funds available to the public.[1] Different funds have different purposes and personalities. They invest in different types of assets. The costs, fees, and expenses of various funds vary widely—to say nothing of their performance. Add to this mix the fact that every investor has different needs, goals, and risk tolerances. With all these factors in mind, this could become a confusing chapter. But I will try my best to keep it simple and clear. To accomplish that goal, I will not be getting into the highly technical aspects of mutual-fund investing. If you want to learn more, there are lots of great books and Web sites that will help you do that. In this chapter I will be making broad assumptions and sharing generalized concepts. Nothing is meant to be the final word or exhaustive. As with everything else in this book, it is your responsibility to get further and more complete information before you invest. In addition to getting competent professional advice, I encourage you never to buy any mutual fund until you understand it. While mutual funds offer many advantages, they have their trade-offs too. Always read the prospectus carefully, ask questions, and get satisfactory answers before you invest.

Sushi and Motorcycles: The Perfect Mutual Fund Analogy

As I tried to hit on the best way to explain mutual funds, it suddenly came to me: mutual funds are a lot like two of my favorite things, sushi and motorcycles! I love Japanese sushi and Harley Davidson motorcycles, but they are both acquired tastes.

The first time I tried sushi was a real learning experience. It was like going through an initiation in a bait shop! I didn't know the difference between a hand roll and a crunchy shrimp roll, and I didn't know wasabi from ginger. I soon learned that, if I planned to eat sushi, I had better learn the language. There were some basic words and terms that I needed to understand. Mutual funds are much the same. To deal with mutual funds, you will need to understand some foundational terms and phrases. So in this chapter I will cover some of the basics of mutual-fund language.

Mutual funds also have a lot in common with motorcycles in that they may all look the same to an untrained observer, but the differences make them interesting—and potentially deadly. As a Harley guy, I love to talk about my bike. It's a gorgeous, black, 1997 Road King with a fuel-injected, 1340cc Evolution engine. Now, don't confuse it with a Harley Sportster 1200 or a Heritage Softail. And, by all means, don't confuse any Harley Davidson with an Indian or a Honda! That's not to say that one is better or worse than another. It's just that they are all different. They do different things. They have different feels. They suit different people.

Mutual funds also fall into a number of categories. Within these categories are subcategories. Different funds invest in different assets. And the funds themselves are owned by numerous fund companies that have their own personalities and investment styles. In this chapter I will also discuss some of these variations and options.

Just the Facts, Ma'am

I always liked *Dragnet*. Joe Friday had a way of finding the bad guy by always asking for "just the facts, Ma'am." I guess when you've got to solve a caper in thirty minutes (minus commercials), staying focused is important. So let's spend a few minutes talking about the facts of mutual-fund ownership.

According to the Investment Company Institute, an estimated 87.9 million Americans own shares in mutual funds. These individuals hold about 80 percent of the money invested in mutual funds. (Most of the remaining 20 percent is held by various fiduciaries— such as banks and individuals acting as trustees, guardians, or administrators.)

And, boy, are these things popular! Between 1990 and 2000, total assets of mutual funds rose from $1.065 trillion to $6.965 trillion.[2] In 1980, less than 10 percent of all U.S. households owned funds. By 2000, that number had grown to 49 percent.[3]

The Investment Company of America has some interesting data about the type of people who buy mutual funds too. On balance, they are a mirror reflection of the U.S. population as a whole. The typical fund investor is age forty-four, married, and in the process of saving for retirement with median household assets of $80,000. Most are willing to accept at least a moderate level of risk in exchange for moderate gain and are not focused on the short-term ups and downs in the market.

Fifty-seven percent have Individual Retirement Accounts (IRAs). Over 75 percent participate in an employer-sponsored defined contribution retirement plan. The typical family in mutual funds has $25,000 invested. This represents almost a third of their assets. Baby Boomers (folks born between 1946 and 1964) are the largest group of mutual fund investors at 51 percent. GenXers (those born after 1964) buy 22 percent of the funds sold. And the Great Generation (those born before 1946) purchase the remaining 27 percent.[4]

Types of Mutual Funds

As they say, the best place to begin anything is at the beginning. So let me start by telling you what a mutual fund is.

Essentially, a mutual fund is an investment that pools your money with the money of numerous other shareholders and invests that money in various securities (like stocks, bonds, and money-market instruments) in the hope of achieving a specified goal. Each investor (shareholder) who owns shares in the mutual fund participates in the fund's gains or losses.

Typically, there is a fund manager (in some cases a group of managers) who plans and executes the fund's investment activities in keeping with the stated aims of the fund. While there are various types of funds that hold an array of different investments, in this chapter we will limit our focus to four primary types of mutual funds:

1. *Stock (equity) funds* are by far the most popular of the four types of funds. As of 2000, $3.96 trillion of the $6.97 trillion invested in mutual funds was in stock funds.[5] Such funds build their portfolios by purchasing the stocks of a number of companies. When you invest in a stock mutual fund you get an indirect equity (ownership) holding in the companies in which the fund invests.

2. *Bond funds* held $808 billion of investors' money as of 2000.[6] A bond is essentially a debt, or an IOU, usually issued by a government, government agency, or a corporation. According to ICI, a bond investor lends money to the issuer; in exchange the issuer promises to repay the loan amount on a specified maturity date, and the issuer usually pays the bondholder periodic interest payments over the life of the loan.[7] Bond mutual funds invest in such instruments.

People who want to live off dividend income frequently invest in bonds or bond funds because of their historical stability.

3. *Money market (cash equivalent) funds* were where investors were storing some $1.85 trillion in 2000.[8] These are usually intended to be liquid funds (readily accessible) that invest in shorter-term instruments (often with maturities of less than ninety days). Money market funds are designed to offer a relatively safe harbor for people concerned about losing money in more volatile investments. But money market funds are generally not insured or guaranteed by the FDIC or any other governmental agency. Such funds may seek to maintain a dollar per share price, but it is possible to lose money even in these funds.

Money market funds offer easy accessibility. Many offer free check-writing privileges (certain minimums and other conditions may apply), and often they pay higher yields than bank accounts.

4. *Hybrid funds* is a smaller category of investment products (holding only $350 billion in assets in 2000)[9] that invest in a mix of stocks, bonds, and/or other securities. Considered by many to be an effective way to make investing simpler, these funds can give you instant diversification across a number of investments. One category of hybrids is *balance funds* that tend to invest in a blend of stocks and bonds. The goal is to smooth out the volatility that often comes with market ups and downs. Another type of hybrid is an *asset allocation fund* that typically combines stocks, bonds, and cash and gradually adjusts the portfolio's mix depending on what the manager expects the future to hold.

Now Let's Get a Little More Specific

Each of the four main categories can be subdivided in a host of ways. Stock funds vary based on the size of the companies they invest in and where the companies are located (i.e., domestic, international). Some invest only in the stocks of a single industry (often called *sector funds*), while others invest broadly in scores of different companies, and on it goes. Bond funds can be categorized by the credit quality of the assets they hold, the average maturity of the bonds in their portfolios (short, intermediate, long-term), whether they hold corporate or government securities, etc.

The Vanguard Group has devised a table that divides the various types of mutual funds. While this is not exhaustive, maybe it will help you visualize how different types of funds might help achieve some of your financial goals.

Types of Mutual Funds[10]

Your Objective	Type of Mutual Fund	What These Funds Hold	Capital Growth Potential	Current Income Potential	Stability of Principal
Current income, stability of principal	Money market	Cash investments	None	Moderate	Very high
Tax-free income, stability of principal	Tax-exempt money market	Municipal cash investments	None	Moderate	Very high
Current income	Taxable bond	Wide range of government and/or corporate bonds	None	Moderate to high	Low to moderate
Tax-free income	Tax-exempt bond	Wide range of municipal bonds	None	Moderate to high	Low to moderate
Current income, capital growth	Balanced	Stocks & bonds	Moderate	Moderate to high	Low to moderate
	Equity income stock	High-yielding stocks, convertible securities	Moderate to high	Moderate	Low to moderate
	Growth and income stock	Dividend-paying stocks	Moderate to high	Low to moderate	Low to moderate
Capital growth	Domestic growth stock	U.S. stocks w/ high potential for growth	High	Very low	Low
	International growth stock	Stocks of companies outside U.S.	High	Very low to low	Very low
Aggressive growth of capital	Aggressive growth stock	Stocks w/ very high growth potential	Very high	Very low	Very low
	Small-capitalization stock	Stocks of small companies	Very high	Very low	Very low
	Specialized stock	Stocks of industry sectors	High to very high	Very low to moderate	Very low to low

The Benefits of Mutual Funds

There are a number of reasons for the popularity of mutual funds. Following are some of the primary advantages:

Professional management. Rich people have always had easy access to professional money management and financial advice. Mutual funds level the playing field for the average investor. When you invest in a good mutual fund, you get the advantage of skilled professionals who make it their business to keep up with what's going on with your money. Think about it; where else could your $5,000 or $10,000 get this level of attention?

Diversification. As we discussed in chapter 16, one of your best protections against risk is diversification. But the trouble is, most small investors (those without at least several hundred thousand dollars in assets) don't have enough money to build a truly diversified portfolio. Yes, you could buy a few stocks from several companies, but what about all the other good company stocks out there? And what about bonds and money-market instruments? By the time you bought a little bit of each security that a fully diversified portfolio should have, the headaches and transaction fees would be driving you crazy.

That's where mutual funds can come to the rescue. Many good mutual funds hold hundreds of securities—all in one convenient, easy-to-buy format. When you invest in a single mutual fund, you are getting the investment potential of all the securities within it. Although diversification does not eliminate risk, it may reduce it.

Diversification: How It Works*	
Supposing you invested $10,000 equally among five companies— it might shake out like this.	Now suppose you invested that same $10,000 in a good stock mutual fund.
Company 1: 50 shares @ $20/share Company 2: 100 shares @ $15/share Company 3: 10 shares @ $150/share Company 4: 60 shares @ $50/share Company 5: 40 shares @ $75/share	Fund shares representing investments in dozens or even hundreds of companies
Since each investment represents 20% of your portfolio, if the stock of even one of your companies hits the skids, you may too!	If this is a good, well-diversified and managed fund, the decline of a single stock (or even several stocks) should not alone have a devastating effect on overall performance.

* See important notes/clarifications/disclaimers at endnote 11.

Convenience. I just got out of a meeting with a friend who is thinking about opening his first mutual-fund account. He has done the research, and now he is ready to transfer money to the mutual-fund company. Understandably, he's a little confused about how to handle the transaction. Since it's a company that I have done business with for a number of years, I was able to tell him just to pick up the phone and let them help him.

Most mutual-fund companies go out of their way to make it easy to do business with them. I have always found them to be helpful professionals intent on taking the confusion out of the transaction. Many mutual fund companies also offer a host of features like electronic funds transfer, automatic investing and withdrawal programs, dividend and capital gains reinvestment programs, telephone or Web transactions, dial-up fund information, and easy ways to move your money from one fund to another.

Quick and easy access to your money. Generally fund shares can be bought or sold on any business day. Of course, some funds may have redemption fees and other provisions; read the prospectus. In some cases (i.e., money in certain retirement plans, when gains have been realized, etc.) taxes and/or penalties may be imposed.

Low minimum investments. Different mutual funds have different minimum requirements. Some require over $20,000 to open an account. But this is not the norm. Most companies have reasonable thresholds—especially for IRA accounts. Many fund families will allow you to invest with only a few hundred dollars.

Performance records and costs information are readily available. Mutual funds distribute prospectuses that are required to give all sorts of pertinent data regarding expenses, performance, returns, and so forth.

Mutual Fund Drawbacks

Guess what? There aren't many perfect solutions in life—or in investing. Despite all their pluses, mutual funds do have some minuses. Following are some of their drawbacks:

Possibility of higher costs. Although a good mutual fund should include cost efficiencies among its attributes, some don't. The various loads, management charges, and other fees imposed on some mutual funds can erode your returns. Always study and compare the funds you are considering.

Possible tax disadvantages. In certain circumstances you may be subjected to taxes that might at least be postponed when you invest in mutual funds instead of individual securities. Check with a competent professional who can assess the fund you are considering along with your personal circumstances.

Diversification "penalty." While mutual-fund diversification can work for you by reducing some of the risk of big losses, it can also work in the reverse by limiting the potential to make a huge gain on a single stock investment.

No FDIC insurance. Unlike most bank accounts, mutual funds don't come with FDIC protection. The Securities and Exchange Commission (SEC) and certain other officials regulate them, but this doesn't guarantee that you won't lose money.

Bookkeeping hassles. Depending on how and when you purchase your mutual fund, you may find some bookkeeping issues (i.e., tax accounting) a bit more complex. Generally, this is not a major problem, especially if you use a qualified pro to do your tax work.

Two Types of Mutual Funds: Load Versus No Load

To begin with, you should know that there are two broad categories of mutual funds:

Load funds are mutuals that have a sales charge. They are usually sold by brokers who make their income from such fees. While a sales charge, or load, can be assessed in various ways, most are charged in one of two ways:

Front-end loads may be imposed on the front end (when you first purchase the fund) in the form of a percentage of the total amount of your investment. Typically, front–end loads range from 3 to 8½ percent.

Back-end loads (sometimes called "contingent deferred sales charges") are fees that are usually charged when an investor sells his mutual-fund shares within the first several years. Typically, a back-end load is charged if the fund is sold within the first six to seven years after it is purchased.

No-load funds do not have a sales charge. With everything else being equal, a no-load fund can reduce your expenses and enhance your return. A trade-off is that you generally will not get the same level of input and advice that you would hope to get from a broker who is selling a loaded fund.

Which Is Best?

Despite the best efforts from proponents of both types of mutual funds, I am unaware of any data conclusively proving that one type of fund is always superior to the other. However, it does stand to reason that, all other things being equal, a no-load fund may increase returns by removing the expense of the load. Here are some points you might want to consider.

First, decide what type of person you are. Do you like advice and input from other people, or do you prefer to do your own reading and research? If you're a do-it-yourselfer, no-loads may fill the bill. If you like a little more hand-holding, you may be more comfortable in the world of loaded funds. However, remember there is such a thing as getting professional advice without paying a load or commission. You might want to consider hiring a professional financial advisor on a fee basis. Some people feel this is a good way to take away the incentive to sell you stuff you don't need.

Don't be misled by people who have conflicts of interest. Commissioned brokers have an incentive to sell loaded funds: Money! Obviously, you wouldn't expect a broker to steer you into a no-load fund that doesn't pay him for his efforts. But the converse can be true also. Although many periodicals and newsletters have squeaky clean editorial policies, some of the financial publications seem to pander too much to their advertisers. Just because a publication writes glowing articles about no-load funds doesn't always mean the advice is totally unbiased. Check to see which type of mutual funds buy the ad space in the magazine. In some cases this may indicate to whom they owe their allegiance.

Understanding Mutual Fund Expenses

When you are looking at a mutual-fund investment, there are at least three issues to consider: return, risk, and expense. Often fund investors who pay close attention to return and risks tend to forget about the expenses. This oversight can cost thousands of dollars through the years. So, as boring as it may seem now, let's spend a few moments looking at how mutual-fund expenses work. As I have already mentioned, the SEC requires that expense information be disclosed in the prospectus that you should receive before buying shares in any fund. But to give you a quick overview, you may find the table below helpful.

Types of Expenses[12]	
Commissions	If the fund is sold through a broker or financial adviser, you may pay a sales charge, called a load. Sales charges can be paid up front (when you buy Class A shares) or paid on a contingent, deferred basis if you leave the fund before a specified period of time (when you buy Class B shares). If you stay in the fund, you pay no sales charge, but annual expenses are higher. No-load funds are mutual funds sold without a sales charge, but you generally will not benefit from the expertise of a financial adviser.
Management Fees	Funds charge this annual fee, which is used to pay the investment adviser(s) for managing the portfolio.
Distribution Fees	These are also called 12b–1 fees. They cover marketing and distribution fees.
Redemption Fees	These charges are designed to encourage long-term investing and to discourage you from selling your shares after only a short period of time. If you're investing for retirement, which means you're probably looking for the long-term, you probably won't have to deal with redemption fees.
Reinvestment Fees	One way to help your investment grow is to reinvest any distributions you receive from it, if such an option is available. If it is, and you reinvest the money, you may have to pay a fee. American Funds does not charge such a fee. Note that in retirement plans, capital gains distributions and dividends are automatically reinvested.

Types of Expenses, *continued*

Exchange Fees   You may have to pay exchange fees if you
move your money from one fund to another
in the same mutual-fund company.

Other Expenses   These include expenses such as transfer agent
fees, custodian fees, and legal fees.

Source: American Funds. Used with permission.

How Do Mutual Fund Expenses Affect Your Return?

When it comes to expenses, mutual funds are all over the board.
Many experts believe that there is no significant correlation between
higher expenses and better returns. Yet, with all other things equal, it
stands to reason that greater expenses can lead to worse bottom-line
returns. Below is a chart that illustrates this point.

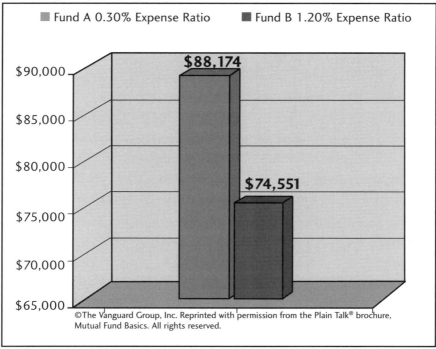

A Word About Index Mutual Funds

While I haven't gone into detail on all the various types of funds, I do want to spend a couple of minutes on one particular category of funds. Despite all the hype about the genius mutual-fund managers of Wall Street, the truth is, a high percentage of actively managed mutual funds don't consistently outperform the market averages. As a matter of fact, after expenses, a significant percentage of funds under-perform various unmanaged stock market indexes like the S&P 500.

Realizing this, a number of years ago, some wise mutual-fund people came up with a new type of product that simply tries to reflect one of the various indexes. Such a fund (creatively called an Index Fund) attempts to buy a basket of stocks that replicates whichever index it is mimicking. Many investors believe this is an ideal way to get broad and efficient market exposure. Today there are dozens of index funds reflecting most of the major indexes.

Since index funds (sometimes called "unmanaged or passive funds") don't involve the expensive research and management fees associated with many managed funds, you save on fund expenses too. Assuming that expenses for many managed funds run from 1 to 1½ percent, index funds offer a real cost advantage; some have total expenses of less than ½ percent.

Although I don't sell or recommend specific mutual-fund companies, you might want to get more information on index funds from some of the companies that promote them most heavily. Among these companies are: The Vanguard Group (800-662-7447), Dreyfus (800-373-9387), and Charles Schwab (800-435-4000).

The Dangers of Chasing Performance

One trap that some mutual-fund investors fall into is the trap of chasing performance. Frequently, people hop from one fund to another trying to get the best returns. While there are times when it makes sense to switch funds, it can easily become a sucker's game. There are at least three things to think about before you take the fund leap:

1. Past performance does not ensure future results. Looking at how a mutual fund has done in a previous period has its place. But making fund decisions based solely on past performance is a little like driving your car by looking in the rearview mirror. Many an investor has jumped to greener grass on the other side of the investment fence just in time to ride the new fund down, as his old fund comes back in favor and begins to gain ground again.

2. Big returns frequently equal big risks. Do you remember what we said earlier about risk and return? Often, the greatest return comes from taking the greatest risk. The same is often true with mutual-fund investing. Frequently the stellar fund that everyone is talking about is investing in highly volatile assets that may go down as fast as they go up.

3. Look out for the expenses. In many cases changing funds is costly on at least two fronts: increased expenses (especially with loaded funds) and, in many cases, negative tax implications.

Pointers from a Pro

One of the most important assets you can have as an investor is a good advisor, someone who is bright and knows his stuff and someone who is honest. Over and over again I have reminded you of the importance of getting qualified, professional help before making investment decisions. I follow that counsel myself. One of my buddies in the financial trenches is Paul Winkler, president of Retirement and Investment Strategies, Inc. The other day I asked Paul to list what he thinks are some of the important considerations for a new investor.

Paul Winkler's Tips on Investing[13]

1. Consider choosing your funds based on which asset class the fund manager is investing in (large U.S., small U.S., short-term fixed, etc.). Academic studies indicate that nothing else is as important to your returns as the portfolio division between asset classes.

2. Keep a close eye on portfolio turnover. Excessive trading in your mutual fund can be costly and add to your fund's level of volatility without necessarily adding to the return.

3. You might consider diversifying internationally. Some studies indicate that risk may actually be *reduced* with international exposure.

4. Think about rebalancing your portfolio to your original allocation from time to time. This may help ensure that portfolio risk doesn't vary excessively and can help investors avoid "chasing performance."

5. You may find that the more intolerant you are to market risk (volatility in the stock markets), the more tolerant you may have to be to inflation risk. Inflation is the great silent tax on portfolio values.

6. Ignore much of the financial media and their predictions. Remember, if they really knew what was going to happen next, they would likely keep that information to themselves.

An Important Closing Word

Unfortunately, writing a book is a little like using a shotgun: you can hit a lot of folks, but the information may not be appropriate for all the readers. Most of my comments in this book are broad-brush in nature, intended for a wide audience. It follows that if your financial situation doesn't fall somewhere in the center of the bell curve, some of this information may not fit your needs. Throughout this book I have reminded you of the need to review all your investments periodically, study tax law changes that may affect you, get competent professional help, and factor in your personal circumstances. This information is simply a summary of best understanding and is not intended to be exhaustive. My examples are hypothetical and are only for illustrative purposes.

However, if you have significant assets, you may find that your needs are best served by an asset management firm that implements the concepts of Modern Portfolio Theory. This Nobel Prize-winning theory is based on the idea that a portfolio should be comprised of asset classes (i.e., U.S. large stocks, U.S. small stocks, international, bonds, cash, etc.) that historically have not always moved in tandem with one another. So when one is down, hopefully others will be up. Some professionals believe this approach may decrease volatility while increasing overall returns. I would encourage you to learn more about Modern Portfolio Theory (MPT). This fascinating approach to investing and money management is widely used by some of the smartest money people out there. Look into it and decide for yourself.

18

Retiring with Dignity

THE FOLLOWING STORY appeared in *The FAX of Life:*

Early on the morning of February 17, 1994, James Rich crawled behind the controls of his plane at an airport near Louisville, Kentucky. The plan was to make a thirty-minute flight to Crossville, Tennessee, where a friend of his was the airport manager. He would arrive just about the time his friend was showing up for work and show off the Piper Seneca he had just finished restoring.

The forty-year-old pilot had not slept much the night before. He had been out late with some friends. So he was still tired when he cleared the runway and pointed his plane south for the quick trip. Climbing to thirty-five hundred feet and putting the Seneca on automatic pilot, he dozed off.

Rich must have slept for three hours. The next thing he knew, he was trying to clear his head while looking through broken clouds onto what he thought was a lake. A closer look revealed that the "lake" extended to the horizon in all directions. Then a glance at the gas gauge told him he was practically out of fuel.

Knowing that he was in trouble, he radioed an SOS. Only then did he discover his true location—188 miles west of Clearwater and

190 miles south of Panama City, Florida. He was over the Gulf of Mexico with only a few minutes of gasoline left!

Still eighty-five miles short of land, the last drop of fuel was gone. His uninsured $70,000 Piper hit the Gulf, sank in about forty-five seconds, and pulled Rich down with its undertow. Two cushions pulled from the plane popped him back to the surface. They would have to keep him afloat until help came, as Rich couldn't swim.

Within fifteen minutes a helicopter was there to drop a rescue basket. Rich scrambled in and was hoisted to safety—still clinging to his seat cushions.[1]

Mr. Rich's humorous, though harrowing, experience reminds all of us to stay alert about the direction our lives are taking. It's easy to get up each day and go about our daily lives on automatic pilot. Then at the worst moment, we are jarred to our senses to realize that things have spiraled hopelessly out of control. My goal in this chapter is to encourage you to reevaluate your retirement plans. Are they on schedule? Have you even started planning for those supposedly "happy golden years"? Or will they be years without enough gold to have any financial happiness? Right now might be the time to rethink, refocus, and retweak. Why? So you won't be left spending your retirement years in the Gulf of Despair, holding onto soggy cushions, hoping for help.

The State of the Retirement World

Folks, the good old days are gone—never to return. No longer do most people begin lifelong careers with a single company immediately after graduation. Today most people change jobs about every five years. And no longer do most companies reward employee loyalty with a defined benefit plan that promises to pay a certain amount of benefits upon retirement. Typically, such defined benefits plans were controlled by the companies that sponsored them. They usually made the investment decisions and decided how much you would receive.

Today most people have to make their own retirement arrangements. And, yes, this frightens some folks. There is a tendency on the
part of many adults to want someone else to protect them. They fear
having to go it alone, making their own plans and decisions. And,
based on the facts, it appears that many people have simply chosen
to do nothing. As I mentioned in chapter 1, 56 percent of U.S. citizens are failing to set aside enough for a comfortable retirement.[2]
Fifty-nine percent of the people surveyed say they expect a lower
standard of living in their retirement years.[3]

But preparing for one's own retirement isn't only a necessity; it's
also do-able. Retirement planning involves two things: knowledge
and self-discipline.

Self-discipline has been one of the undergirding topics of this
entire book. So much of our success in life depends on our willingness to control our baser desires and fears. Maturity involves learning to control one's self. It means having the strength to say no to the
here and now, in order to enjoy a more fruitful future. As it pertains
to retirement planning, self-discipline requires the dogged determination to earn a reasonable amount of money and then the mental
toughness not to spend it on other things. Assuming you have made
the decision to do what you must to accomplish your retirement
goals, we can turn our attention to some of the knowledge you will
need to accomplish the task.

To begin, unless you are far smarter than the average guy or gal,
you probably don't feel particularly knowledgeable when it comes to
annuities, IRAs, 401(k)s, and the like. That's all right; you aren't
alone. I have seen many smart folks' eyes glaze over when I started
talking about this stuff! Essentially, there are two ways to get smart
in this area: study for yourself and/or hire a pro.

Frankly, my best results have come when I've done a little of
both. There is nothing like self-study. I would urge you to read good
Web sites and books. I especially commend you for reading this

book! Go to reputable seminars. Watch the financial news. Generally expose yourself to the great material that is so abundant these days. Compare what different people teach. Always confirm the accuracy and appropriateness of everything. As I've said before, people's risk tolerances, time horizons, and goals vary. Investment options and tax laws change. Pay attention and double-check everything; after all, it's your retirement!

For me, there comes a time when I need to sit and discuss things with smart people. That's why I often talk with several professionals (i.e., legal, investing, financial, accounting, etc.) before I make major decisions. Often they are able to help me evaluate the various options and their appropriateness for my situation.

Three Ways to Prepare for Retirement

Most people draw their retirement funding from one (or a combination of three) sources: Social Security, employer-sponsored programs, and various types of personal savings/investments. I want to give you enough data to whet your appetite to study and get more details on these options.

Social Security. Sadly this is a major source of funds for many retirees. The Social Security Administration tells us that Social Security makes up about 40 percent of the average individual's retirement income. The average recipient gets about $800 per month. But since your lifetime earnings and circumstances vary, your benefits may be different.

Far too many people have reached retirement expecting a lot more from Social Security than they got. If you haven't already gotten the information, I encourage you to contact the Social Security Administration for an idea of what you can expect at retirement. Check with them on-line at http://www.ssa.gov/statement/ or call them at 800-772-1213. When you get the information, be sure to review it carefully, making sure all data and amounts are correct.

Although the future of the system isn't certain, the following chart may be helpful in determining when you should begin receiving full benefits based on the present standards. You can start as early as age sixty-two, but benefits will be greatly reduced.

The Year You Were Born	Retirement Age
Prior to 1938	65
1938 to 1942	65*
1943 to 1954	66
1955 to 1959	66*
1960 and After	67

* Full benefits require an additional 2 months for each birth year.
(That is, if you were born in 1938, your retirement age would be 65 years and 2 months; for 1939, 65 years and 4 months.)

Confirm and check these details and information with a trusted professional or the Social Security Administration before taking action.

Employer-sponsored programs. Company retirement plans typically fall into one of two broad categories: defined benefit plans and defined contribution plans. Today most companies no longer offer defined benefit plans. In recent years many companies have changed their approach to retirement planning. Today a large percentage of companies offer what are known as defined contribution plans. In such plans the money available at retirement is based on how much you (and, in some cases, your employer) contribute and on how your investments perform. American Funds breaks down some of the defined contribution plans this way:

- **401(k) Plans** allow an employee to make pretax contributions. Your boss may also contribute to your plan. The amount that can be contributed is determined by your employer and limits established by federal law (and may be adjusted annually). Earnings on contributions grow tax-deferred until withdrawn. The company generally offers a group of investment options that may include various types of mutual stock, bond, and/or cash funds.

- **403(b) Plans** are much like 401(k) plans but are generally available to employees of nonprofit organizations which qualify under IRS Code Section 501(c)(3).

- **SIMPLE Plans (Saving Incentive Match Plan for Employees)** are designed to help employees at smaller companies (fewer than one hundred employees) plan for retirement. SIMPLEs can be set up as IRAs. Contributions are vested at 100 percent immediately. Employers are required to make certain contribution matches.

- **Profit-Sharing Plans** allow for a company to make a discretionary contribution to the employee's account. Employee contributions are not permitted. The employer's contributions are typically tied to the firm's success.

- **Simplified Employee Pension Plans (SEPs)** are designed for self-employed people and small businesses. Similar to a traditional IRA, an instrument permitting the opportunity for tax-deferred growth is set up for each participant.

- **Money Purchase Plans** can be used when an employer promises a fixed contribution to eligible employees. This contribution is based on a formula. Such plans do not allow for participant contributions.

Individual savings and investments. Any retirement income you want, beyond Social Security and employer-sponsored plans, will have to come from your own planning and savings programs.

Broadly speaking, such investment vehicles fall into two camps: taxable and tax deferred.

By far the most popular type of personal retirement savings plan is the Individual Retirement Account, or the IRA. Federal tax laws may permit you to establish an IRA and get the benefits of tax-deferred accumulation for retirement living. IRAs were created by Congress to help average people supplement their Social Security and employer retirement income. For our purposes here, IRAs fall into two categories: traditional and Roth. At this writing (provisions are subject to change), they generally shake out as follows:

- **Traditional IRAs** allow you to contribute up to $3,000 yearly, which may be deductible on your taxes, depending on your income. Other wonderful spiffs in the new tax laws make IRAs even more attractive. For example, the limit is due to increase even further until 2010. Also there is a new "catch-up" provision that allows qualified individuals fifty years or older to make even higher contributions. The money grows tax deferred until it is taken out. You must be under 70 and a half to open an account. If you withdraw money before age 59 and a half, you may have to pay a 10 percent penalty plus taxes unless there is an exception that applies to you. Money will generally be taxed as it is withdrawn.

- **Roth IRAs**, which are similar in some ways to traditional IRAs, began with the Taxpayer Relief Act of 1997 when Congress opened the door to this new type of account. With contribution limits like those of traditional IRAs, Roth contributions are made on an after-tax basis. Since you've already paid taxes on the money before it went in, the law says you won't have to pay federal taxes when you take it out. While qualified withdrawals may be tax free, there may well be financial downsides if you withdraw your money in less than five years, or before age 59 and a half.

Consider getting qualified professional advice to determine which type of Individual Retirement Account makes the best sense in you situation.

Some Other Ways to Save for Retirement

There are other options in the retirement-saving idea bag. Some of them are:

Annuities are a popular way to save for retirement. While I would encourage you to study the pros and cons of annuities fully, here are a few basic points that you may find interesting. To begin with, many experts suggest that you consider an annuity only after fully funding all other tax-deferred options available (i.e., IRAs, 401(k)s, etc.).

I believe, under certain circumstances, annuities can be useful retirement planning tools. Some of the typical benefits of an annuity are unlimited contributions, the option of a guaranteed life income, and a death benefit.

Since annuities are insurance products, they may come with high fees and high-pressure sales pitches. Do your own reading and research. Don't hesitate to get competent, unbiased, professional advice before you buy. Also be sure to check out the insurance company's rating. You don't want to reach retirement age with an insurance company that has already succumbed!

Personal investments are another way many people pave the road to retirement. Of course, there are all sorts of personal investments. Probably the most popular are mutual funds that invest in stocks, bonds, and/or cash equivalents (see chapter 17). Although you may not be able to defer taxes on the earnings of such mutual-fund holdings, there are still some things you can do to minimize current tax consequences. Today many mutual fund companies offer tax-advantaged or tax-managed funds that strive to invest in ways that reduce your present tax obligations. But even if it isn't tax advantaged, the income and growth from a mutual fund spends just fine during the retirement years.

Another way some people plan for retirement is by gradually building a portfolio of rental real estate during their working years. This is an ideal way for some people to build a solid retirement income. But beware! Managing investment real estate isn't as easy as some of its promoters make it sound. Unless you pay for professional management, get ready for hassles with renters, broken toilets, pet problems, etc. I don't recommend entering the rental real estate business using a lot of borrowed money and leverage. Debt of this sort can destroy the joy of retirement!

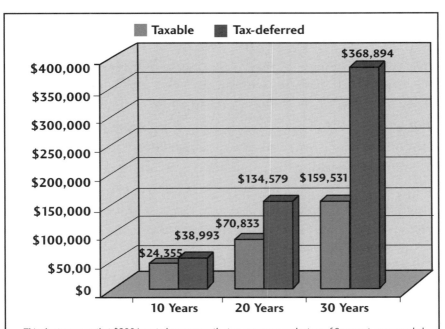

This chart assumes that $200 invested once a month at an average annual return of 8 percent, compounded monthly. For illustrative purposes only and does not reflect actual returns of any fund. A tax rate of 28 percent is assumed. If taken in a lump sum distribution at 28 percent, the amount left in a tax-deferred account after 30 years would be $265,604. Withdrawals may be subject to tax and, before age 59 and a half, may also be subject to a 10 percent federal penalty. Source: American Funds. Used with permission.

Tax-Deferred Versus Taxable Investments

One of the great things about many retirement plans is the favorable tax treatment they receive. *Tax deferral* means your retirement savings may grow faster. Notice how a monthly investment of $200 might grow in a tax-deferred account as compared to a taxable account.[4]

How Much Does It Take to Retire?

Of course, we all have different circumstances, cost-of-living issues, and lifestyles. Some people get by on far less than others. But my advice is not to be unrealistic here. Too many people have assumed that retirement living would cost less than it actually has.

Some experts in the field suggest that a good rule of thumb may be to expect retirement living to cost approximately 70 to 90 percent of what preretirement living costs. They reason that, after you leave the workplace, overall costs will come down. You may use less gas and have lower car expenses without the drive into work. You may not have to buy as many clothes or eat lunch out as often.

But let me make the case for the other side. Who says you won't be traveling as often? After all, if you are healthy, you may want to spend more time visiting the grandkids, going on mission trips, and traveling with friends. And, if your health fails, what about medicine and medical costs? Remember, also, that the cost of living and inflation will both probably continue to increase. While the 70 to 90 percent approach may fit you just fine, don't approach your retirement with a one-size-fits-all mentality. Think through what you will do with your time and what it will cost.

How Does Inflation Affect Your Savings?

When I was a boy, my dad often regaled me with stories of how much less expensive things were when he was a kid. Today, some forty years later, I'm doing the same with my offspring. Surely you can identify with this. Don't you remember buying Cokes for a quarter? Ice cream treats and candy bars used to cost less than a dime. And how about that McDonalds' meal that cost less than 50 cents? (Hamburger, fries, and a milkshake—all for 47 cents!)

One undeniable fact of life is that the cost of living continues to increase. If this trend continues into the future, which is probably a safe assumption, our money will continue to buy less and less. Today candy bars cost most of a dollar, and a soft drink can set us back more than a buck.

That is inflation at work. It slowly eats away and erodes the buying power of our money. Over the past several decades, inflation has averaged roughly 3 to 5 percent yearly. Of course, as with investment returns, the past is no guarantee of the future. But whether future inflation runs at 4 or 2, 7 or 12 percent—it will have a real impact on the quality of your retirement lifestyle. And, believe me, if you

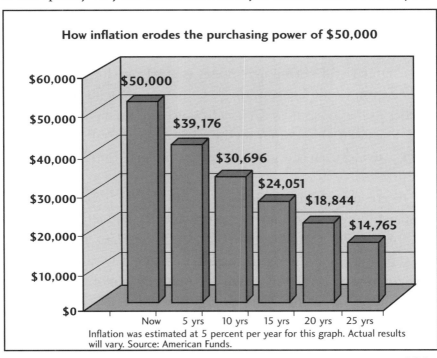

How inflation erodes the purchasing power of $50,000

Inflation was estimated at 5 percent per year for this graph. Actual results will vary. Source: American Funds.

don't factor inflation into your retirement plans, buying candy bars and soft drinks will be the least of your problems.

As you make retirement plans, ask your advisor about inflation. Look for investments that stand a good chance of beating inflation. Following is a little table prepared by American Funds that shows how inflation would erode the purchasing power of a hypothetical $50,000 if inflation ran at 5 percent.[5]

Think about this: In round numbers, an inflation rate of 4 percent will cut your buying power in half in about eighteen years; at 5 percent it would take only about fourteen years.[6]

More Options

If you hit retirement age without enough dollars to do it with dignity, there are other options that don't involve cookbooks with pet food recipes. Today's retirement population is the strongest and healthiest in the history of the world! Sixty-five used to be old age. Today many folks are living full, productive lives well into their eighties and even their nineties.

Granted, without enough money you may not have as much flex-time as you would like. But since you haven't done the tough things earlier in life to assure a financially solvent retirement today, now's the time to do a checkup from the neck up. Your challenge now is to find activities that are not only enjoyable and fulfilling but, also, profitable.

There are lots of options here. Many retirees have gone back to work with their old companies as consultants. Some have found the flexible schedules and fees to be a dream come true. Other folks have used retirement as the launching pad to start a new career in a fresh, invigorating setting. Still others have turned lifelong dreams into new business start-ups. Remember, Colonel Sanders was in his sixties when he started his fried chicken empire!

Review Your Plan!

Over time things change. As the years pass, market conditions, investment options, tax laws, personal goals, and a host of other things change. What may have been a great idea when you established your retirement plan may not make sense today. I don't encourage people to become overly obsessive, but I do encourage them to stay engaged and involved in their retirement master plan. Many experts suggest that you review your plan at least once a year, if not more often. Ask yourself (or your advisor) questions like:

- How is inflation impacting my investments?
- Have I gotten any raises or promotions or started a new job?
- Has my type of employment changed (i.e., from government to private sector, etc.)?
- Has my marital status changed (i.e., death, marriage, etc.)?
- Have tax laws changed that might impact me?
- Am I contributing enough to meet my needs?
- Are my investments performing as they should?
- Am I getting close enough to retirement to begin reconfiguring my investment allocation?
- Have I experienced any illness, injury, or disability that might affect my plans?

Two Retirement Plan Warnings

There are some things to beware of as you plan for retirement. Following are some comments about two of the most frequently made retirement planning mistakes.

Don't let panic make matters worse. Over the years I've talked with a number of people who were concerned about their retirement nest eggs. I remember a friend who had some real estate ventures go sour and leave him in a tough spot just a few years prior to retirement. And, of course, we have all known people who simply waited too long to begin saving for retirement. Sometimes when people get into such a predicament, they make matters worse by trying to fix the problem the wrong way. If you are in a similar situation, beware of the temptation to try to catch up by putting what money you do have into overly risky, highly speculative investments. Just as a compulsive gambler is always trying to get even with the house on the next bet, following such a frantic approach to your investing is likely to make matters even worse.

Don't get too conservative too early. Unlike years ago, when many people didn't live much past retirement, today the chances are good that you may live twenty, thirty, even forty years after the gold-watch ceremony. This means that old ideas about converting stock-based investments into bonds or cash at retirement may need to be rethought. As the illustration in chapter 16 (comparing the returns of stocks, bonds, and cash) indicated, most long-term investors agree that stock-based investments are one of the best ways to grow their money and stay ahead of inflation. Accordingly, you may want to consider keeping a portion of your assets in stock-based investments even after retirement. However, remember that it may serve you best to have a sizable percentage of your dollars in fixed-income investments (i.e., bonds, cash, etc.) that tend to have more predictable returns.

About Retiring from God

Despite what our culture says about retiring and living a life of leisure, as Christians, we need to consider another option. There is certainly nothing wrong with slowing down, spending more time relaxing, and fulfilling some lifelong dreams. But, for the Christian man or woman, retirement from our profession shouldn't mean retirement from our God. Retirement can be a time of spiritual growth and service to others. Assuming your health is good, retirement years can be some of the most productive of your entire life. After all, you don't have to spend as many hours making a living, and, hopefully, your finances are in order. Your maturity and knowledge can be used to bless and mentor younger Christians.

Today there are thousands of retired Christians all over the country like my friend Al Daugherty who invests hundreds of hours each year at Disaster Relief. This incredible ministry keeps up with disaster points around the country from its Nashville headquarters. When a major flood, hurricane, or other natural catastrophe hits, Disaster Relief is able to hit the road with a truckload of food, clothes, and spiritual support. Although Al has been an active Christian all his adult life, I would venture to guess that his greatest efforts for the kingdom have come since his retirement.

Jesus said, "The harvest is plentiful but the workers are few. Ask the Lord of the harvest, therefore, to send out workers into his harvest field" (Matt. 9:37b–38).

Maybe this is your time.

19

Before We
Say Good-bye

 *WHAT DO OLD FRIENDS* do before they say good-bye? What happens at bus stops, piers, family reunions, and deathbeds? Usually people who love one another speak of important things at such moments. They don't waste time on the trivial or mundane. They make the parting minutes count. It's the last time they may be together, so they share their hearts.

I realize that you and I may not know each other intimately. But, after nineteen chapters (and several Diet Cokes), I consider you to be my friend. So, in that context, I ask myself, *What do I really want to communicate before we part?*

I suppose if there was only one thing left to say, it would be this: Please don't sacrifice the eternal for the temporal. There is a real danger in books like this to lose our heavenly focus while talking about the here and now. While there is an appropriate place for things financial, we can easily let money become our focus and forget that one day each of us will stand before God to give an account of how we invested the time and talents he gave us.

Jesus spent much of his ministry dealing with money issues. Over and over again he warned his followers not to put their trust in things that won't last. He asked them, "For what will it profit a man if he gains the whole world and forfeits his soul?" (Matt. 16:26 NASB). And in the Sermon on the Mount, he urged his followers:

> *"Do not store up for yourselves treasures on earth, where*
> *moth and rust destroy, and where thieves break in and steal.*
> *But store up for yourselves treasures in heaven, where neither*
> *moth nor rust destroys, and where thieves do not break in*
> *and steal; for where your treasure is, there will your heart be*
> *also" (Matt. 6:19–21 NASB).*

Then, in verse 24, He drives a stake in the heart of today's secularized Christianity: "No one can serve two masters; for either he will hate the one and love the other, or he will be devoted to the one and despise the other. You cannot serve God and wealth."

Part of the Family

To follow Jesus we must first know him. We have to be part of his family. The Bible says, "For all have sinned and fall short of the glory of God." Unless you have made a personal, gut-level decision to accept Christ as your Savior, you are not one of his. Jesus said, "I am the way and the truth and the life. No one comes to the Father except through me" (John 14:6a).

Becoming part of Christ's family is simple yet profound, easy yet demanding. In a phrase, it is a free gift that will cost all you have. This may be why Jesus urged prospective followers to count the cost of discipleship:

> *"If anyone would come after me, he must deny himself*
> *and take up his cross and follow me. For whoever wants to*
> *save his life will lose it, but whoever loses his life for me will*
> *find it" (Matt. 16:24–25).*

You may wonder, *If it is so tough, why does anyone do it? If it costs so much, why would anyone be interested?* I can't speak for anyone else, but I would like to tell you what Jesus has done for me.

Jesus has brought balance and purpose into my life. When I acknowledged my own worthlessness, he redeemed me and gave me new value. Daily he washes all the filth and sin from my life so I can smile at the guy in the mirror. He has opened my eyes to my own shortcomings while simultaneously showing me his ability to mend all my flaws. He has carried me over roads too dark and dreadful to handle alone and always returned me to the sunlight. He has answered untold scores of prayers in our family. He has blessed my marriage, healed my daughter, and given us love within. When I wake up in the middle of night with a chest pain, I prayerfully reach out to him. He is always there; he's never asleep. Gently he reassures me that all is well. And like the apostle Paul, he reminds me that if I continue living, it will be for him; and if not, I'll be in his glorious presence before my heart has completed its last beat.

Coming to Jesus

Whether you call it "getting saved," "accepting Christ," "coming to Jesus," or "being born again," it's all the same thing. It's that time in your life when you lay it all down at the cross and accept Jesus on his terms. No excuses. No hedging. No arguing. If you are ready to get serious with Jesus, let me share the basics with you.

Begin by understanding that salvation and forgiveness are free gifts from God. There is absolutely nothing you can do to earn your salvation; it is a free gift from God. Paul told the early church, "For it is by grace you have been saved, through faith—and this not from yourselves, it is the gift of God—not by works, so that no one can boast" (Eph. 2:8–9).

The Bible tells us how we can accept this free gift of God's grace:

1. It begins by hearing and believing (having faith) that Jesus is who he says he is, the Son of God and our Savior. Romans 10:17 tells us that faith comes by hearing the word of God. In Hebrews 11:6, we learn the importance of belief, for "without faith it is impossible to please God."

2. We must be willing to repent (sorrowfully turn away from) our past sins. In Acts 17:30, the Bible says that God "commands all people everywhere to repent" (also see Luke 13:3; Acts 2:38; 2 Peter 3:9).

3. We need to be willing to acknowledge our acceptance by confessing that Jesus is Lord, the Son of God. In Matthew 10:32, Jesus said, "Everyone who confesses Me before men, I will also confess him before My Father who is in heaven."

4. Finally, the Bible teaches that we step into Christ through a symbolic burial called baptism. This is when we are immersed in water, allowing our old self to be buried and arising a new creature in Christ! What a beautiful moment! In Acts 2:38, when a crowd of people asked what they had to do to be saved, the apostle Peter told them, "Repent and be baptized, every one of you, in the name of Jesus Christ for the forgiveness of your sins. And you will receive the gift of the Holy Spirit" (also see 1 Peter 3:21).

Different Strokes for Different Folks

Different people respond differently. Some folks are motivated by the realization that someone else was willing to die for them. Some people respond out of joy and love. Others don't look up to God until they are flat on their backs. Others never accept Jesus.

I hope you know Jesus and have accepted him as your personal Savior. If you have, great! If we don't meet in this world, we'll spend some real quality time together in the next world.

But, if you haven't come to Jesus, maybe today is your day. He's already waited a long time for you. There is no guarantee of tomorrow. You probably will never know the day they cut the flowers for your funeral or the day your coffin arrives in town. Why put it off any longer? Two months ago one of my dear friends was baptized into Christ after putting him off for forty-one years. We buried Wayne two weeks ago. His wife told me he held her one night just before he died and said, "Sweetheart, I'll never know why I waited so long."

This Is Now Yours

I hope you have found some of the things we have talked about in this book to be helpful. Maybe you'll do a better job investing for retirement, buying a car, or planning for college. That's all fine and good. But most important, I hope you remember to invest for eternity. Please live for, and serve, Jesus.

Hold the torch high!

Appendix 1

Important Things to Know and Accept Before You Read This Book

1. This publication is designed to provide accurate information with regard to the subject matter covered. It is sold with the understanding that neither the publisher nor the author is engaged in rendering legal, accounting, investing, or other professional advice. If legal advice or other expert professional assistance is required, the services of a competent professional person should be sought (developed from a declaration of principles jointly adopted by a Committee of the American Bar Association and Committee of Publishers and Associations). The author and publisher specifically disclaim any risk, loss, or liability that may be incurred as a consequence, whether direct or indirect, of the application and/or usage of any of this material.

2. Everything in this book is simply for your consideration. These are only ideas for your review—thought starters, if you will. The material is general in nature and is not intended to be an exhaustive presentation on the topics covered. It should be read simply as a part of a broader study program. Other materials on these same topics may be beneficial in giving the reader a more informed, accurate, timely, and balanced understanding. In many cases the materials herein may give the pros or the cons of an issue or concept without fully discussing the other side of the issue. My hope is to inspire you and help you catch a vision. I'm not suggesting that any given idea is going to be right for everyone. We all have different circumstances,

priorities, and philosophies. Feel free to read and ponder these concepts. Then accept, modify, or reject them as you see fit.

3. In the various examples, case studies, and stories throughout this book, I have often changed names and modified some details and quoted remarks to protect privacy and enhance some of the points being made.

4. If financial, legal, tax, investing, securities, accounting, or other professional and/or expert assistance/advice is needed, the services of a competent professional should be sought. You are urged not to act upon anything within this book without the advice of a competent professional and/or expert who is also familiar with your individual needs and circumstances.

5. The information contained herein has been obtained from sources believed to be reliable, yet while every reasonable effort has been made to ensure the accuracy of all numbers, interpretations, calculations, data, and/or other information at the time of writing, be aware that mistakes are sometimes made and changes occur. Accordingly, we cannot guarantee its accuracy, timeliness, or completeness. The accuracy, completeness, and applicability to your circumstances are not guaranteed or assured. Various assumptions (for calculations and other data) were made throughout the work that probably would not be fully duplicated in your situation, thus probably changing your results. Always recalculate and confirm the accuracy and applicability for your own purposes. In some cases I have depended on various third parties for stats, calculations and advice that I cannot guarantee.

6. Information herein is simply for use as a comparative tool to give you a point of reference. Various assumptions have been made in calculations, life situations, and a host of other things that may not be duplicated in your experience. As always, review all your investments periodically. Further, neither the author nor the publisher assure the accuracy or assume responsibility for statements, figures, facts, or other data in this publication including, but not limited to, typographical errors, omissions, etc., regarding financial, legal, tax, investing, accounting, securities, and other related matters.

7. Examples are hypothetical and are only for illustrative purposes and should not to be used or construed as recommendations. No warranties are made regarding the results obtained from use of any material herein. There is no guarantee to the suitability or potential value of any particular investment or information source. Past performance does not guarantee nor does it assure future results. There is no assurance that your investments will have similar returns. Yours could be more or very possibly less. Nothing herein constitutes the solicitation for the purchase or sale of any security or other

product. Never purchase an investment without first carefully reading all available information (i.e., the prospectus, etc.) and getting competent professional help. Pay special attention to all notes and endnotes as they may include important explanations, disclaimers, etc., vital to the text and data herein.

8. In certain places the book discusses various market indexes. The performance of an index is not an exact representation of any particular investment, as you cannot invest directly in an index. Stocks of small- and mid-cap companies often fluctuate more than those of large companies. Emerging markets and foreign stocks are frequently more risky than major U.S. stocks. All references, assumptions, data, and other content herein are applicable to the United States of America and may not hold true or be applicable elsewhere or in other time frames.

9. The author attempts to apply a Christian worldview throughout this book. Consequently his comments and overall presentation may not in all cases be based strictly on what makes the best financial and/or legal sense. His overriding goal is to remain faithful to what he perceives to be biblical, and his writing reflects that viewpoint.

Appendix 2

Web Site Smorgasbord

I started to title this section "Favorite Web Sites." But it occurred to me that it's really more of a Web site smorgasbord. Just like a smorgasbord restaurant, there are a lot of different things to choose from here. You may find some sites tastier than others. Some will be filling and nutritional, while others may leave you hungry. Some will be as fun as eating a piece of cherry pie, while others will be more like stewed okra—good for you but painful on the taste buds. Since each individual's needs and situations vary, feel free to pick and choose as you wish.

You'll notice that there are several options under most of the headings. Some of these Web sites are personal favorites, while others would receive a less enthusiastic review from yours truly. The inclusion of a Web site on this list should not be considered an endorsement of that site. The real strength of this sort of information is that it allows you to learn, study, and compare for yourself. It allows you to read broadly. As you peruse the following sites, remember that many of them have their own agendas. Some are going to try to sell you stuff—whether you need it or not. You probably won't agree with all of the advice and data at every site. I don't! But, hopefully, at the end of the smorgasbord line, you'll have a tray of healthy information to digest.

One Web site that I hope you will feel especially welcome at is our own: www.nodebtnosweat.com. We try to present a fun site that combines useful financial and life-skill information—all with an eternal focus.

Banking (On-line)

www.etradebank.com

Cars

www.autobytel.com
www.autoweb.com
www.carpoint.com
www.carbargains.com (one of the popular car-buying services)
www.edmunds.com
www.intellichoice.com
www.kbb.com (Kelly Blue Book)

Charitable Giving

www.give.org (Affiliated with the Council of Better Business Bureaus, this site reports on nationally soliciting charitable organizations.)

College

www.collegeboard.com
www.savingforcollege.com

Consumer Rankings and Information

www.consumerfed.org
www.gomez.com

Credit Card Information

www.cardweb.com
www.creditcardfreedom.com

Credit Reporting

www.equifax.com
www.experian.com
www.transunion.com

Financial Information and Products

www.americanfunds.com
www.barrons.com (Barrons Business Publication On-line)
www.crown.org
www.finance.yahoo.com
www.fidelity.com
www.financialengines.com
www.forbes.com (*Forbes* Magazine)
www.ici.org (Investment Company Institute)
www.mfea.com (Mutual Fund Investors' Center)
www.moneycentral/msn.com
www.morningstar.com

www.quicken.com
www.savingsbonds.gov
www.smartmoney.com
www.stevediggs.com
www.tiaacref.com
www.vanguard.com
www.wsj.com (*Wall Street Journal*)

Insurance

www.answerfinancial.com
www.insurance.com
www.insweb.com (offers comparison quotes from multiple providers)
www.quickquote.com (focuses on term life insurance quotes)
selectquote.com
www.term4sale.com

Legal

www.legaldocs.com
www.nolo.com

Miscellaneous

www.quackwatch.com (bills itself as "your guide to health fraud, quackery, and intelligent decisions")

Phone Rates

www.abtolls.com

Real Estate

www.homeadvisor.com
www.homestore.com
www.monstermoving.com
www.nar.realtor.com
www.realestate.yahoo.com

Social Security

www.ssa.gov

Tax Information

www.irs.gov (Internal Revenue Service)

Things to Buy

www.ebay.com
www.goto.com

Travel

www.expedia.com
www.priceline.com
www.travelocity.com

Web Designers and Hosts

www.JabezNetworks.com

Notes

Chapter 1: Failure, the First Step to Success

1. Elizabeth Razzi, "Retailers' Siren Song," *Kiplinger's Personal Finance,* November 2000, 130–34.

2. Ibid.

3. Ibid.

4. Ibid.

5. Paul J. Lim and Matthew Benjamin, "Digging Your Way Out of Debt," *U.S. News & World Report,* 19 March 2001, 54.

6. Ibid.

7. www.CardWeb.com.

8. Ibid.

9. "New Study: Typical American Household Has Net Financial Assets of $1000," Consumer Federation of America (consumerfed.org) and Primerica, October 1999 press release.

10. "CFA Research Reveals Most Americans Have Built Little Wealth," Consumer Federation of America, February 2001 press release.

11. "New Study: Typical American Household Has Net Financial Assets of $1000," Consumer Federation of America (consumerfed.org) and Primerica, October 1999 press release.

12. Ibid.

13. "More Than Half of Americans Behind in Saving for Retirement," Consumer Federation of America (consumerfed.org) and DirectAdvice.com, April 2000 press release.

14. Ibid.

15. "CFA Research Reveals Most Americans Have Built Little Wealth," Consumer Federation of America, February 2001 press release.

Chapter 2: The Great Balancing Act

1. *The Word in Life Study Bible* (Nashville, Tenn.: Thomas Nelson Publishers, 1996), 2, 190–92.

Chapter 3: Acknowledge Who Owns Your Money

1. Loosely paraphrased from Ecclesiastes 6:15.

2. See Exodus 13:2, 12; 22:29; Leviticus 2:12–16; Numbers 18:8ff; Deuteronomy 18:4; Jeremiah 2:3; Romans 8:23; 1 Corinthians 15:20, 23; 16:15.

3. Leviticus 5:6.

4. Alger Fitch, *What the Bible Says About Money* (Joplin, Mo.: College Press, 1987), 74–84.

5. See Genesis 14:17ff and Hebrews 7:1ff.

6. See 2 Corinthians 9:7.

7. Barry L. Cameron, *The A,B,C's of Financial Success* (Joplin, Missouri: College Press, 2001), 113–14.

8. See Luke 10:30ff.

Chapter 6: The Fine Art of Buying a Car

1. Sarah Breckenridge, "Ten Things Your Auto Dealer Won't Tell You," *Smart Money,* March 2001, 89–92.

2. Jerry Edgerton, *Money's Car Shopping Made Easy* (New York: Warner Books, 1997).

3. Consumer Reports, *New Car Buyers' Guide 2001,* 17.

4. Autopedia, "Lease vs. Purchase Comparison," www.autopedia.com.

5. While deemed accurate, this calculation is based on a number of assumptions that may or may not hold true in your case. Figures are estimates. Mistakes in calculations/assumptions can be made. Be sure to reconfirm all calculations and assumptions for yourself to ensure accuracy. This information is simply a summary of best understanding and is not intended to be full or exhaustive. All examples are hypothetical and are only for illustrative purposes. Consult with a competent professional before spending money.

6. Jerry Edgerton, *Money's Car Shopping Made Easy* (New York: Warner Books, 1997), 47.

Chapter 7: Buying Insurance

1. QuickQuote Life Insurance Resource Center, www.quickquote.com.

2. InsWeb, "Defining Universal and Whole Life Insurance," www.insweb.com.

3. QuickQuote Life Insurance Resource Center, www.quickquote.com.

4. InsWeb, "Defining Universal and Whole Life Insurance," www.insweb.com.

5. QuickQuote Health Resource Center, www.quickquote.com.

6. Insurance Information Institute, "How to Insure Your Home and Personal Belongings," www.iii.org.

Chapter 8: How to Buy a Home

1. Wendell Cox and Ronald D. Utt, Ph.D., "Smart Growth, Housing Costs, and Home Ownership," *The Heritage Foundation Backgrounder Executive Summary,* www.heritage.com, 6 April 2001.

2. As cited by Marc Robinson, *Buying the Best Home* (New York: Dorling Kindersley Publishing, 2000).

3. "Is Home Ownership Right for You?" www.RealEstate.com.

4. Ibid.

5. "How Much Home Can You Afford?" National Association of Realtors, www.REALTOR.com.

6. "How Big a Monthly Payment Can You Afford?" www.RealEstate.com.

7. Notes/Clarifications/Disclaimers: While deemed accurate, the accuracy of these calculations (including but not limited to tax calculations) and their applicability to your circumstances are not guaranteed. There is always a possibility of miscalculation. Always recalculate and confirm accuracy for your own purposes. As always, you should obtain personal advice from qualified professionals. These are hypothetical calculations for comparison and/or illustrative purposes only. No rate is assured, and no specific performance is represented. Various assumptions were made that may or may not coincide with others in your experience. This is not intended as investment or other advice; it is simply a comparative tool to give you a point of reference. Tax laws and/or their changes may affect these assumptions and factor in your personal circumstances. Interest rates and the value of money may impact these illustrations. This information (tax, legal, and/or other) is simply a summary of best understanding and is not intended to be full or exhaustive. Neither this book, nor its author, gives legal or tax advice.

8. Same as notes/clarifications/disclaimers in endnote 7 above.

9. Same as notes/clarifications/disclaimers in endnote 7 above.

10. Same as notes/clarifications/disclaimers in endnote 7 above.

11. Same as notes/clarifications/disclaimers in endnote 7 above.

12. Mike Hardwick, "What Every Home Owner Should Know About Refinancing," Nashville, Tenn.: Churchill Mortgage Corp., www.churchillmortgage.com.

Chapter 9: Kids, Cash, and Character

1. As cited in Janet Bodnar, "Unspoiled Little Rich Kids," *Kiplinger's Personal Finance,* kiplinger.com, December 2000.

2. Ibid.

3. Ibid.

4. As cited on the www.kidsmoney.org Web site.

5. As cited in "Average Allowances," by www.factmonster.com

6. Cindy Bond, "Labor Pains: After-school Jobs Get a Bad Review," www.familyeducation.com.

7. As cited in "The Five Worst Jobs for Teens," www.familyeducation.com.

8. Paul J. Lim and Matthew Benjamin, "Digging Your Way Out of Debt," *U.S. News and World Report,* 19 March 2001, 54.

9. CardWeb.com as cited in "Managing Your Money," *USA Today,* 5 January 2001, 3.B.

10. Lucy Lazarony, "Marketing Plastic to Students Causes Lawmakers, Educators to Melt Down," www.bankrate.com.

11. Ibid.

12. Ibid.

13. Shepard Smith, "The Fox Report," Fox News Channel, 27 August 2001.

Chapter 10: Planning for College

1. As cited on WPLN Radio, Nashville, Tenn., on "Market Place" (produced by Minnesota Public Radio, Public Radio International, 6 June 2001).

2. "College Costs Facts and Myths," 2001, www.collegeboard.com.

3. Ibid.

4. As cited in "Sources of Financial Aid," T. Rowe Price, 2000, www.troweprice.com.

5. This data was supplied by third parties. While deemed accurate, the author does not assure its correctness, accuracy, completeness, or appropriateness for your situation. It is based on a number of assumptions that may or may not be duplicated in your experience. This is not intended as investment advice. As always, review all your investments

periodically; study tax law changes, which may affect these assumptions; get competent professional help; and factor in your personal circumstances. This information is simply a summary of best understanding and is not intended to be full or exhaustive. All examples are hypothetical and are only for illustrative purposes. Your investment may or may not perform as you might wish. Neither this book, nor its author, gives legal, investing, tax, or other professional advice. This is not an offer to buy or sell any security(s). This is not intended as investment advice; it is simply a comparative tool to give you a point of reference for your unique situation. This disclaimer applies to all data in this chapter.

6. "Frequently Asked Questions," www.Savingforcollege.com, LLC.

7. Sarah Breckenridge and Michele Marchetti, *Smart Money*, December 2001, 108–15.

8. "Frequently Asked Questions," www.Savingforcollege.com, LLC.

9. Sarah Breckenridge and Michele Marchetti, *Smart Money*, December 2001, 108–15.

10. While deemed accurate, the accuracy of these calculations and their applicability to your circumstances are not guaranteed. As always you should obtain personal advice from qualified professionals. These are hypothetical calculations for comparison and/or illustrative purposes only. No rate of return is assured and no specific security's performance is represented. Various assumptions were made, one of which is the frequency of compounding that could be different in your case. If you are investing in a fund that taxes you on capital gains and/or dividends, expect the future value to be lower. Regular investing does not assure a profit or always protect against loss. Remember that rates of return can vary over time and that higher return potential also involves a higher degree of risk. This is not intended as investment advice—it is simply a comparative tool to give you a point for reference for your unique situation. As always, review all your investments periodically, keep up with tax law changes that may affect these assumptions, get competent professional help, and factor in your personal circumstances. This information (tax, legal, and/or other) is simply a summary of best understanding and is not intended to be full or exhaustive. Since it is, of course, always possible for there to be miscalculations, the accuracy of these interpretations and calculations are not assured—have them checked for yourself. Performance is historical and does not necessarily reflect future performance. This book, nor its author, give legal or tax advice. This is not an offer to buy or sell any security(s). Neither this book nor its author give legal or tax advice.

11. See endnote 10 above.

Chapter 11: Finding Great Bargains

1. *NBC Nightly News*, 10 July 2001.

Chapter 13: Debt and Credit Cards

1. Paul J. Lim and Matthew Benjamin, "Digging Your Way Out of Debt," *U.S. News & World Report*, 19 March 2001, 54.

2. www.CardWeb.com.

3. Travis Plunkett or Stephen Brobeck, "Credit Card Issuers Aggressively Expand Marketing and Lines of Credit on Eve of New Bankruptcy Restrictions," Consumer Federation of America, 27 February 2001.

4. Ibid.

5. www.CardWeb.com.

6. Shepard Smith, "The Fox Report," Fox News Channel, 27 August 2001.

Chapter 14: A Do-It-Yourself Credit Repair Kit

1. Larry Burkett, "Dealing with Creditors," www.crown.org, 2001.

2. Larry Burkett, *The Complete Financial Guide for Young Couples* (Colorado Springs: Victor Books, 1989), 37–38 and as cited at www.crown.org in "Establishing Credit."

3. www.CardWeb.com.

4. www.CardWeb.com.

Chapter 15: What I Wish They'd Told Me About Investing

1. A third party supplied this data. While deemed to be accurate, the author does not assure its correctness, accuracy, or appropriateness for your situation. Check them for yourself. It is based on a number of assumptions that may or may not be duplicated in your experience. This is not intended as investment advice. It is simply a comparative tool to give you a point of reference for your unique situation. As always, review all your investments periodically, study tax law changes which may affect these assumptions, get competent professional help, and factor in your personal circumstances. This information is simply a summary of best understanding and is not intended to be full or exhaustive. All examples are for illustrative purposes only. Performance is historical and does not reflect the future. There is no assurance that your investment will have similar returns. Yours could be more but possibly less. Neither this book nor its author gives legal, investing, tax, or other professional advice. You cannot invest directly into an index. This is not an offer to buy or sell any security(s). This disclaimer applies to all scenarios in this chapter.

2. Notes/Clarifications/Disclaimers: As always, you should obtain personal advice from qualified professionals. These are calculations for comparison and/or illustrative purposes only. No rate of return is assured and no specific security's performance is represented. Various assumptions were made that may or may not coincide with others' or with future rates/returns. Regular investing does not assure a profit or always protect against loss. Remember that rates of return can vary over time and that higher return potential also involves a higher degree of risk. This is not intended as investment advice—it is simply a comparative tool to give you a point for reference for your unique situation. As always, review all your investments periodically, keep up with tax law changes that may affect these assumptions, get competent professional help, and factor in your personal circumstances. This information (tax, legal, and/or other) is simply a summary of best understanding and is not intended to be full or exhaustive. Since it is, of course, always possible for there to be miscalculations, the accuracy of these interpretations and calculations are not assured by the author—have them checked for yourself. Their applicability to your circumstances is not guaranteed. Performance is historical and does not necessarily reflect future performance. Neither this book, nor its author, give legal or tax advice. You cannot invest directly in an index. This is not an offer to buy or sell any security(s).

Chapter 16: Six Secrets of the Great Investors

1. This calculation is based on a number of assumptions (some of which include that no withdrawals are made before age sixty-six, 10 percent return with annual compounding, contributions made at first of year, possible tax impact is not taken into consideration, dividends and/or capital gains are reinvested, etc.). Any distributions will affect the total. This is not intended as investment advice. It is simply a comparative tool to give you a point for reference for your unique situation. As always, review all your investments periodically, study tax law changes that may affect these assumptions, get competent professional help, and factor in your personal circumstances. This information is simply a

summary of best understanding and is not intended to be full or exhaustive. While deemed accurate, the accuracy of these calculations and/or interpretations, and their applicability to your circumstances is not guaranteed—have them confirmed for yourself. All examples are hypothetical and are only for illustrative purposes. Performance is historical and does not reflect the future. There is no assurance that your investment will have similar returns. Yours could be more, but very possibly less.

2. See endnote 1 above.

3. This calculation assumes no withdrawals are made from the account before age 70. Remember, certain IRA withdrawals may be subject to taxes and penalties. Any distributions will affect the total. Assumes first of year contributions and annual compounding. This is not intended as investment advice—it is simply a comparative tool to give you a point for reference for your unique situation. As always, review all your investments periodically, study tax law changes that may affect these assumptions, get competent professional help, and factor in your personal circumstances. This information is simply a summary of best understanding and is not intended to be full or exhaustive. While deemed accurate, these interpretations and calculations may or may not be correct—have them confirmed for yourself. All examples are hypothetical and are only for illustrative purposes. Performance is historical and does not reflect the future. There is no assurance that your investment will have similar returns. Yours could be more, but very possibly less.

4. While deemed accurate, the accuracy of these calculations and their applicability to your circumstances are not guaranteed—have them confirmed for yourself. As always, you should obtain personal advice from qualified professionals. These are hypothetical calculations for comparison and/or illustrative purposes only. No rate of return is assured, and no specific security's performance is represented. Various assumptions were made, some of them include that you invest monthly, your investment is tax-deferred, compounds monthly, reinvests dividends and capital gains, and no withdrawals are made before age sixty-five. If you are investing in a fund that taxes you on capital gains and/or dividends, the future value may be lower. Regular investing does not assure a profit or always protect against loss. Remember that rates of return can vary over time and that higher return potential also involves a higher degree of risk. This is not intended as investment advice—it is simply a comparative tool to give you a point of reference for your unique situation. As always, review all your investments periodically, keep up with tax law changes that may affect these assumptions, get competent professional help, and factor in your personal circumstances. This information (tax, legal, and/or other) is simply a summary of best understanding and is not intended to be full or exhaustive. Since it is, of course, always possible for there to be miscalculations, the accuracy of these interpretations and calculations is not assured—have them checked for yourself. Performance is historical and does not necessarily reflect future performance. Neither this book, nor its author, give legal or tax advice. This is not an offer to buy or sell any security(s). Neither this book, nor its author, give legal or tax advice.

5. Certain IRA withdrawals may be subject to taxes and penalties. Any distributions will affect the total. Various assumptions have been made. Some include: Calculations assume annual compounding and that contributions are made at the first of each year. Assumes that there are no withdrawals made from this IRA until retirement. There are some IRA withdrawals that may be subjected to penalties and/or taxes. The accuracy of these calculations and their applicability to your circumstances are not guaranteed—have them confirmed for yourself. These are hypothetical calculations for

comparison and/or illustrative purposes only. No rate of return is assured, and no specific security's performance is represented. Regular investing does not assure a profit or always protect against loss. Remember that rates of return can vary over time and that higher return potential also involves a higher degree of risk. This is not intended as investment advice—it is simply a comparative tool to give you a point of reference for your unique situation. As always, review all your investments periodically, keep up with tax law changes which may affect these assumptions, get competent professional help/advice, and factor in your personal circumstances. This information (tax, legal, and/or other) is simply a summary of best understanding and is not intended to be full or exhaustive. Since it is, of course, always possible for there to be miscalculations, the accuracy of these interpretations and calculations is not assured—have them checked for yourself. Performance is historical and does not necessarily reflect future performance. Your results could be better or worse. Neither this book, nor its author, give legal or tax advice. This is not an offer to buy or sell any security(s).

6. Same as endnotes 5 above.

7. Source: www.strong.com. Used with permission. These are hypothetical tables/calculations for comparison and/or illustrative purposes only. No rate of return is assured, and no specific security's performance is represented. Regular investing does not assure a profit or always protect against loss. Remember that rates of return can vary over time and that higher return potential also involves a higher degree of risk. This is not intended as investment advice—it is simply a comparative tool to give you a point of reference for your unique situation. As always, review all your investments periodically, keep up with tax law changes which may affect these assumptions, get competent professional help/advice, and factor in your personal circumstances. Your results may be better or worse. This information (tax, legal, and/or other) is simply a summary of best understanding and is not intended to be full or exhaustive. While deemed to be accurate, it is of course always possible for there to be miscalculations. The accuracy of these interpretations and calculations is not assured—have them checked for yourself. Neither this book, nor its author, give legal or tax advice. This is not an offer to buy or sell any security(s). DCA does not assure positive returns.

8. Same as endnote 7 above.

9. Same as endnote 7 above..

10. Asset allocation planning tools are designed to help you determine and pursue your investment goals. Such tools may help you assess your risk tolerance, time horizon, financial situation, etc. The goal should be to help you achieve adequate risk-adjusted returns over a period of time—not necessarily maximize returns. None of this material should be considered investment advice or used as the sole or primary basis for your decisions. Instead it should be considered only as part of all the other information you deem important in investment decision-making. Remember that this information is constantly changing and adapting. What makes sense at the time of this writing may change in time, which means that target asset mixes may also need to change from time to time. Review your models, plans, investments, etc. periodically. This information (tax, legal, and/or other) is simply a summary of best understanding and is not intended to be full or exhaustive. While deemed to be accurate, it is of course always possible for there to be miscalculations. The accuracy of these interpretations and calculations is not assured—have them checked for yourself. As always, get competent professional advice. It is totally your decision and responsibility to implement any given asset mix that you choose. Nothing herein is given as investment advice and/or as an offer to sell any product and/or security. Asset allocation does not ensure positive returns.

11. www.tiaa-cref.org. Used with permission.

12. Same as endnote 10 above. These are sample portfolio allocations only. Depending on your tolerance for risk or your individual circumstances, you may wish to choose a more conservative or a more aggressive allocation plan than any of the tables shown. Also, remember that some of these allocations are for longer-term financial goals. You may well choose to hold cash and/or cash equivalents for shorter-term goals and emergencies. Return data may be premised on the reinvestment of income dividend and capital gains distributions. They don't include the effects of investment expenses and taxes, nor do they represent the performance of any particular investment. Asset allocation does not insure positive returns.

13. Retirement and Investment Strategies, Inc., Goodlettsville, Tennessee, supplied this material. Used with permission. Although author and publisher believe this information to be correct, they make no assurance and/or guarantee of such accuracy/ correctness/appropriateness/etc. Refer to Endnote #10 and #12 of this chapter.

14. American Funds, www.yourretirementsource.com. Used with permission. Same as endnotes 10 and 12 above.

Chapter 17: Mutual Funds, Motrocycles, and Sushi

1. Investment Company Institute, www.ici.org.
2. Ibid.
3. Ibid.
4. Ibid.
5. Ibid.
6. Ibid.
7. Ibid.
8. Ibid.
9. Ibid.

10. Source: Vanguard Group. This data was supplied by a third party, and while deemed accurate, the author does not assure its correctness, accuracy, or appropriateness for your situation. Check the information for yourself. It is based on a number of assumptions that may or may not be duplicated in your experience. This is not intended as investment advice; it is simply a comparative tool to give you a point of reference for your unique situation. As always, review all your investments periodically, study tax law changes that may affect these assumptions, get competent professional help, and factor in your personal circumstances. This information is simply a summary of best understanding and is not intended to be full or exhaustive. All examples are hypothetical and are only for illustrative purposes. Performance is historical and does not reflect the future. There is no assurance that your investment will have similar returns. Yours could be more but very possibly less. Neither this book nor its author gives legal, investing, tax, or other professional advice. This is not an offer to buy or sell any security(s). This disclaimer applies to the entire contents of this chapter.

11. This is not intended as investment advice—it is simply a comparative tool to give you a point of reference for your unique situation. As always, review all your investments periodically, study tax law changes that may affect these assumptions, get competent professional help, and factor in your personal circumstances. This information is simply a summary of best understanding and is not intended to be full or exhaustive. All examples are hypothetical and are only for illustrative purposes. There is no assurance that your investment will have similar returns. Yours could be more, but very possibly

less. Neither this book nor its author gives legal, investing, tax, or other professional advice. This is not an offer to buy or sell any security(s).

12. Source: American Funds. Notes/disclaimers/explanations from Endnote #10 above apply.

13. See endnote 10 of this chapter.

Chapter 18: Retiring with Dignity

1. Rubel Shelly, "Time To Check Your Direction?" *The FAX of Life*, 5 August 1996. Used with permission.

2. "More Than Half of Americans Behind in Saving for Retirement," Consumer Federation of America (consumerfed.org) and DirectAdvice.com, April 2000 Press Release.

3. Ibid.

4. Source: American Funds. A third party supplied this data. While deemed to be accurate, the author does not assure its correctness, accuracy, or appropriateness for your situation. Check them for yourself. It is based on a number of assumptions that may or may not be duplicated in your experience. This is not intended as investment advice. It is simply a comparative tool to give you a point of reference for your unique situation. As always, review all your investments periodically, study tax law changes that may affect these assumptions, get competent professional help, and factor in your personal circumstances. This information is simply a summary of best understanding and is not intended to be full or exhaustive. All examples are hypothetical and are only for illustrative purposes. Performance is historical and does not reflect the future. There is no assurance that your investment will have similar returns. Yours could be more but very possibly less. Neither this book, nor its author, gives legal, investing, tax, or other professional advice. This is not an offer to buy or sell any security(s). This disclaimer applies to everything in this chapter.

5. Same as endnote 4 above.

6. American Funds, www.yourretirementsource.com.

If you liked the book,
you'll *love* the seminar!

Now you can bring the **No Debt No Sweat Seminar** to your church or organization. Steve Diggs will personally teach you:

$ 3 great principles of godly living
$ How to get out of debt forever!
$ 10 keys to a successful budget
$ What the Bible says about money
$ 3 ways to achieve financial freedom
$ A do-it-yourself credit repair kit
$ 6 secrets of the great investors
$ How mutual funds work
$ Stop fighting over money!
$ How to use God's money God's way
$ How to buy a car
$ How to prepare for retirement

For details, call **615-834-3063**
or visit us at **www.ndns.org**.

Our Web site is powered by JabezNetworks.com.